P9-CDV-417

OUACHITA TECHNICAL COLLEGE

# HUMAN SEXUALITY

# HUMAN SEXUALITY
## New Directions
## in
## American Catholic Thought

**A Study**
**Commissioned by**
**The Catholic Theological Society of America**

**Anthony Kosnik, Chairperson**
**William Carroll**
**Agnes Cunningham**
**Ronald Modras**
**James Schulte**

**PAULIST PRESS**
New York/Paramus/Toronto

Acknowledgments

Quotations from *The Documents of Vatican II*. Reprinted with permission of America Press. All Rights Reserved.©1966 by America Press, 106 W 56 Street, New York, NY 10019.

Library of Congress
Catalog Card Number: 77-074586

ISBN: 0-8091-0223-4

Published by Paulist Press
*Editorial Office:* 1865 Broadway, N.Y., N.Y. 10023
*Business Office:* 545 Island Road, Ramsey, N.J. 07446

Printed and bound in the
United States of America

# Contents

# Foreword

The pages that follow constitute the final report of a committee established by the Board of Directors of the Catholic Theological Society of America in 1972. At the meetings of June 10 and October 15, 1976, the Board voted to "receive" the report and to arrange for its publication. These actions imply neither the approval nor disapproval by the Society or its Board of Directors of the contents of the report. The publication is intended as a service to the membership of the Society and a wider public of interested persons by making available the results of this research. The Board wishes to express its gratitude to the committee for its theological effort that promises to contribute to the further reflection and discussion that is called for on a topic of such moral and pastoral significance.

Board of Directors
Catholic Theological Society of America

# Preface

Human sexuality has become in recent years a subject of extensive study, research, reflection, and debate. Profound changes in sexual attitudes and behavior patterns in America and elsewhere have led to serious questions regarding the adequacy of traditional Catholic formulations and pastoral responses to sexual matters. In the fall of 1972, recognizing its responsibility to the American Catholic community and its pastors, the Board of Directors of the Catholic Theological Society of America commissioned the establishment of a committee to do a study on human sexuality in the hope of "providing some helpful and illuminating guidelines in the present confusion."

One of the first tasks of this committee was to clarify the precise meaning of the charge given it and to determine the nature of the study desired. Was it to be a work of speculative or pastoral theology? Was it to be directed primarily to professional theologians or to practicing pastors and counselors, those active in pastoral ministry? How ambitious should it be? Should the completed report consist of twenty pages outlining some new directions or twenty volumes exhausting and synthesizing every aspect of human sexual behavior?

The limited time and resources allotted the committee precluded at the outset any consideration of a comprehensive study. Yet the complexity, importance, and sensitivity of the subject seemed to demand more than a simple statement of new orientations. The call for "helpful and illuminating guidelines" suggested a study that would be primarily pastoral in nature. We were convinced, however, that helpful guidelines could not be effectively formulated or communicated without providing some understanding of the biblical, historical, empirical, and theological sources that constitute the foundation for good pastoral theology and practice. This background seemed particularly necessary to provide greater understanding of our past attitudes and approaches, to show the basis for current misconceptions, and to open the way to new directions. As a result, the final form of our study takes a position somewhere between that of a highly technical, cumbrously footnoted work of speculative theology and a practical, experience-oriented work of pastoral theology. We have attempted to harmonize the best elements of both approaches. This means, however, that a professional theologian may find certain positions insufficiently elaborated and argued whereas the pastoral minister or counselor may become impatient with some of the minutiae and apparently unnecessary detail. The purpose of this study and its unavoidable limitations should help to explain both reactions.

The nature and scope of this study has led us naturally to divide it along the following lines: the Bible and human sexuality; Christian tradition and human sexuality; the empirical sciences and human sexuality; toward a theology of human sexuality; and pastoral guidelines for human sexuality.

As followers of Jesus Christ, we begin our study by looking to the Scriptures as a primary witness to the revelation of God and insight into the divine plan for the human race, specifically as it pertains to human sexuality. The first chapter, therefore, reviews the pertinent biblical material of the Old and New Testaments. With the help of contemporary critical biblical scholarship, special effort has been made to separate what is revealed and lasting in the Bible from what is culturally conditioned and subject to change.

To assure continuity with Catholic tradition, the second chapter is largely historical. We recognize our indebtedness to the tradition from which we speak as Catholics. We are convinced that there can be no genuine theological development that does not flow from the past. This section attempts to review the rich tradition that constitutes our Catholic Christian heritage. At the same time, it tries to distinguish the constant values from changing historical and cultural influences that have shaped particular Catholic attitudes or formulations regarding sexuality.

With sensitivity to the present, the third chapter summarizes the empirical data available from the social and behavioral sciences and attempts to interpret their significance. We have sought broad consultation from recognized experts in a variety of fields in order to take due note of new developments and information which recent studies have afforded in the area of human sexuality.

The fourth chapter attempts to integrate the biblical, historical, and anthropological data into a theological synthesis. Theological and cultural experiences of the past and present provide a source from which to discern the basic human values and principles that have been constant in Catholic teaching. These values furnish the foundation from which we have attempted to elaborate principles for interpreting and evaluating sexual behavior. We have strived to accomplish this task by taking cognizance of the plurality of theological opinions and approaches that have characterized Catholic tradition in the past and that constitute the state of Catholic theology today.

The fifth chapter of this study addresses itself to particular situations or questions in the area of sexual morality. It attempts to provide information and assistance for leaders in pastoral ministry to help them form and guide consciences in this area according to the mind of Jesus. We wish to acknowledge once again and emphasize the limitations of our study and of the present state of theological and scientific research; many questions will certainly continue to demand more complete and satisfying answers.

Given the nature of the task assigned to us, we have addressed the phenomenon of human sexuality from a perspective that is specifically Roman Catholic and North American. We acknowledge gratefully that our study has benefited considerably from consultation with specialists in various sciences and of various theological convictions. In November 1974, the initial draft of the first four chapters was forwarded to some twenty-five theologians and other experts for their review and criticism. In June 1975, a summary report of these chapters was presented to the members of the Catholic Theological Society of America at their annual meeting and subsequently published in the proceedings. In the fall of 1975, a second draft including the entire report was again circulated for critical review by the same group of experts. Many of their recommendations were incorporated into the study. In May of 1976 the report was presented to the Board of Directors of the Catholic Theological Society and officially received by the Board at their executive meeting in June 1976. At the Board's request, three additional theologians, unrelated to the previous consultations, were invited to review the study and submit their recommendations. These were received by our committee for consideration and incorporation in October 1976. Authorization for publication of the study as a report commissioned by and submitted to the Catholic Theological Society of America was granted at an Executive Board meeting in October 1976.

It should be noted at this point that this study is not a collection of separate essays authored by different members of this committee. Although individual members may have prepared initial drafts and contributed more to certain sections because of their particular expertise, the entire work was discussed, modified, reviewed in detail, and approved by the committee as a whole. Our rules for procedure allowed for the inclusion of dissenting or minority positions. Much to our surprise and satisfaction, however, the mutual openness and sharing that prevailed throughout our collaboration resulted in a final product that was acceptable to every member of the committee without substantial disagreement or objection.

This study, as we have indicated, was commissioned and received by the Catholic Theological Society of America. Although many members of the Society were consulted, the finished report does not necessarily reflect the official position of the Society or its Board nor a consensus of its members. Nor do we as a committee presume in any way to put forth our conclusions as the official magisterial teaching of the Catholic Church. We have attempted simply to bring Christian theological reflection to bear on the complex phenomenon of human sexuality in the hope of providing some helpful pastoral guidelines to beleaguered pastors, priests, counselors and teachers. In the spirit of the Second Vatican Council, we trust that our efforts will foster an attitude of openness and cooperation and encourage others to join us in the continuing search for more satisfying answers to the mystery of human sexuality.

William Carroll
Agnes Cunningham
Anthony Kosnik
Ronald Modras
James Schulte

# Acknowledgments

The Committee wishes to acknowledge and express a profound debt of gratitude to the following for their special role in bringing this study to completion:

To the Catholic Theological Society of America and Canada for its courageous vision in commissioning and financially underwriting this study.

To the Board of Directors of the CTSA for their steady encouragement, gentle prodding, and patient endurance throughout the project.

To the many consultants and reviewers whose constructive recommendations have contributed greatly to this report. We are especially grateful to the following: Gregory Baum, Charles E. Curran, John Dedek, Dennis J. Doherty, Margaret Farley, R.S.M., Eugene J. Fisher, John Glaser, A. Regina Hall, George Kanoti, Mrs. H. June Kuczynski, R.N., Richard A. McCormick, S.J., Giles Milhaven, Timothy E. O'Connell, Michael Prieur, and Cornelius J. van der Poel, C.S.Sp. Their consultation does not necessarily imply full agreement with all our statements and conclusions.

To our families, friends and the institutions we serve for the many personal sacrifices our commitment to this study required of them as well as for their generous understanding and support of our efforts.

To Sr. Irene Doman for her careful and expert editing of the manuscript.

To Sr. Elizabeth Ozdych, S.J., for countless hours of freely contributed secretarial services, typing and retyping the manuscript into its final form.

May their greatest reward be an ever-deepening appreciation among all of God's people for the beauty, power and richness of the tremendous gift that is human sexuality.

# Introduction

The Catholic attitude toward human sexuality appears at first sight not simply complex but even contradictory. An ambiguity lies at the heart of Catholic tradition giving rise to ambivalence.[1] On the one hand, marriage is regarded as a sacrament that intensifies one's relationship with God; sexual intercourse is seen as cooperating with divine creativity; and the union of husband and wife is held symbolic of the union of Christ and the Church. On the other hand, much is made of the fact that Jesus was celibate; for many centuries virginity was considered superior to marriage; and the conditions under which sexual pleasure is "permitted" as "legitimate" are still restricted to a degree found in few other cultures, ethical systems, or religions.

There are several reasons for the complexity of the Catholic attitude toward sex. The Church's tradition is marked by an historical development extending some three thousand years. It has been subject to a plurality of religious, cultural, and philosophical influences. Although rooted in the Bible, which itself witnesses to a moral evolution and comprises a variety of theologies, Catholic teaching comes down to us from the Church Fathers and medieval schoolmen, bearing the limitations of their pre-scientific historical condition. Inadequate knowledge of biology, as well as religious taboos, the tradition of subhuman treatment of women, and a dualistic philosophy of human nature have all left a distinct imprint upon Catholic thinking.

In addition to the complexity of the subject itself, there is the complexity of Christian anthropology. At the very core of being human, sexuality can be viewed properly only within the context of the whole person and the whole of human life. Behind any attitude or moral opinion on sex lies a particular anthropology, a particular view of the meaning of life, of human nature and destiny. Sexuality should not be studied in isolation. Unless it is seen as integrated into the whole of human life with

*1*

all its relationships, sexuality can too easily degenerate into a naive biologism. A proper understanding of the Catholic tradition on sex, therefore, requires that it be viewed within the context of Christian anthropology, which is itself a complex synthesis of both biblical and classical anthropology.[2]

Despite differing emphases that may have distinguished Platonic, Aristotelian, and Stoic conceptions, it was a common conviction of classical antiquity that the human species should be viewed primarily as *animal rationale*, that is, from the standpoint of human reason. Along with this prevailing rationalism, classical anthropology was often characterized by dualism, explicit in Plato, implicit in Aristotle. Rationality constituted the essentially human and identified the human with the divine. Matter was regarded as the principle of individuation and hence of separation. The body was an encumbrance, identified if not with evil then at least with inferiority, a prison that prevented the truly human and good in man, the spirit, from returning to where it belongs.[3]

Biblical anthropology differed sharply from that of classical Greece. To recognize God as Creator and Lord is to acknowledge human creatureliness and dependence. The human spirit, while related to the divine, is not identical with it. There is no body-soul dualism in the Bible, no disparagement of the body as if it were evil or inferior; we are "living beings" that God has created good.[4] The Bible takes a unitary view of human nature. We are our bodies, living bodies, not incarnated spirits. Even less are we Cartesian ghosts in a machine.[5]

Furthermore, it is not the rationality or immortality of the soul that constitutes our greatness or uniqueness as human beings but the fact that we have been created in the image and likeness of God (Gen 1:26, 27). The original meaning of human likeness to the Creator was most likely our human participation in God's dominion over creation. Only later, under the influence of Hellenistic philosophy, was the likeness interpreted as immortality (Wis 2:23). The most important implication of being created in the divine image, however, is relatedness to God. Humanity in the Bible is never seen as autonomous. It is always in relationship to God that people are viewed, their actions judged, and achievements evaluated. As a consequence, both Scripture and Christian tradition take serious cognizance of human sinfulness.

From the myths of Genesis to the images of the Apocalypse, the Bible views the human race as falling short of the mark. Adam (literally, mankind) attempts to be like God, to raise independent claims for himself and ultimately dispose of his own existence (Gen 3:5). The psalmist proclaims that no one does good, all have gone astray (Ps 14:3; 53:3). The gospels present Jesus as critical of the deceptive self-righteousness that presumes to boast before God (Lk 18:9-14). Even the most faithful of his disciples is taught to pray "forgive us our trespasses" (Mt 6:12). St. Paul looks into himself and recognizes sinfulness at war with his best intentions. "I do not do the good I want but the evil I do not want is what I do" (Rom 7:19).

Biblical anthropology speaks not only of human sinfulness but also the tendency in us to cover over that sinfulness through self-deception. Satan, the archetypal symbol for evil in the world, is described as "the father of lies" (Jn 8:44), "the deceiver of the whole world" (Rev 12:9). Jesus accuses his critics among the Pharisees of blindness in not recognizing their own need for divine mercy (Mt 23). St. Paul describes the human condition as marked by exchanging the truth of God for a lie, a deception that leads to self-dishonor (Rom 1:24-25).

Christian tradition had to struggle against opposing anthropologies and world-views, but ultimately it succeeded in maintaining the paradoxical view of human nature found in the Scriptures. In its first centuries of missionary expansion, the Church could not help but be affected by the culture and categories of classical antiquity, its dualism, sometimes its pessimism. Christian tradition has attempted, with sometimes greater, sometimes less success, to steer a middle course between an optimism that neglects the reality of sin and a pessimism that neglects the essential goodness of creation and the reality of grace. Expressive of this middle course are three principles basic to Christian anthropology each of which necessarily colors the Christian view of human sexuality.

First, human nature is essentially good. "God saw everything that he had made, and behold, it was very good" (Gen 1:31). In virtue of the biblical doctrine of creation, the Church rejected as heretical any identification of matter with evil. Despite the influence of dualism upon early Christian thinking, Christian anthropology insists that the body and its sexuality must be viewed as good.

Second, human nature is in need of healing. "All men have sinned" (Rom 5:12). The universality of human sinfulness, symbolized by the myth of the Fall, the radical need for healing grace, was expounded and developed most explicitly by St. Augustine. Both he and St. Thomas Aquinas after him saw human sinfulness rooted ultimately in pride, the arrogation to oneself of the central place in life rightly held only by God (*City of God*, bk. XII, ch. 13). From pride there follows concupiscence; selfishness gives rise to sensuality and the misuse of creation (*Summa Theologiae*, I-IIae, q. 77, a. 4). Despite the essential goodness of human sexuality, its use and expression can be rendered sinful by egotism.

Third, human nature has an example and source of healing in Jesus Christ. Jesus constitutes for Christian faith not only the revelation of God, but also the ideal of what human nature can become, the exemplar of unselfish love. "Behold the man" (Jn 19:5). Jesus' life, death, and resurrection reveal for Christians that God's yes to creation has not been rescinded by human pride. Despite our sinfulness, we are accepted. Healing is possible, reconciliation is a reality, albeit in a relationship marked by dynamic process. The Christian doctrines of justification and grace provide the basis for a Christian ethic that is essentially eucharistic, that is to say, a moral stance that is a response of gratitude to a gracious God. The virtues and values exemplified by Jesus, above all his unselfish love, are espoused by his disciples in thanksgiving for the love God has revealed (Jn 13:35; 1 Jn 4:19). Those virtues and values, above all, that faithful and unselfish love, pertain to every sphere of Christian life, not the least of which is human sexuality.

This peculiar juxtaposition of the doctrines of creation, universal sinfulness, and grace constitutes the hallmark of Christian anthropology.[6] It is the framework necessary to appreciate Christian tradition regarding human sexuality. The essential goodness of creation, its abuse through selfishness, the human proclivity to self-deception, the call to live lives of unselfish love as disciples of Jesus—all this cannot help but affect the Christian attitude toward sexual behavior. Paradoxical as biblical anthropology is in itself, the Christian view of human nature involved still further tensions when the convictions of Jerusalem came to be joined to the philosophies of Athens. Conflicts occurred that have yet to be fully resolved. The polar tensions that mark contemporary Catholic attitudes toward sexuality are related to the very roots of Christian anthropology. Within this complex view of human nature, the complex Catholic view of human sexuality has evolved.

# I

# The Bible and Human Sexuality

Although there are numerous allusions to sexuality in the Bible, the Sacred Scriptures are not concerned with sexuality as such. There is no single word for this concept in either the biblical Hebrew or Greek language. The allusions to sexuality, however, are often quite frank. The social importance of reproduction constitutes a basic reason for early biblical teaching on sex-related matters.

At the very outset, however, two important caveats need to be made. The Bible should not be seen as giving absolute prescriptions with regard to sex. Specific culturally conditioned instructions cannot claim validity for all time. The teaching of the Bible must be seen against the background of its time, against the cultural and sociological conditions that characterize its era. The Bible is an historical document bearing the limitations of all historical records.[1]

Furthermore, one should not look to the Bible for a systematic presentation on sex. The Scriptures are not a textbook of ethics. The Bible contains a variety of statements on sex and some concrete demands that have the character of models. Only a few general lines or directions can be abstracted, and these must be interpreted historically, combined with the more adequate scientific knowledge of our times. Simply lining up a catalogue of texts does violence to biblical theology and accomplishes little of value.

## THE OLD TESTAMENT

As a document of a thousand-year period in the history of a people and their religious evolution, the Old Testament contains a variety of theologies and attitudes regarding sexuality.

The prominence of sex in the pagan cults, at least as viewed by the biblical authors, constrained Israel's prophets and religious leaders to take emphatic stands on any sexual practices that seemed related to cult. Especially after the exile, the preservation and propagation of the chosen people made sexual intercourse more than simply a private affair. Sons were viewed as a gift of God (Ps 127:3) and children as a blessing (Ps 128:4). Although eventually spiritualized within a cultic framework, the very word "blessing" seems to have referred originally to the power of fertility (Gen 1:22).[2]

## GENESIS

The opening chapters of Genesis present two quite different traditions, each with its own theology, anthropology, and attitude toward sex. However, both the older Yahwist tradition (dated circa 950 B.C.) and the later Priestly tradition (dated circa 550 B.C.) take a unitary view of the human race. In contrast to the mythologies of other ancient cultures, the Old Testament makes no suggestion that sexual duality results from some primeval fall. Both creation accounts assure us that from the very beginning humanity consisted of male and female.

Sexuality is described as willed by God, created as something good, about which human beings need not be embarrassed or ashamed in any way. The creation accounts in Genesis show no trace of contempt for the human sexual nature, as if it pertained somehow to a lower order of nature, inferior to the spiritual or intellectual. Sex is but one aspect of human life, neither despised nor dominant,[3] because never viewed in isolation. Sex is seen in a broader context, together with all the other aspects of human life.

In this regard, the older Yahwist tradition sets the sexual nature of men and women within the framework of our nature as social and relational beings. The Yahwist associates sexuality with the human problem of loneliness. "It is not good that man is alone; I will make him a helper like himself" (Gen 2:18). Solitude is not good. To be solitary constitutes a state of "helplessness," which can be overcome only by companionship. The first purpose of sex, as described by the Yahwist, is mutuality, our belonging to one another.[4] When a man clings to his wife and the two become one flesh (Gen 2:24), their sexual relations are expressive of a union deeper than physical contiguity. For the Yahwist, sexuality was a gift from God, drawing people from loneliness to relationship.[5] Some four hundred years later, the Priestly tradition came to relate sexuality with procreation, regarding the power to propagate as the direct result of God's blessing. The context for the blessing and the command to be fruitful and multiply (Gen 1:28) is the responsibility incumbent upon mankind for stewardship of the earth. Sharing in God's creative activity and dominion over life, men and women are called likewise to share in his providence.

A particularly striking feature of the Old Testament is its refusal to divinize sex. Although God was depicted in human form (Ezek 1:23), the thought of sexuality in God was alien to Israel. Yahweh stood beyond the polarity of sex. Sexual duality belonged to the sphere of creatures, not of the Creator. This view of creation is most "astonishing,"[6] when one considers Israel's religious environment. Her Canaanite neighbors regarded the copulation and procreation of their gods mythically as a pattern for the very process of creation. Possibly for this reason, temple personnel such as the *kedushim* and *kedushoth* (usually translated as temple prostitutes, male and female) were prohibited in the cult of Yahweh (Dt 23:18-19); to this day, though, their precise function has been difficult to determine.

## CULTIC PURITY

As in other religions of antiquity, the experience of the awesome holiness of God led Israel to adopt the concepts of pure and impure, clean and unclean. Along with birth and death, sexual discharges were seen as linked with divine power. Unless strictly regulated, they could render a person unclean and hence unfit to participate in the ritual worship of God[7] (Am 2:7; Hos 4:14; Jer 2:20ff). Since uncleanness was an external ritual fault, not a moral failing in our sense, the means of regaining purity consisted of washings and other rituals (Lev 11-15).

Demands for cultic purity in the Old Testament can be explained at least in part by the awe that Israel shared with the ancient world in regard to birth, death, and sexual discharges. In these occurrences, ancient peoples saw themselves as coming into contact with uncanny powers beyond human control. Possessed by these forces, a person could not enter into communion with God. The awe of blood (Lev 15:19-24) helps to explain the taboo against having intercourse with a woman during her menstrual period (Lev 15:24; 18:19; 20:18). Likewise, the awe manifested toward the male seed can shed some light on the Old Testament prohibition against homosexual activity between men (Lev 18:22; 20:13), with no reference to similar behavior between women.

Another taboo of the Old Testament was the exposure of the sex organs. Nakedness was shameful and abhorrent to many ancient Semitic groups except under strictly defined circumstances; it was a sign of humiliation and degradation (Gen 9:21-23; 2 Sam 6:20; 10:4). War captives were subjected to it (Is 20:2-4), and a hated nation was described as a virgin whose nakedness will be displayed to all (Is 47:3). The Hebrews also had a horror of deformed sex organs (Dt 23:2), and forbade a priest to function if he was maimed (Lev 21:20).

Along with the prohibitions against sowing a vineyard with two different kinds of seed, plowing a field with two different kinds of work animals, and wearing cloth made of two different kinds of thread, women were forbidden to wear men's clothes and men were forbidden to wear women's clothes (Dt 22:5-11).[8] The taboos against incest (Lev 18:6-16; Dt 27:23) extended even to the excommunication of any offspring from an incestuous union (Dt 23:3). Sexual uncleanness was viewed as polluting not only the offenders but even the land (Lev 18:25, 28; 19:29; Num 5:3; Dt 24:4; Jer 3:2, 9). The motivation of the biblical legislators probably did not involve or imply a morality of sexuality in itself. Rather, their outlook should be interpreted in the context of the ancient view of divine order, closely associated with the Egyptian notion of ma'at (harmony) or even possibly with the Hebrew notion of shalom (wholeness).

## PATRIARCHAL SOCIETY

Together with the demand for cultic purity, Old Testament attitudes toward sex were influenced by the patriarchal form of marriage and the family. Though women were included in some genealogies (Gen 4), descent was basically reckoned from the father's line (Gen 5). As head of the household, the father usually arranged the plans for marriage on behalf of his son, even to the point of selecting his wife. The role of the bride was that of a passive participant; in return for the man's payment of a bride price (mohar), the woman's father gave her away to become the man's wife (Gen 24:4; 29:23, 28; 34:8). The contracting parties were not the bride and groom but the families of the spouses, specifically the fathers; if the bride's father was dead, her brothers acted in his stead.

As a consequence of Israel's patriarchal society, **women** were kept in an inferior legal and social position. A blunt indication of woman's status can be found in the Exodus version of the decalogue, which lists a man's wife together with his property (Ex 20:17). Jeremiah, too, classified a man's wife with his chattel (Jer 6:12). The very word for "husband" in Hebrew, *baal*, also means "owner of property." The verb "to marry" also means "to possess." Terms such as "give in marriage" (Gen 29:28; 34:8; Jos 15:16-17) and "take a wife" (Gen 4:19; 6:2; 11:29) indicate that a girl was an object whose fate was determined first by her father and then by her husband. Further evidence of the subordination of women to men in the Old Testament can be found in the legislation permitting a man to revoke a vow made to God by his wife, if he saw fit to do so (Num 30:10-14).

On the other hand, one of the most significant, and difficult, Old Testament passages dealing with the position of women is Gen 2-3, in which the original condition of woman seems to be described as one of relative equality: a man leaves his father and mother to live with his wife, a "helper" like himself.

More than one view of woman is expressed by the authors of Scripture.[9] Many important biblical figures were women such as the mother of Lemuel (Prov 31), Miriam the Prophet (Ex 15:21), and Deborah the Judge (Jgs 5). In Wisdom literature, women are variously praised for their many "homely" virtues (Prov 18:22; 19:14; Sir 26:1-4) or castigated for their quarrelsomeness, seductiveness, and promiscuity (Sir 25:16ff; 9:3-20; 26:6-12). It is to Sirach, a true misogynist, that we owe the preservation of the midrash on Gen 3: "Sin began with a woman, and thanks to her we all must die" (Sir 25:23); this interpretation was to become much a part of the New Testament tradition (Rom 5:12; 1 Cor 15:22; 1 Tim 2:14).

The book of Deuteronomy offers a surprisingly positive approach to women, with important insights into the customs of the day. The passage in Dt 5:21, for example, through a change in the wording of the Decalogue, removes the wife from the list of property and affirms her nature as person rather than chattel. While most Pentateuchal and even many Deuteronomic laws dealing with women were in fact designed to protect the rights of the husband or father rather than those of the woman (e.g. Dt. 22:29), Deuteronomy contains laws designed to some extent in her interest. Dt. 21:15-17 provides for the inheritance rights of an unloved woman's child. Dt. 22:13-19 protects the wife's honor from slander. Dt. 24:5, in granting a draft exemption to a newlywed, shows consideration for a young wife's feelings as well as for the husband's need for an heir. Dt. 21:10-14 is almost unparalleled in the ancient world in the protection afforded the woman taken captive. A comparison of Ex 22:15-17 with Dt 22:22-29 should make this point even more clear. Deuteronomy greatly expanded the terse code of Exodus, by distinguishing the circumstances of rape or seduction and by viewing the acts as a violation of the woman's honor, and not merely a threat to the father's economic interest, as in Exodus.

Deuteronomy thus seemed to raise the legal status of women, both by the changes it made in individual laws and, specifically, by making women legal members of the covenant community. Deuteronomy consistently included women in its listing of participants in covenant ceremonies, often in places where other biblical traditions just as conspicuously left them out of the narrative (Dt 29:10, 17; 31:12; 12:12, 18; 16:11, 14). While the male-dominated customs of the people and much of the legislation remained intact despite the efforts of Deuteronomy, the radical implications of the Deuteronomic approach must be seen as an integral part of the whole biblical tradition.

Fundamental to the patriarchal society of the Old Testament and the generally inferior position of women was the functional character assigned to marriage. The social purpose of marriage in Israel, as in other ancient societies, was not so much the legitimation or regulation of sexual intercourse as the procreation of children. Romantic, exclusive love between man and wife, of course, is often portrayed, even in the midst of the polygamous setting of the Genesis narratives (e.g., Abraham and Sarah, Jacob and Rachel). And those few later passages that give us a glimpse into the intimacy of family life invariably show the wife as loved, listened to, and treated as a person of responsibility, e.g., Song of Songs, Ruth, Esther, Judith, 1 Sam 1, 2 Kgs 4, and the Book of Tobias, with its two aged couples.

Yet the need to bear children, especially male heirs, was so crucial an aspect of the institution of marriage that a barren wife would not hesitate to provide her husband with a concubine to produce an heir in her stead (Gen 30:1-13). By Davidic times, monogamy became the general practice, though it is not clear whether this development was based on moral or merely economic grounds. Kings, on the other hand, regularly practiced polygamy and concubinage, mainly for reasons of diplomacy (2 Sam 5:13-16; 1 Kgs 11:1-3). It should be noted that the rebuke of this practice in Dt 17:17 is not on grounds of sexual misbehavior, but rather for fear that polytheism may be introduced by the "foreign" wives.

The prevailing double sexual standard in ancient Israel quite possibly resulted from the social functions of marriage: the bearing of children and the maintenance of the household. In Israel's agricultural society, a large family meant a large working force to tend the fields. In a society without a clear concept of an afterlife, sons were a guarantee that a man's name would be remembered. Israelite society thus permitted men great latitude in sexual relations, as long as they respected the rights of their countrymen to a clear line of inheritance. Women, however, were bound to unconditional fidelity. They were not permitted extramarital sex relations, lest they endanger the legitimacy of their husbands' progeny. Virginity in women, but not in men, was considered a prime quality in the choice of a partner, and the marriage fee was fixed accordingly, with laws to enforce compliance. Polygamy, concubinage, and extramarital intercourse with slaves and prostitutes were legally countenanced for the male.

Adultery was prohibited to Israelite men (Ex 20:14, 17; Dt 5:18, 21) but only when the wife or betrothed of a fellow Israelite was involved (Dt 22:22; Ezek 16:40). No penalty was attached to having intercourse with a Gentile woman. According to Ex 22:15-16, the man who had intercourse with an unbetrothed Israelite virgin was required to pay the standard marriage price to the father and to marry the woman unless her father objected. Only later, in Deuteronomy, was the injury considered as having been done against the woman as well; the violator was required to marry her (whatever the father's wishes), and could never divorce her (Dt 22:28-9).

Clearly, the motivation behind Old Testament legislation had nothing to do with sexuality in itself. It stemmed rather from social and economic considerations and in some cases from respect for the personhood of women. A reflection of this is to be seen in the flexibility of Jewish practice in both postbiblical and biblical times. Certain communities of Jews in Asia and Africa countenanced polygamy from its Old Testament origins to our own time; in the meantime, Jews settling in Europe followed the laws prevailing in that area and maintained monogamy. While the social position of women, even in the period of the Deuteronomic reform, was in many ways inferior to that enjoyed by women in Egyptian and Mesopotamian cultures, the Elephantine colony of Jews in Egypt accorded the Jewish wife the same civil rights as enjoyed by her Egyptian sisters. She was able to obtain a divorce on her own action, to own property, to be a party to contracts, to inherit in her own name, and to pay taxes.¹⁰ Just how much the Old Testament took polygamy for granted may be seen from Ezechiel's parable, in which he describes God as the husband of two wives, Jerusalem and Samaria (Ezek 23).

The practice of levirate marriage in the Old Testament can also be explained largely by economics and the desire for progeny. Levirate marriage (*levir* = husband's brother) required that if a man died without leaving a male heir, his brother was bound to marry the widow and raise up a son, who would bear the dead man's name and his right to the family inheritance (Dt 25:5-10). The exact extent to which levirate marriage was practiced is unknown, but the purpose of the law is clear enough: to preserve the homogeneity of the family group and the name of its male members, as well as to safeguard the family estate and to ensure the welfare of the widow (Gen 38; Ru 4; Josephus). Levirate marriage and the provision of an heir for the deceased Israelite were meant to prevent dispute and litigation, which would be more likely to occur if a widow were to marry outside the family.¹¹

Against this background, one can understand the proper significance of the story of the punishment of Onan, formerly proposed as a divine prohibition against masturbation, birth control, and any "wasting" of the male seed. The sin of Onan, for which his premature death was seen as God's punishment, was not simply the fact that he "wasted his seed on the ground" (Gen 38:9). Neither was he punished simply because he refused to fulfill his levirate obligation to father an heir for his dead brother. The punishment for refusing to perform the obligation was to be degraded and insulted ceremonially (Dt 25:7-10). The issue, however, was ostensibly one of justice. By feigning to perform his levirate obligation, while actually preventing the possible conception of a male heir, Onan was trying to steal his dead brother's inheritance.¹²

## FIDELITY AND PERSONHOOD

The Old Testament paid its highest tribute to marriage when it presented the union of husband and wife as a symbol of the covenantal union and love between Yahweh and Israel. First appearing in Hos 2, the theme was taken up and developed by later prophets. At times the image was used to emphasize the dominion of God and the faithlessness of Israel (Ezek 16:23). In the light of the Covenant, Israel's infidelity was logically equated with adultery (Is 1:21) or with playing the harlot (Jer 3:6). In other passages, the symbolism is that of God's patient and enduring love (Hos 2; Is 54:4ff; 62:4ff; Jer 2:2), in testimony to the fact that love and tenderness were also integral to the Old Testament understanding of marriage and sexuality. Further evidence of this view is offered by the Canticle of Canticles. Although later interpreted as descriptive of the love between Yahweh and Israel, the Canticle is a collection of secular lyrics, affirming and even celebrating the goodness and joy of sexual love.

Extending over a period of some one thousand years, the Old Testament represents not only a plurality of attitudes toward sexuality but also a distinct development, particularly with regard to the dignity of the person. Since in the minds of the biblical authors secular prostitution was not easily distinguishable from the cultic practices associated with it, the prophets came to combat both with similar vigor (Jer 3:2). As a result, the original prohibition of sacred intercourse (Dt 23:18ff)[13] was interpreted in the Greek Septuagint translation as a general proscription of all prostitution among the chosen people. Wisdom literature equated secular prostitution with practices of ritual intercourse, and the wise men of Proverbs directed their longest and most dire warnings against prostitutes (Prov 6:23-35; 7:1-27; 9:13-18). It is not altogether clear that these warnings were morally based. In fact, as one commentator has observed, "It is remarkable that the entire Old Testament never manages a clear and unambiguous moral condemnation of prostitution."[14]

But neither does the Old Testament reach the moral neutrality of some ancient societies in which prostitutes were regarded as performing a useful and acceptable service. On the contrary, the Old Testament encouraged fidelity, urging the remembrance of the wife of one's youth and the joy that was shared (Prov 5:15-20). The state described in Genesis, in which a wife was meant to be a helper (Gen 2:18), became in Tobit an ideal to be striven for (Tob 8:1-10); a couple was to approach marriage not in lust but in a spirit of prayer. The mutual love of husband and wife was praised as pleasing to the Lord (Sir 25:1). And Malachi, underlining the personal meaning of marriage, warned against breaking faith with the wife of one's youth, for she is a "companion" and "wife by covenant" (Mal 2:14).

An underlying theme in the Old Testament, significant for the Christian attitude toward sex, is the notion of the "law of the heart" (Dt 6:4-6). Under the impact of the prophets, cultic notions of purity were interiorized and transformed into profound moral concepts. Without lessening the need to observe all the laws of the Torah, ritual precepts became subordinated to moral requirements (Is 1:11-17; Ps 15:2-5; 18:21-27; 24:4; Job 17:9; Prov 15:26). Jesus entered into and continued this prophetic tradition with his call to purity of heart (Mt 5:8; 23:25-26).

## THE NEW TESTAMENT

The New Testament, like the Old, does not attempt to provide a complete systematic ethics on sexual conduct. The sayings of Jesus and the writings of the New Testament Church on sexuality are all occasional, conditioned by particular questions arising from particular circumstances. Consequently, St. Paul's moral judgments or statements on sexuality cannot simply be taken out of context and applied to the situations of the present time. They represent the application of the gospel to the circumstances of the first century Christian community within the necessarily limited vision of that time. The lasting value of his directives is paradigmatic. Like the apostolic Church, the Church of today needs to apply the same gospel with its same values to very different circumstances, employing the broader vision and more accurate scientific information that two thousand years have since come to offer us.

It is also important to recognize the influence that natural philosophical ethics had on the New Testament. Just as Greek philosophy had an impact upon Hellenistic Judaism, so the ethics of the Stoics affected the thinking of St. Paul. The morality of the New Testament cannot simply be identified with that of the Old Testament. Cultural and social circumstances and religious viewpoints had changed. The moral directives of the New Testament have distinctive traits. There are values not found in the Old Testament, new insights derived principally from a new horizon, and a new motivation for moral activity. In interpreting the New Testament, therefore, we need to distinguish between what is original and what is derived, between declarations of essential importance and those of a peripheral quality. There is considerable difference between the letter of a law and the intent of the law, between the means used to protect a value in a moral decision and the moral value itself.

The theology of the New Testament regarding human sexuality, like that of the Old, is historically conditioned. The fundamental presupposition for all ethical statements in the New Testament, including sexual ethics, is that the Church is the community of the last days. Jesus preached that the Kingdom of God is at hand (Mk 1:15). St. Paul was convinced that "this world as we see it is passing away" (1 Cor 7:31).

Any exegesis of the New Testament, therefore, must be historical and critical. The total thrust of the New Testament teaching must be taken into consideration, with special attention given to the values and intentions that lie behind its ethical injunctions. Jesus himself practiced this kind of exegesis with respect to the question of divorce (Mt 5:31-32). He contradicted an explicit divine statute (Dt 11:1-4; 30:16) on the basis of the intent of the law and the fundamental values that it was meant to protect (Gen 1:27; 2:24).

## JESUS

The gospels witness not only to the Jesus of history but also to the post-Easter Church's faith in him as the Risen Christ. They contain not only factual information about him but also theological interpretation of his significance. Critical New Testament scholarship has come to recognize that it cannot produce a biography of Jesus or even in many instances guarantee his exact words. We do not have an in-depth portrait of him. But critical biblical scholarship is able to discern the outstanding features that distinguished Jesus most sharply from his contemporaries. Among these distinctive features of Jesus' teaching and attitudes, several have particular significance for a Christian ethics regarding sexuality.

As we know him from critical historical examination of the gospels, Jesus vigorously opposed the reduction of Jewish law to mere externals. He interiorized the law. Morality for him was more than the external observance of legal prescriptions (Mt 5:8). It is not by external actions that a person is rendered unclean, but by what comes out of the heart (Mt 15:1-20). Not only the action but adulterous intention is sinful (Mt 5:27-28). In taking this stance, Jesus stood within the tradition of the Pharisees, with whom the New Testament shows him in constant contact.

Like the prophets and some of the greatest Pharisees, such as Rabbi Hillel and later Rabbi Akiba, Jesus consistently resists the temptation to lose sight of the spirit of the Law amid technicalities and distinctions. For Jesus the intent of the Law was the welfare of people. Jesus subordinated the letter of the Law to human needs: "The Sabbath was made for man, and not man for the Sabbath" (Mk 2:27). This dictum was pronounced by Jesus in a passage in which he upheld the more lenient ruling of Hillel against the stricter interpretation of Shammai on the permissiveness of plucking and eating corn on the Sabbath (Shabbat 7, 2; 128ab).[15] Jesus stood for humanizing the law. For him, it is precisely our joy, our healing and wholeness (salvation), the happiness here and hereafter of people that constitutes the will of God (Jn 15:11). Such were the "weightier matters" of the Law on which he insisted (Mt 23:23).

Jesus, the "man for others" (Bonhoeffer), struggled in defense of the defenseless. He championed the cause of the oppressed and despised (Mk 2:15; 3:10-11; 8:2; 10:13-16; Jn 8:1-11). It is in this context that his affirmative attitude toward women can best be understood.[16] Jesus openly associated with women (Lk 8:2ff), took compassion on them (Mk 1:29-31;

5:21-43; 7:24-30; Lk 7:11-17; 13:10-17), spoke of them in his parables (Mt 13:33; Lk 15:8ff; 18:1ff), and numbered them among his intimate friends (Lk 10:38-42; Jn 11). He showed little trace of the common ancient (and modern) assumption that women are inferior. While there is no single statement of Jesus that can be taken as a definite program in this respect, his behavior spoke louder than any words.

Jesus' egalitarian attitude toward women and concern for the oppressed explain his revolutionary stand on divorce (Mk 10:2-12; Mt 5:31-32; 19:3-9; Lk 16:18), one of his most distinctive moral teachings and one of the surest we can ascribe to him. If a man found adequate cause—"something indecent"— the Mosaic Law permitted him to dismiss his wife with a bill of divorce (Dt 24:1). The rabbis argued over what exactly constituted adequate cause for divorce.[17] Jesus interpreted the Law in terms of its purpose, which, indirectly at least, was to circumscribe the arbitrariness of a husband and protect his wife; the law prevented a husband from divorcing his wife on caprice, by demanding grounds and orderliness. Jesus' prohibition of divorce was a means of protecting women from exploitation. He forbade treating women as chattel, disposing of them at will and leaving them without financial support. He regarded them instead, as partners in marriage (Mk 10:2ff). As recognized earlier by the prophet Malachi (Mal 2:13-14, 16) and by some rabbis,[18] one value which the Law was meant to protect was marital fidelity. Thus Jesus required obedience to the spirit and intent of the Law.[19]

Jesus did not proclaim a new sexual ethic as such; rather, he centered attention on the best thinking of his day by placing men and women on the same level not merely in theory but also in real life. The golden rule applied to all, not only to men (Mt 7:12). A Talmudic saying likewise posited an equality of male and female before God:

> The compassion of God is not as the compassion of men. The compassion of men extends to men more than to women, but not thus is the compassion of God. His compassion extends equally to all (Sifre, Nm, Pinehas, 133).

This divine compassion characterized Jesus' whole ministry. For both Rabbinic Judaism and the New Testament, there was to be no distinction between male and female before God (Gal 3:28; Seder Eliyahu Rabbah IX, XIV). Jesus was thus able to break through the androcentric double standard of ancient society.

Taking the insights of Deuteronomy to their logical conclusion, Jesus made the same requirements of both sexes. He placed men and women equally under the same double law of love (Mk 12:30-31, taken by Jesus from Dt 6:4-9 and Lev 19:18). Jesus would have agreed with, and in fact lived out, the principle underlying the Talmudic dictum, which praises the man who "loves his wife as himself, and honors her more than himself" (Yeb 63a; San 76b). Had Judaism and Christianity ever fully implemented such a notion, the ancient world would have been revolutionized from within.

The gospels present Jesus as an ethical model, and the Christian life as one of following Jesus (Mk 8:34; 10:21; Jn 13:15), especially in his unselfish love (Jn 13:34), service (Mk 10:44-45; Jn 13:1-15), and forgiveness (Mt 6:12; Lk 17:3-4). The personalism of Jesus and the primacy that he gave to the law of love (Mk 12:28-34) have profound implications for sexual ethics (Lk 7:36-50).

Jesus' teaching on marriage is limited for the most part to his affirmation of fidelity in prohibiting divorce. The gospels build on this in describing Jesus and his mission with the image of a wedding feast. In the tradition of the rabbis who were accustomed to use the wedding feast as a sign of messianic fulfillment, Jesus is compared to a bridegroom (Mt 25:1-13; **Mk** 2:19), and the kingdom of God to a marriage banquet **(Mt** 22:1-14). In viewing the union of man and woman as a messianic symbol, the gospels demonstrate an affirmation of marriage and of the joy that accompanies it. The same attitude can be seen in the story of Jesus at the wedding feast in Cana (Jn 2:1-12).

On the other hand, the New Testament shows Jesus as unmarried and presenting as an ideal to be emulated those who have "made themselves eunuchs for the sake of the kingdom"

(Mt 19:12). There is a long-standing tradition in the Church of interpreting these words in Matthew as an invitation to consecrated virginity. The context for the saying, however, is Jesus' teaching on marriage and divorce. A good case can be made for interpreting this dictum on celibacy for the kingdom not as an insert, but as a continuation of the preceding teaching on divorce, referring to those who have separated from their wives because of adultery.[20] Jesus' call, in this case, is not to consecrated virginity but to marital fidelity. If this interpretation is correct, the reason for the amazement of Jesus' hearers becomes clear: the ideal of loyalty and dedication to one marriage partner should withstand even infidelity and separation. This interpretation fits into the tendency in Matthew to omit anything like a call to virginity.[21]

Unlike Matthew or Mark, Luke speaks explicitly about renouncing marriage. To the list of home, brothers, sisters, and parents, who are to be renounced for the sake of the gospel (Mt 10:37; 19:29; Mk 10:29), Luke adds the wife (Lk 18:29). In doing so, the evangelist cannot be accused of falsifying the mind of Jesus. Even though Jesus' immediate disciples were married (Mk 1:29-31; 1 Cor 9:5), marriage could only be seen as this-worldly (Mt 24:37-39). With the advent of the kingdom, a new age was in the offing. Marriage was seen as only a temporary condition of a world that was passing away (Mk 12:25).

## St. Paul

Following the events of Jesus' death and resurrection, the disciples became the Church. The messenger became the message, and the preaching about the kingdom became a preaching about the Christ. Jesus' followers regarded Easter as the divine affirmation of his gospel, but only as a beginning (1 Cor 15:20); the Church looked forward to a final consummation with Christ's second coming, this time in glory. In its eager anticipation the New Testament Church expected the consummation to come quickly (1 Thes 5; 2 Thes 2). The time was short (1 Cor 7:29ff).

It is important to keep in mind this expectation of Christ's imminent return in order to understand the teaching of St. Paul on sexuality. St. Paul has been unfairly accused of a Hellenistic antipathy toward the body and its sexuality. But regarding sex St. Paul was very much a Jew of his day: sex is a fact of creation, and hence it is good (1 Cor 7:5). It was his conviction that this world was passing away (1 Cor 7:31); as a result, St. Paul encouraged the unmarried to prepare for Christ's impending return without the encumbrances of marriage (1 Cor 7:26-27).

Another factor to be kept in mind in interpreting St. Paul is the moral climate that constituted the background of his ministry and the context of his epistles. The Greeks of the ancient world distinguished between love and sexual pleasure. Theirs was a depersonalized and depersonalizing attitude toward sexuality, summarized succinctly in a citation out of Attic Greece:

> We have prostitutes for our pleasure, concubines for every day needs, and wives to raise our legitimate children and to have as dependable guardians of the home.[22]

Prostitution was rampant at the time of St. Paul. Men, married and unmarried, could have sexual intercourse with slaves and prostitutes without qualm or scandal. The degeneracy of the Hellenistic-Roman world explains the many New Testament allusions to prostitution and warnings against it (Rom 1:24; Gal 5:19ff; Eph 5:3, 5; Col 3:5; 1 Thes 4:3ff) particularly in St. Paul's epistles to the church at Corinth (1 Cor 5:9-12; 6:9; 6:15-20; 2 Cor 12:21). Even to the pagans of the time, the harbor city of Corinth was notorious for vice. Its temple to Aphrodite was serviced by a thousand prostitutes, and a common Greek name for a prostitute was a "Corinthian girl."

The Greek word for prostitution (*porneia*), derived from a verb meaning "to sell," was a term used especially of slaves; Greek prostitutes were usually purchased slaves. Although its original meaning was limited, the term broadened gradually and came to be identified with extramarital relations, adultery, sodomy, unlawful marriage, and even sexual intercourse in general without further precision. At times in the New Testament (Acts 15:20, 29; 21:25; 1 Cor 5:1ff), the word is used to prohibit marriage within the degrees of kinship forbidden by the Old Testament (Lev 18:6-18). Elsewhere (1 Cor 6:9; Gal 5:19; Eph 5:5; Col 3:5; Heb 13:4; Apoc 2:14), the condemnation referred to intercourse with prostitutes. In each of these instances, however, the Greek *porneia* was translated into the Latin vulgate as *fornicatio*, a translation which led many to interpret the New Testament condemnation of prostitution as including all forms of premarital sexual intercourse. Only in two instances (1 Cor 6:9; Heb 13:4) does the New Testament distinguish prostitution from adultery. The two concepts had become closely identified already in Old Testament wisdom literature (Prov 2:16ff; 6:26ff). In Malachi, God demanded that husbands be faithful to their wives (Mal 2:14). And Jesus wiped away the Old Testament double standard altogether: infidelity is adultery for husbands as well as for wives (Mk 10:10-12). But not only extramarital intercourse constitutes adultery. Fidelity for Jesus is a value to be maintained in attitude as well as in action, a matter of the heart (Mt 5:28).

Jesus interiorized the Law, and his interiorization of fidelity finds a parallel in St. Paul's use of the concept "passion," "lust," or "desire," expressed in the word *epithumia*. Originally the word denoted the direct impulse toward food, sexual satisfaction, or simply desire in general. This usage is frequently seen in New Testament references to hunger (Lk 15:16), longing (Lk 22:15), and even a desire for God's word and revelation (Mt 13:17). Under Stoic influence, however, passion and desire took on pejorative connotations. Indifference, aloofness from the sensual world, *apatheia*, became the virtues of the true philosopher. The wise man was counseled to struggle against his passions, which were regarded as the source of sin.[23]

The Old Testament was not unaware of the need for discipline of the senses (2 Sam 11:2; Job 31:1); after the exile, an emphasis on bodily discipline was conjoined in Hellenistic Judaism with Stoic moralism (4 Mac; Philo). The merger finds expression in St. Paul, who, like the Church after him, saw the Stoics as allies against libertinism. The alliance was a fateful one for Christian ethics, particularly in its evaluation of pleasure and the emotions. In the tradition of the Stoics, St. Paul warned against the passion of desire (1 Thes 4:5) and summed up the tenth commandment with a simple "You shall not covet" (Rom 7:7; 13:9). Unlike the Stoics, however, St. Paul saw obedience to the will of God, not reason, as the antithesis of *epithumia*. Often translated in the Latin as *concupiscentia*, passion was shown as arising from sin (Rom 1:24) and leading to sin (Rom 7:7ff). Although paralleled with the desires of the will (Eph 2:3), passion was related to pleasure (Tit 3:3): passion is seeking of pleasure, and pleasure is the satisfaction of passion. The Stoic aversion toward both has influenced Christian ethical thinking from the time of St. Paul to our own.

In St. Paul's mind, sensual license (*aselgeia*) and impurity or uncleanness (*akatharsia*) were associated with prostitution (Gal 5:19; 2 Cor 12:21) and passion (1 Thes 4:5, 7). The opposite of Christian holiness (Rom 6:19; 2 Cor 12:21; 1 Thes 4:7), *aselgeia* and *akatharsia* were listed among the works that prevent entrance into the kingdom of God (Gal 5:19, 21). But impurity is not limited to the sexual domain; it can pertain to motivation as well (1 Thes 2:3). Although the concept was derived from the Old Testament cultic views of clean and unclean, the New Testament continued the tradition of the prophets, in which purity pertains to interior morality. Impurity for St. Paul denoted the condition of unredeemed man, whose commitment is to his own desires instead of to God (Rom 1:24; Eph 4:19).

Likewise open to misunderstanding, are St. Paul's warnings against inclinations of the flesh (Rom 8:6) and the works of the flesh (Gal 5:19). The word "flesh" (*sarx*) meant something quite different to St. Paul than it does to us. The Old Testament used the term to designate all that is temporal and passing, all that is weak, corruptible, and therefore mortal. Standing in the Old Testament tradition, St. Paul included among the sins of the flesh not only immorality (*porneia*), impurity (*akatharsia*), and sensual license (*aselgeia*), but also jealousy, anger, and even an exaggerated zeal for the Mosaic Law (Gal 5:19; 3:3). Similarly, among those who will not enter into the kingdom of God, he listed not only those who engaged in prostitution, adultery, and homosexual behavior,[24] but also the intemperate and greedy (1 Cor 6:9-10).

The biblical notion of flesh embraces the total human person with all his physical and moral corruptibility. St. Paul's references to the flesh are by no means synonymous with the body or its materiality, as if contrasted to the soul, the spiritual component of human nature. This reading of Platonic dualism into the biblical ideas of spirit and flesh has led in the past to a false ascetical ideal, in which the body was despised and spirituality or holiness were identified with a rejection of physical pleasure, including the pleasure of sex.

The most extensive teaching on sexuality in St. Paul, and in the entire New Testament is found in 1 Cor 7, dealing with problems of marriage and celibacy. The whole chapter is dominated by St. Paul's expectation of Christ's imminent return in glory. Another possible influence on Paul's views may have been the new ascetical movements at Corinth, which required complete sexual abstinence even for the married (7:1). In the light of Christ's impending return, Paul prized celibacy above marriage (7:7; 34:38, 40); the time was short (7:29), and he would have the Corinthian Christians free from care (7:32). Paul recognized, however, that not everyone had the gift of celibacy (7:7), and, for those who did not, marriage was preferable to "being aflame with passion" (7:9). Paul rejected the contention of those zealous ascetics who held that marriage is a sin and that the married should abstain altogether from sexual relations (7:2-3). If a husband and wife mutually agree to abstain from sexual intercourse for the sake of prayer, it should be only for a time (7:5). Recognizing that prolonged continence can lead to temptation, Paul encouraged regular intercourse within marriage.

In the same passage Paul acknowledged Jesus' prohibition of divorce. Fidelity is a command of the Lord (7:10-11). In the light of that command, Paul counseled Corinthian Christians to remain together with their spouses, even if they were non-Christian. There were certain other values, however, which Paul considered of equal importance with marital fidelity. "If a peaceful life together is not possible, then the Christian spouse is no longer bound" (7:12-16); the marriage may be dissolved. Paul did not say whether, in such a case, remarriage was to be regarded as permissible; he took it for granted.[25]

After encouraging maintenance of the status quo in socio-economic as well as marital matters (7:17-24), St. Paul gave his reasons for preferring celibacy over marriage. Both Jewish and Christian apocalypses (Mk 13:5ff; Apoc 6:8-9) invariably described the tribulation that would precede the beginning of the messianic age. This "impending distress" (7:26) led Paul to counsel detachment, for the world, as they knew it, was passing away (7:27-31). In such a state of affairs, Paul considered marriage as a distraction from service to the Lord (7:32-35). Yet, despite his personal preferences, he acknowledged the lawfulness and goodness of marriage (7:36-38). Widows likewise could remarry if they wished to do so (7:39-40). St. Paul refused to lay down restraints curtailing Christian liberty (7:35). The champion of the freedom of the sons of God (Gal 4) refused to make his opinions into ordinances. Everyone had his own gift from God (7:7), and God's gifts cannot be legislated.

Even after the time of St. Paul and not only in Corinth, the New Testament Church was constrained to uphold the honorableness of marriage against an exaggerated asceticism (Heb 13:4). John the Baptist was an ascetic, and Jesus spoke of him with high regard (Mt 11:7-14). But Jesus was not noted for strenuous asceticism himself (Mt 11:19). His Jewish faith emphasized the goodness of creation (Gen 1:31). In going out to the Gentiles, however, the early Church had to confront ascetic currents, probably Gnostic in origin (Col 2:8, 16, 20-23). The deutero-pauline letters indicate that there were Christians who required abstinence from certain foods and prohibited marriage (1 Tim 4:3). The New Testament Church resisted these demands in the name of the goodness of creation (1 Tim 4:4; cf also 2:15; 5:14); but the trend continued. St. Irenaeus in the 2nd century spoke of false teachers who maintained that "marriage and procreation are spawn of the devil" (Adv. haer., 1, 23, 2).

Against those who would disparage marriage and sexuality, the epistle to the Ephesians exalted married life into a symbol of the union of Christ and the Church (Eph 5:22-33). That a man and his wife become one is a great "mystery," not in the sense of an enigma, but as a revelation of profound significance. The unity pronounced by God in the beginning between a husband and wife was taken as prophetic of the unity between Christ and the Church (Eph 5:32; cf also 2 Cor 11:2). This comparison enjoined upon every Christian couple the task of witnessing by their mutual love and respect the abiding presence of Christ in the Church. "If celibacy is the sign of the Church's expectation of her Lord, then one can and must say of marriage that it is the sign already present of the already realized union of Christ and the Church."[26]

Besides unity and love, however, the comparison of marriage to the relationship of Christ and the Church also speaks to another aspect of sexuality: the subordinate position of women. As Christ is the head of the Church, a husband is "head" of his wife; wives are to be "subject" to their husbands as to the Lord (Eph 5:21ff; Col 3:18; 1 Pet 3:1-6).

There is evident in the early Church a growing divergence between theory and practice in the matter of woman's status. The New Testament Church accepted Jesus' revolutionary attitude toward women in theory. Women were "co-heirs" of the grace of life (1 Pet 3:7). St. Paul's affirmation that there is no difference between male and female is the clearest statement of the dignity of women in the entire New Testament (Gal 3:28). Women took an active role in the life of the New Testament Church, rendering practical assistance (Acts 9:36ff; 16:15), instruction (Acts 18:26), and diaconal leadership (Rom 16:1ff). Social custom, however, militated against the original feminist impulse in Christianity, and Jesus' revolutionary personalism toward women was gradually submerged. Silence and submission came to be imposed on women (1 Cor 14:34; 1 Tim 2:11ff). Marriage in the first century was too patriarchal to allow for any other outcome. With the elevation of marriage to a symbol of Christ and the Church, the socio-cultural status of women became canonized into an ideal; a state of affairs was seen as sanctioned by the divine will. Women were to be honored, but precisely as the "weaker" sex (1 Pet 3:7).

If the Bible is characterized by conflicting motifs with respect to women, it is no less so in regard to humanity in general and sexuality in particular. There is a tension in Scripture, not only regarding specific issues, such as celibacy or asceticism, and not merely because of extrinsic influences, like those of Greek philosophy or cultural forms. Together with the clear development toward personalism, fidelity, and the primacy of love, there are also opposing principles lying at the very heart of biblical anthropology.

On the one hand, the Bible pronounces the world and all that is in it as good, including humanity and its sexuality (Gen 1:31). It is not good for a man to be alone (Gen 2:18). Sexual fertility is a blessing (Gen 1:28). Humankind is created in the image and likeness of God, sharing in God's dominion over the earth (Gen 1:26). Although dominion is the original significance of humanity's likeness to God, it does not exhaust the meaning; Scripture reveals a God who is not only Lord but Love (Dt 7:8; 1 Jn 4:8). Humanity mirrors God not through individuals but precisely through men and women in relationship (Gen 1:27). Incomplete in themselves, men and women are made for relatedness; human sexuality is a dramatic expression of that relatedness (Gen 2:18).[27]

While the biblical doctrine of creation affirms sexuality and sexual pleasure as good, biblical eschatology, on the other hand has led sexual pleasure to be viewed as problematic. Christianity looks forward to a fulfillment in which sexuality and sexual pleasure are explicitly excluded (Mk 12:25). As adopted sons and heirs (Rom 8:17), partakers of the divine nature (2 Pet 1:4), Christians see themselves called to a happiness greater than any that can be conceived (1 Cor 2:9), a happiness utterly transcending pleasure of any kind, particularly sexual pleasure. Ever since St. Paul, abstinence from sexual pleasure has been seen as an anticipation of that future fulfillment (1 Cor 7), and passionate desire for pleasure as contrary to holiness (1 Thes 4:5). As a result, Christian tradition and spirituality have tended to see a certain incompatibility between sexual pleasure and sanctity. Living a sex life somehow does not seem to fit into living the divine life fully.[28]

## SUMMARY

The foregoing survey, schematic as it is, demonstrates clearly that the Bible does not provide us with a simple yes or no code of sexual ethics. No single text or collection of texts constitutes anything like a coherent biblical theology of human sexuality. Scripture is not even concerned with sexuality as such, regarding it instead as one aspect of life, properly viewed only within the context of the whole person and the whole of human life with all its relationships and responsibilities.

The Old Testament contains such a plurality of customs, laws, and insights related to sexuality, that no single voice can be said to prevail. Throughout the Old Testament, however, one can clearly perceive the influence of taboos regarding cultic purity and of the patriarchal form of marriage and society. While monogamy seemed to be held up as an ideal state (Gen 2:24), polygamy and, for the male, even concubinage were tolerated. Only adultery with the wife or betrothed of a fellow Israelite was consistently condemned, and this in such a way as to make clear that the reason for the condemnation is to be found not in the nature of human sexuality but in the familial and societal responsibilities owed to members of the same community. The Old Testament view of women ranged from regarding them as chattel (Exodus) or objects of disdain (Sirach) to the affirmation of their personhood (Deuteronomy). Women function in the biblical narratives in a variety of ways from leaders, prophets, and judges to mere sex objects. Recognized as good in itself, sexual activity was condemned when even remotely associated with the fertility rituals of Israel's heathen neighbors. Yet marriage and erotic imagery were often used (Hosea, Canticle of Canticles) to describe the sacred covenantal union between God and Israel.

As in the Old Testament, every statement in the New Testament regarding human sexuality is historically occasioned and conditioned. Jesus did not proclaim any new sexual ethic as such. Of indirect but profound significance for any Christian ethics of sexuality, however, are Jesus' teaching on the essential equality of men and women, his prohibition of divorce affirming fidelity within marriage for both sexes, and the primacy he gave to the law of love; in short, his personalism. Jesus' affirmation of human dignity led him to resist legalistic casuistry and to insist on the "weightier matters" of the Law, namely, its spirit and intent. Jesus humanized the Law in the sense that, for him, it was precisely our joy, our holiness as wholeness, human welfare and well-being, that constituted the will of God.

Jesus' affirmation of human dignity and his attitude toward law resounded in St. Paul, particularly in his championing of Christian equality (Gal 3) and freedom (Gal 4). In opposition to exaggerated asceticism, St. Paul affirmed the goodness and lawfulness of sex (1 Cor 7) but unhesitatingly expressed his personal preference for celibacy in light of the return of Christ in glory, which Paul regarded as imminent. St. Paul's eschatology, the depraved moral climate of his day, and the influence of Stoic philosophy on his thought must all be kept in mind for the correct interpretation of his references to marriage and sex related matters.

Employing the historical critical method of interpretation, contemporary biblical scholarship makes it clear that we cannot validly abstract statements regarding sexuality out of their biblical context and use them as proof texts to validate any twentieth-century theology of human sexuality. It is not that Scripture has failed to answer current problems and questions regarding premarital sexual intercourse, masturbation, birth control, and the like. Our questions simply were not asked by the biblical authors; hence, answers to these questions should not be expected from them.

Looking at the plurality of the statements and attitudes on human sexuality in the Bible, the inconsistencies among them, and the historical circumstances that gave rise to them, critical biblical scholarship finds it impossible on the basis of the empirical data to approve or reject categorically any particular sexual act outside of its contextual circumstances and intention. In view of the weight of contrary historical evidence, anyone who maintains that the Bible absolutely forbids certain forms of sexual behavior, regardless of circumstances, must likewise bear the burden of proof.

This is not to say, however, that the Bible leaves us without ideals or any guidance whatever. Scripture provides us with certain fundamental themes as a basis on which to construct a modern theology of human sexuality. Despite changing historical circumstances and perspectives, the biblical authors consistently give common witness to the nature of God as gracious and loving, and to the ideal of fidelity as a foremost expression of our loving response. While the Bible does not provide absolute dictates about specific sexual practices, it declares that sexual intercourse is good, always to be seen, however, within the larger context of personhood and community.

## II

# Christian Tradition and Human Sexuality

### THE FATHERS OF THE CHURCH (2nd to 5th Century)

The Fathers of the Church, following the tradition of Jesus and his apostles, did not resolve the prevailing ambivalent attitude of Christians toward sexuality. They reaffirmed what had been taught in an earlier age regarding the unity and indissolubility of marriage,[1] the reciprocal duties of spouses,[2] the purity of heart and fidelity that should characterize conjugal relations.[3]

The patristic doctrine of marriage, however, was influenced by several factors proper to this era. There were: (1) errors resulting from current pagan religious and philosophical thought; (2) the increasing priority accorded virginity and celibacy as evangelical, Christian values; (3) the development of a concept of sacramentality of marriage and the emergence of ecclesiastical legislation in the domain of sexual discipline. The manner in which the Fathers addressed each of these challenges helped to shape their attitude and teaching on sexuality in general.

### The Fathers in a Pagan World

The Fathers reacted to a way of life marked by decadence attributable to several factors: a too anthropomorphic concept of the deities, sexual practices associated with idolatry and with the matriarchal divinities, and certain sophisticated speculations in Greek thought. Within paganism, serious philosophers and poets inveighed against the widespread corruption that signaled the deterioration of state and religion in the Graeco-Roman world.

Within the Christian community, the Fathers combated two excessive tendencies developing out of a dualistic *Weltanschauung*, which perceived spirit and matter either as totally incompatible or as inseparably identified. On the one hand, Encratites,[4] Gnostics,[5] Montanists,[6] Novatians,[7] and Priscillianists[8] vied with one another in the pursuit of ascetic extremes. For Christians influenced by these groups, marriage was a state of lesser or greater sin, continence was an obligation, and second marriages were to be avoided. On the other hand, another view of Gnosticism[9] led to an erroneous confusion of virginity and marriage, general sexual laxity, and such practices as the curious institution of the *syneisaktoi* (cohabitation of celibates).[10]

Confronted by extremes of rabid asceticism and antinomian eroticism, the Church Fathers found inspiration in Stoicism. Here, again, a certain exaggeration prevailed, as in the emphasis, for example, on the ideal of the emotionless wise man who does not move even his finger without a purpose.[11] Following this train of thought, sexual intercourse was to be engaged in only for the procreation of children. Sexual abstinence was held to be as praiseworthy after marriage as it was before. Under the influence of the Stoa, the Fathers taught that sexual intercourse was forbidden when a man's wife was already pregnant. It was regarded as unreasonable to sow seed in a field that had already been planted.[12]

As a result of such views, there arose in time a double standard of morality: one for weaker, "ordinary" Christians and another for those called to a "higher" life.[13] A more positive view is represented by Clement of Alexandria, who defended marriage against Gnostic attempts to reject it. For Clement, the purpose of marriage was not restricted to the procreation of children. The mutual love, support and assistance that the partners extend to each other unite them in an eternal bond.[14]

*The Fathers on Marriage and Virginity*

In the early fourth century, as Christianity achieved recognition and acceptance in the Roman Empire, virginity and the ascetic life replaced martyrdom as a way to complete Christlikeness.[15] Discussions of marriage were marked by a comparison, not necessarily disadvantaged, with virginity. If marriage is the sign of the union between Christ and his Church (Eph 5:22-32), virginity is the reality by which the virgin signifies that the *ekklesia* is the bride of the Lord.[16]

By and large, the doctrine of the Fathers at this time remained balanced. An unfaithful monk or virgin was never considered superior to a faithful husband or wife, father or mother. However, the treatises of the Fathers on the virginal life seem to express a certain disregard for marriage.[17] The preeminence attributed to virginity in this period laid the foundation for later exaggerations in the teaching on marriage.[18]

Despite this ambivalence, the consistent teachings of the Fathers reaffirmed the value of marriage and rejected those positions that favored virginity by holding marriage in contempt.[19] The doctrine of both the Greek and Latin Fathers is removed from such errors.[20] It is only when the polemical, occasional, rhetorical style of the patristic argument is recognized that the patristic view of marriage can be rightly evaluated.[21]

*Sacramentality and Legislation of Marriage During the Patristic Age*

The Fathers contributed to a slowly developing concept of Christian marriage as a symbol of the mystical union between Jesus and his bride, the Church. Ignatius of Antioch taught that the *episcopos* ought to preside at marriages between Christians.[22] Tertullian was the first to bear witness to a ceremony of marriage following an accepted, fixed ritual.[23] Both he and Cyprian used the word, *sacramentum*, although the meaning is less precise than that to be developed later by Augustine.

In the Ante-Nicene period there was clearly general agreement that marriage had been "instituted" by Christ. Christian marriage assured to the spouses special graces for mutual support and sanctification. Marriage between Christians was far superior to the union of pagans because the former was the sign and symbol of Christ's union with his Church.[24] This early attitude was reflected in a later period as, for example, in Jerome's reminder to Christian spouses that their relations are to be holy, since their very union is holy.[25]

The earliest Church legislation concerning Christian marriage is found in the canons of the Council of Elvira (AD 306).[26] The laws enunciated at this and following councils or synods point to the consciousness of the Church in regard to the power she held to maintain and apply the teachings of Jesus on Christian marriage. Over and above this responsibility, the Church felt empowered to add, according to circumstances, other necessary prescriptions in this matter. By the time of St. Augustine, a list of "impediments" was already in existence and the practice prevailed of imposing penalties, particularly in the case of marriages contracted in opposition to the laws of unity and indissolubility.

The attitude of the Fathers toward Christian marriage was, in the last analysis, manifested in practice rather than in theory. The Fathers looked on Christian marriage as that union which had been instituted by Jesus Christ and sanctified by him. It was blessed by the Church. Thus, it was the "sacrament" that became a source of holiness and of grace, symbolizing the relationship between Jesus Christ and his Church.

## The Teaching of St. Augustine

Research into the origins of Christian attitudes toward sexuality tends to identify St. Augustine as the thinker whose teaching has largely prevailed into our own times.[27] Augustine's teaching on sexuality and marriage is contained in several of his works: *De continentia, De bono conjugali, De sancta virginitate, De bono viduitatis, De nuptiis et concupiscentia.* In these writings, the patristic doctrine of the Ante-Nicene period is preserved and condensed.

Augustine's thought, however, surpasses that of the earlier Fathers, especially in reference to the moral value of the conjugal act. Because the procreation of children is the end of marriage, the conjugal act, for Augustine, is sinless even though he cannot identify any other human act which provides an occasion for the transmission of original sin.[28] It is legitimate[29] and honorable.[30] The conjugal act is a duty.[31] Like food and study, which are the necessary means to such goods as health and wisdom, the conjugal act is good, insofar as it is directed toward the end to which it is naturally ordered.[32]

For Augustine, the goods of marriage are found in its end —children; in its law—the mutual fidelity of the spouses; in its sacramental significance—the indissoluble union between the spouses.[33] There can be no doubt but that the doctrine of marriage was furthered through St. Augustine.

Nevertheless, his teaching was both paradoxical and ambiguous.[34] Augustine's personal experience of sinfulness in his own sexuality had a strong bearing on his attitude toward this dimension of human life. Strains of an earlier Manichaeism were reflected in his arguments to combat the errors of the Pelagians,[35] and inevitably filtered into Christian thought. It must be noted, too, that later thinkers made selective use of Augustine's theology, concentrating primarily on his pessimism.[36] Such selectivity led, for example, to the identification of the very feeling of sexual pleasure as the consequence of man's fall and as a sin.[37]

At the end of the patristic era, the Christian attitude toward human sexuality was generally pessimistic.[38] Although sexuality of itself was recognized as good because of its procreative function, the pleasure attached to sex was viewed as a consequence of original sin. The experience of sexual pleasure, therefore, even indeliberate, and even within marriage for the purpose of procreation, was regarded somehow as tainted with sin.[39] This attitude, however, did not necessarily reflect the full experience of the total Church.[40] To a lesser extent, the Fathers also recognized the values of mutual love and support between husband and wife.[41] Gregory Nazianzen, Cyril of Jerusalem, and John Chrysostom, among others, have left inspiring considerations and instructions on the divine origins of marriage[42] and the fruits that shared love bears in the lives of children.[43] A conjugal spirituality developed as Christians were exhorted to contemplate the ecclesial and Christological dimensions of the mystery of marriage,[44] ratified by the Holy Spirit of God.[45]

The understanding of "the role of sexuality . . . as a vital element in the full development of the individual person"[46] was necessarily limited, during the patristic era, to the scientific perceptions of the age. This limitation further influenced the attitude of the Fathers toward women—an attitude expressed in ways which, at times, seem to contradict one another. The Fathers were neither as anti-feminist as some authors would claim nor as pro-feminist as some others would hope. They praised the exemplary wife and faithful virgin even as they supported the diminishment of woman's participation in the mission and ministry of the Church.

In conclusion, it must be affirmed once again that no clearly defined or consistent theology of sexuality marks the patristic period. The early Christians, like those who came after them, lived realities before they theorized about their value and essential qualities.[47] They left unfinished for future ages the task of considering "human sexuality . . . in its appropriate relationships with the whole person" and of recognizing that "the concept of Christian love and the interpersonal values it represents must contribute to our understanding of sexuality itself."[48]

## EARLY MIDDLE AGES (6th to 10th Century)

An interesting insight into the prevailing sexual attitudes and values of the early Middle Ages is provided by the "penitentials," i.e., handbooks containing penances for various offenses intended to guide confessors in their pastoral care of penitents. Many of the attitudes found in the writings of the patristic period continued to find echo in the more concrete and specific provisions of these penitentials.

Sexuality was viewed fundamentally as a creation of God and hence basically good. Procreation was the dominant, though not exclusive, value for which sexuality was intended. Sexual intercourse to fulfill one's marital duty was accepted on the authority of the Apostle Paul. A majority of writers, however, rejected the opinion that married couples could engage in intercourse simply to avoid temptation and prevent infidelity. This attitude obviously reflected a carry-over of the Stoic distrust of pleasure as evil because it impaired and weakened the mind's power of judgment, and for this reason was regarded as an affront to human dignity.

The fact that the writers of the penitentials were not completely convinced of the Stoic principle against pleasure is reflected in the pastoral clemency with which transgressions were treated. Even though continence was enjoined upon the partners in a barren marriage, no penalty was indicated for a violation of this injunction—an indirect and tacit recognition that sexual expression, even when procreation is impossible, is not always a serious violation of man's nature and dignity.[49]

Other cultural and historical influences are reflected in various prohibitions concerning sexuality. Married couples, for instance, were forbidden to engage in intercourse during menstruation in the belief that this would result in malformed children.[50] The concept of ritual purity led to prohibition against sexual relations at various sacred times. Illustrative of the latter notion are precepts to refrain from the marriage act on Sunday, holy days, and other sacred seasons of the year as well as before receiving communion.[51]

Even in their somewhat elementary approach to morality, however, the penitentials were not simplistic in pretending that they could assign an absolute moral evaluation to every sexual act. They reflect, rather, a somewhat sophisticated appreciation of the various considerations that must enter into a judgment on the gravity of any sexual offense. Among the more important factors of evaluation cited in the penitentials are the following:

(1) The degree of consciousness or malicious intent of the offender proportionately increased the gravity of any offense. For example, for unintentional pollution, the

penitent was assigned the recitation of 15 psalms; if pollution resulted from deliberately entertained provocative thoughts, this penance was increased to seven days of fast on bread and water.

(2) The repetition of forbidden acts or a habitual disposition to perform them was regarded as far more serious than an isolated offense. For example, a penance of one hundred days for the first offense of masturbation was extended to a year if the action was repeated.

(3) The misdeeds of clerics were treated far more severely than those of the laity on the assumption that the state of life of the person contributed much to the evil of the action and hence made it more destructive of the community. For offenses of fornication, clerics of lower rank were assigned a penance of three years; deacons, five years; priests, seven years; and bishops, twelve years.

(4) The possible or actual consequences resulting from any action increased the seriousness of the moral offense. For example, a layman who had committed fornication received a penance of one year on bread and water; if a child was begotten from the union, the penance was increased to three years.

The attitudes toward human sexuality reflected in these prescriptions were undoubtedly heavily influenced by the limited understanding of biology prevalent at the time, by the sense of cultic purity, by the Stoic mistrust of pleasure, and by a dominant emphasis on the procreative purpose of sexuality. Beneath the surface, however, we can discern, especially in the intricate rules for regulating sexual conduct, an appreciation of human sexuality as a powerful force in maintaining personal dignity and in building human community. Whatever threatened or violated these fundamental values was regarded as immoral and sinful. The social and cultural influences of the times may have resulted in some misplaced emphases and unwarranted prohibitions. The concern for individual dignity and the common good, however, reveal some appreciation, albeit imperfect, of the more basic, constant and unchanging moral principle for evaluating human sexuality. The eventual disappearance of sanctions for sexual activity among elderly married couples was indicative of a slow, gradual movement away from the pleasure-fearing and procreation-dominated outlook to a more positive and person-oriented appreciation of human sexuality.

## HIGH MIDDLE AGES (11th to 14th Century)

In the High Middle Ages, attitudes toward sexuality were profoundly influenced by (1) the scholastic systematization of theology, (2) the development of a unified Church law, and (3) the reality of medieval life. These factors converged in the work of the Council of Trent, which in turn has had a profound effect on Catholic morality up to the present, particularly through the Roman Catechism.

The movement to accept marriage as fully sacramental was completed with the work of Albert the Great and Thomas Aquinas. Thomas' synthesis of the human reality of marriage as both a civil and sacramental institution was unparalleled in previous writings,[52] and it marked a high point in the scholastic discussion of marriage and sexuality. Thomas also departed from the Augustinian tendency to be suspect of all pleasure, viewing it as natural insofar as it was ruled by reason. However, since sexual pleasure was so strong, it was more removed from reason than other powers; hence, Thomas did not include it in his generally positive theology of the role of the passions.[53] As a result, the positive aspects of the medieval development were generally overshadowed by the continuation of the rather negative earlier tendencies.

In the tradition of the Fathers, the schoolmen taught that sex was permitted only within marriage and primarily for the sake of procreation. The male seed was the active principle, and its procreative end governed all speculation on sexual ethics.[54] Women were of no real value except as receptacles for the seed—gardens, as it were, for human reproduction.[55] The fact that most theological thinking took place within monasteries resulted in the exaltation of virginity at the expense of marriage.

With the exception of Abelard, Albert,[56] and to some extent Thomas Aquinas, who taught the natural goodness of sex, the bulk of theological opinion favored the rigorism of Augustine. Some authors suggested a more spiritual approach to marriage[57] but the conviction prevailed that the pleasure of sex was associated with concupiscence, so that, even within marriage, sinlessness was rare.[58] The emergence of marriage as one of the seven sacraments complicated the issue, since then the grace-giving aspect of marriage had to be integrated into the question; while no one said every sexual act was intrinsically sinful, all were agreed that some evil element was present in every sexual act since the Fall. A major question posed by the schoolmen was the marriage of the aged and sterile, a practice permitted since the earliest times. How it could be reconciled with the view that sexuality was primarily for procreation remained a much discussed problem.

The unification of Church law as initiated by Gratian (c. 1150) tended to deemphasize and dismiss any precedents that went contrary to the generally rigorist bent of the canonists. Its emphasis of the objective over the subjective elements removed any consideration of sexuality even further from the realm of a human interpersonal or secular reality.

Life in medieval Europe also made its impact on the development of attitudes toward sexuality. The advent of courtly love had no small influence on the popular approach to sexuality. The landless peasant, forbidden to marry, had to content himself with the admiration and pursuit of the lady of the manor, who often found this admiration a happy sport. This arrangement contrasted sharply with the loveless marriages of convenience arranged largely for economic or political motives that prevailed among the landed gentry and nobility. The resultant widespread practice of clandestine unions led to Church legislation requiring the observance of canonical form as essential for Christian marriage, further deemphasizing the interpersonal element expressed through sexuality. Confusion was added to the age by extremist groups like the Catharii, who while purporting to be against all forms of sexual exchange were accused of living very loose lives in practice. Although the penitentials of the day provide some insight into the medieval concepts of sexuality, there is ample evidence that confessors were urged not to question too closely in these areas lest they teach people to sin.

With William of Occam (c. 1349), there arose the practice of teaching moral theology negatively, that is, according to the Ten Commandments rather than according to the virtues, as St. Thomas had done. For Occam, God imposed exterior obligations arbitrarily. Man was viewed statically instead of in relationship to others. Occam's view of man affected the subsequent teaching of all morality in the Catholic tradition and provided a negative perspective for all moral teaching on sexuality.

## EARLY MODERN PERIOD (15th to 19th Century)

The appearance of the "moral manuals," intended primarily for the training of confessors and focusing heavily on sin, further confirmed the negative approach to sexual matters. Since these manuals served as the almost exclusive source of moral teaching, they had a particularly profound impact on the formation of values and attitudes regarding human sexuality. The dominance of the procreative criterion is reflected in the basic distinction found in most treatises on sexuality during these centuries, that is, the division between sexual sins "in accordance with nature" and those "contrary to nature" (unnatural).[59] The former (fornication, adultery, incest, rape, and abduction) preserve the procreative possibility and are consequently regarded, apart from other considerations, as a lesser violation of the moral order. The latter (masturbation, sodomy, homosexuality, and bestiality) violate this procreative purpose and therefore are looked upon as the more radical abuse of human sexuality.

Such an approach led quite naturally to a highly negative, juridical, and act-centered morality, which all too easily proclaimed moral absolutes with little regard for person-oriented values. Certain laxist tendencies of the seventeenth and eighteenth centuries, which provoked an extremely vigorous reaction in the form of the Jansenist and Puritan movements, only intensified this development. These movements were particularly harsh and negative in their views on human sexuality, and they set in motion attitudes that have continued right into the twentieth century.[60]

To be sure, there were many attempts during these centuries to question the preeminence of the procreative purpose of sexuality and to assert a concern for person-oriented values. As early as the fifteenth century, Martin Le Maistre (1432-1481) advanced his bold thesis that "not every copulation of spouses not performed to generate offspring is an act opposed to conjugal chastity."[61] The sixteenth-century specialist on marriage, Thomas Sanchez (1550-1610) was able to assert, contrary to prevailing opinion, that "there is no sin in spouses who intend to have intercourse simply as spouses."[62] In the eighteenth century, St. Alphonsus Liguori added his authority to this growing movement away from dominant procreative justification of sexuality with his clear assertion that one of the purposes of marriage was to provide an outlet for sexual impulses.[63] Throughout these centuries there was also a growing recognition of the impact of poverty and of the educational welfare of offspring as important considerations restricting the procreative priority of sexuality and justifying the practice of *amplexus reservatus*[64] (penetration without ejaculation).

The nineteenth century found the Sacred Penitentiary attempting to respond to the growing practice of onanistic intercourse by espousing acceptance of Lecomte's (1824-1881) recommendations regarding the use of the sterile period.[65]

## CONTEMPORARY PERIOD (20th Century)

With the advent of the twentieth century, prominent Catholic theologians, Herbert Doms, Bernhardin Krempel, and Dietrich von Hildebrand elaborated in their treatises on marriage a far more comprehensive approach to the personalist values in Christian sexuality. Their writings undoubtedly had an impact not only on the thinking of individuals but even on the official formulations of the Church regarding sexuality.[66]

In 1930, the issue was brought into the open when the Anglican Bishops meeting at the Lambeth Conference approved by a vote of 193-67 the following resolution:

> Where there is a clearly felt moral obligation to limit or avoid parenthood, the method must be decided on Christian principles. The primary and obvious method is complete abstinence from intercourse (as far as may be necessary) in a life of discipline and self-control lived in the power of the Holy Spirit. Nevertheless, in those cases where there is such a clearly felt moral obligation to limit or avoid parenthood, and where there is a morally sound reason for avoiding complete abstinence, the Conference agrees that other methods may be used, provided that this is done in the light of the same Christian principles. The conference records its strong condemnation of the use of any methods of conception-control from motives of selfishness, luxury or mere convenience.[67]

This statement, rejected twice previously in 1908 and 1920, marked the first time that a major Christian group had publicly gone on record favoring such a separation of the procreative and unitive ends of marriage. It occasioned a strong response from Pius XI in the form of his encyclical on Christian marriage, *Casti Connubii* promulgated in December of that same year. In the words of Pius XI:

> But absolutely no reason, even the most serious, can turn something which is intrinsically against nature into something conformable to nature and morally good. Since, therefore, the conjugal act is designed by its very nature for the generation of children, those who in performing it deliberately deprive it of its natural power and capacity act against nature and commit a deed which is shameful and intrinsically immoral . . . Our voice promulgates anew: any use of marriage whatever, in the exercise of which the act is deprived of its natural power of procreating life, violates the law of God and nature, and those who commit anything of this kind are marked with the stain of grave sin.[68]

The encyclical, however, also at the same time gave full official support of the Church to the use of rhythm as a legitimate means of exercising responsible parenthood.

> Nor are those considered as acting against nature who in the married state use their right in the proper manner, although on account of natural reasons either of time or of certain defects, new life cannot be brought forth. For in matrimony as well as in the use of the matrimonial rights there are also secondary ends, such as mutual aid, the cultivating of mutual love, and the quieting of concupiscence which husband and wife are not forbidden to consider as long as they are subordinated to the primary end and so long as the intrinsic nature of the act is preserved.[69]

The growing consciousness of the official Church toward the personalist ends of human sexuality is reflected even more clearly in the following passage of this same encyclical:

> This mutual inward molding of a husband and wife, this determined effort to perfect each other, can in a very real sense, be said to be the chief reason and purpose of matrimony, provided matrimony be looked at not in the restricted sense as instituted for the proper conception and education of the child, but more widely as the blending of life as a whole and the mutual interchange and sharing thereof.[70]

These passages reveal a keen awareness and support of the dual purpose of sexuality—a giant step forward from the narrowly procreative framework of the earliest centuries. But their separate treatment indicates that a harmonious integration of the two had yet to be achieved in the Church's official teaching.

In October 1951 in his *Address to the Midwives*, Pius XII reinforced Pius XI's condemnation of artificial contraception in no uncertain terms:

> Our predecessor, Pius XI, of happy memory, in his encyclical *Casti Connubii*, December 31, 1930, solemnly proclaimed anew the fundamental law governing the marital act and conjugal relations: that any attempt on the part of mar-

ried people to deprive this act of its inherent force and to impede the procreation of new life either in the performance of the act itself or in the course of the development of its natural consequence, is immoral; and no alleged "indication" or need can convert an intrinsically immoral act into a moral and lawful one. This precept is as valid today as it was yesterday; and it will be the same tomorrow and always, because it does not imply a precept of the human law but is the expression of a law which is natural and divine.[71]

The strong language of Pius XII's statement led some theologians to conclude that this was close to a definition of faith and that the Church's official teaching on this matter was for all practical purposes now "irrevocable."[72]

The fact that Pope John XXIII saw fit in June 1964 to establish a special "Papal Commission for the Study of Population, the Family, and Birth" to investigate this whole matter proved that the conclusion of some theologians may have been a bit premature. In fact, the Majority Report of that Commission recommended a position that marked a considerable departure from the statement of Pius XII:

The morality of sexual acts between married people takes its meaning first of all and specifically from the ordering of their actions in a fruitful married life, that is, one which is practiced with responsible, generous, and prudent parenthood. It does not then depend upon the direct fecundity of each and every particular act. Moreover the morality of every marital act depends upon the requirements of mutual love in all its aspects. In a word, the morality of sexual actions is thus to be judged by the true exigencies of the nature of human sexuality, whose meaning is maintained and promoted especially by conjugal chastity, as we have said above.[73]

So the Church, particularly through the teaching of Pius XII, has come to realize more fully that marriage has another meaning and another end besides that of procreation alone, even though it remains wholly and definitely ordered to procreation, though not always immediately.

What has been condemned in the past and remains so

today is the unjustified refusal of life, arbitrary human intervention for the sake of moments of egotistic pleasure; in
short, the rejection of procreation as a specific task of marriage. In the past, the Church could not speak other than
she did, because the problem of birth control did not confront human consciousness in the same way. Today, having
clearly recognized the legitimacy and even the duty of regulating births, she recognizes too that human intervention in
the process of the marriage act for reasons drawn from the
finality of marriage itself should not always be excluded,
provided that the criteria of morality are always safeguarded.[74]

The Vatican II *Constitution on the Church in the Modern
World* promulgated in December 1965 clearly rejected the hierarchical ordering of the purposes of sexuality in terms of primary and secondary. It recommended that the integrating principle for harmonizing both ends of marriage be "the nature of
the human person and his acts."[75]

More specific conclusions regarding the implications of
this principle for artificial contraception were not permitted to
be drawn, due to a special intervention of Paul VI, who was
awaiting the completion of the report of the special Papal
Commission.[76]

In July 1968 Pope Paul VI issued his encyclical *Humanae
Vitae* rejecting the findings of the Majority Report of the Commission and reaffirming the position of Pius XI and Pius XII.

The Church, calling men back to the observance of the
norms of the natural law, as interpreted by her constant
doctrine, teaches that each and every marriage act must
remain open to the transmission of life.[77]

There can be no question that the encyclical *Humanae
Vitae* represents the official position of the Church's highest
teaching authority. It is important to note, however, that Pope
Paul in promulgating this Encyclical purposefully refrained
from designating its teaching as infallible; his spokesman,
Monsignor Ferdinand Lambruschini explicitly stated that it
was not irreformable.[78] The diversity of responses received

from various Episcopal Conferences,[79] the theological ferment which followed upon the encyclical[80] and a host of recent surveys[81] of clergy and faithful indicate that there remains a wide divergence between official Church teaching and the actual practice of the faithful.

It was the decade of the sixties that marked a decisive turning point in the attitudes and practices of many Catholics regarding sexual matters. Among the factors that helped influence this profound change in attitude and practice are the following:

(1) developments in biblical, historical and systematic theology leading to a more wholistic and person-oriented approach to moral matters;

(2) advances in the behavioral and social sciences providing new understanding and insights into the purpose and meaning of human sexuality;

(3) a deeper societal appreciation of the dignity, uniqueness, and freedom of each individual human being;

(4) the personalist-oriented theology of marriage and sexuality such as expressed in the majority report of the Papal Commission and in the Vatican II document, *The Church in the Modern World*;

(5) an increased sense of personal freedom and responsibility for the determination of one's own life that has made the uncritical conformity to authoritative pronouncements an unacceptable response;

(6) easy availability of sophisticated means of birth regulation such as oral contraceptives, the IUD, and other measures;

(7) a growing awareness of the problem of overpopulation and its possible threat to the overall quality of human life.

Vatican II's treatment of sexuality and marriage in the document on *The Church in the Modern World* highlights some of the most significant characteristics of this new approach to sexuality. It rejects the primacy of the procreative over the unitive aspects of sexuality insisting on their proper harmony and integration.[82] It rightfully suggests the human person as the integrating center of these distinctive values giving explicit recognition to the personal[83] and interpersonal values at the core of human sexuality. It calls attention to the human quality of expressions of sexuality and how they must contribute to the growth and development of the person.[84] It reflects a keen sensitivity to the social and communal dimensions of human sexuality and marriage.[85] Finally, in recognizing the Creator as the source and summit of human sexuality sanctified in a special way in the sacramental union that is marriage, it brings a transcendent perspective to a reality that is too often considered from a limited and temporal vantage point.[86]

With Vatican II a new era has been ushered in with regard to the Church's understanding of and approach to sexuality. A new appreciation of the personal dimension of human sexuality and a new principle for integrating the procreative and unitive purposes of sexuality in marriage have been introduced.

These basic insights of Vatican II were extended beyond the context of marriage to other areas of human sexuality in a December 1975 document issued by the Sacred Congregation for the Doctrine of the Faith entitled: *Declaration on Certain Questions Concerning Sexual Ethics.*[87]

Although not intended to be a comprehensive statement of the Church's teaching on sexual matters, the document does contribute to the developing Church teaching in this area.

The nature and meaning of human sexuality is presented in a way that goes far beyond the "primarily for procreation" or "merely for pleasure" approaches still current in some statements on the subject. It expresses the purpose of human sexuality in terms of its radical importance for the development of the person and integration into the human community:

The document declares:

> The human person is so profoundly affected by sexuality that it must be considered as one of the factors which give to each individual's life the principal traits that distinguish it. In fact it is from sex that the human person receives the characteristics which on the biological, psychological and spiritual levels, make that person a man or a woman, and thereby largely condition his or her progress towards maturity and insertion into society.[88]

This new appreciation of the depth and meaning of human sexuality is of no small significance and prepares the way for a far more positive and wholistic approach to sexual questions. Such an understanding reveals the woeful inadequacy of attempting to approach the subject exclusively from either extreme of procreation or pleasure.

For this reason the Declaration is able to extend the personalist principle, "the nature of the person and his acts," that Vatican II advanced for the evaluation of sexual conduct in marriage to sexual questions outside the context of marriage as well.[89] It implies a rightful role for human sexuality at all stages of human development and not something merely restricted to the married state. Within and without marriage, however, human sexuality must serve the radical purpose of promoting growth toward personal maturity and integration into society. The application of this principle rejects both the extremely subjective criterion of sincere intention alone as well as the exaggerated objective criterion of act alone as unacceptable.

Further, the Declaration recalls some too frequently forgotten fundamental priorities that have relevance with regard to evaluating moral conduct, namely:[90]

(1) That genuine moral behavior must proceed from internal conviction rather than external imposition; simple conformity to a rule because someone says so is not mature moral response in keeping with the nature and dignity of the human person.

(2) That for the believer, Christ is the supreme and ultimate test of the moral rectitude of any behavior; any rules, directives, norms must be subject to Christ as the ultimate norm of morality for the Christian.

(3) That the nature of the human person provides the proximate objective norm for determining which behavior is appropriate and moral; the complexity and mystery of man requires that the conscientious moral person will be continuously open to all insights from science and revelation that will enable him to better interpret and apply this norm.

Contrary to much current theological thought, the Declaration suggests that the moral exigencies flowing from the nature of man can be readily reduced to certain absolute and immutable prescriptions regarding particular actions but the argumentation here is far from conclusive.

Finally, even though its treatment of specific issues (premarital sex, homosexuality and masturbation) appears to be exaggeratedly absolute and legalistic far more attention is given pastoral considerations[91] than was customarily the case. Counselors and confessors are repeatedly cautioned against simplistic judgments regarding imputability. Serious consideration must be given to various subjective factors that can profoundly interfere with and affect the objectively ideal moral response.

Thus this most recent document on human sexuality from the Church's universal magisterium reflects both a continuity with the tradition of the past and a development of that tradition. On the practical level, it follows the tradition closely in its treatment of specific sexual questions in the simple objective-subjective framework (objectively evil though not always subjectively sinful). Even so it modifies this approach considerably by calling for greater attention to the subjective elements in pastoral judgments. On the theoretical level, it develops the past tradition substantially, in presenting an understanding of human sexuality as radically rooted in the very nature of the human person and important to growth at every stage of being and not merely in the context of marriage. It extends the principle of Vatican II—"the nature of the human person and his acts"—to evaluating human sexual conduct even outside the context of marriage. This provides a far more adequate criterion than approaches that focus on procreation or pleasure. These developments will continue to influence Catholic thought for a long time to come as the implications and significance for human sexual behavior are gradually unfolded.

# III
# The Empirical Sciences and Human Sexuality

The methodology employed by Catholic moralists through the recent past placed little emphasis on empirical data despite the natural law orientation of most of them (Curran 1975).* Catholic natural law ethics characteristically proceeded deductively from a metaphysical analysis of man's individual and social nature. Normative behavior was arrived at syllogistically. The moral imperative was fundamentally a logical imperative flowing from an a priori premise. The actual behavior of people and their moral appreciation of this behavior was considered irrelevant to the determination of moral norms.

From time to time opinions of select theorists and practitioners in the behavioral sciences who might warn against the harmful consequences of, for instance, masturbation were noted when they supported the deductive reasoning (Renshaw 1976). Radically, however, empirical conduct had no systematic role in the fashioning of the more characteristic moral theory. The discrepancy observed between Catholic principles and Catholic behavior was easily explained by human frailty, by sin and the ubiquitous "spirit of iniquity." For this very reason actual behavior could never be a source of normative behavior.

The discrepancy between theory and actual behavior posed no serious systematic problem for Catholic moral theology.

---

*This chapter was originally prepared utilizing a style and a system of references peculiar to the social sciences. It has been decided to leave the arrangement unchanged since it suits the matter under discussion and the need for uniformity throughout the text does not seem compelling. The references for this chapter will be found with the other footnotes at the rear of this work, arranged according to author and year of publication in accord with *The Publication Manual of the American Psychological Association,* 1967 revision.

There remained the problem, however, that humanists and other conscientious thinkers within and without the Church often failed to agree with the Catholic analysis of man's individual and social nature and the moral behavior logically required by the analysis. It could hardly be argued that intellectual ability and integrity were the private preserve of Catholic moralists. So once again the role of sin was invoked. Sinful men were attempting to analyze sin-touched human nature. Catholic theologians argued that the Church in its official teaching has the advantage of the special divine assistance of revelation and the grace of the corrective teaching authority (McCormick 1974). These aids were considered not as displacing the rational analysis (except for those moralists who sought a more express biblical foundation for Christian ethics) but rather as supplementing and elevating it, thereby purging the destructive influence of sin.

A criticism leveled against the foregoing argument is that it is naive. The argument fails to acknowledge sufficiently the pre-reflective, historical embodiedness of every thinker and every moralizing human community (Gustafson 1975). No thinker or body of thinkers pursues rational reflection as a purely intellectual exercise. Pre-reflective subjectivity can never be totally bracketed when rational analysis is undertaken. The affective and experiential dimension is always present and must always be taken into account. These are lessons that have been driven home by the great critiques of the last two centuries as well as by insights into human functioning illuminated by the work of thinkers like Freud. To discard systematically history and experience as mere sin and source of error, the argument continues, is gratuitously to render more difficult our stumbling efforts to discern God's will for man.

Further, the assistance of revelation and of the teaching tradition is not so sweeping as to exorcise the influence of history and culture on Catholic thought. Ignoring pre-reflective data does not eliminate it. On the contrary, ignoring it allows such data to exercise an uncontrolled and unanalyzed influence on the would-be rational product. More importantly, some would argue, far from being pure sin and error, history and experience may be forms of divine assistance to the rational process (Gustafson, McCormick 1975). If *agere* is to follow *esse*, if ontology is to be the basis of behavioral norms, then we must be aware that being, including human fallen-redeemed being, reveals itself through time and experience as well as through rational reflection.

We do not presume to resolve here the debate over the function of empirical data in ethical norm making. However, it can be said that Catholic moralists in the past have been unduly influenced in their thinking by certain unexpressed and perhaps unconscious assumptions about the effect of some behavior on human existence. Untested assumptions about empirical facts may well have played an unacknowledged role in the thinking of moralists, thus subtly prejudicing what moralists thought to be unencumbered logical (if not divinely assisted) reasoning.

For this reason, we deem it necessary to survey the results of research in those areas of human behavior germane to this study. We are well aware that empirical research is an ongoing project. Today's findings may be overthrown by tomorrow's. A once impressive study may be shown to be vitiated by a systematic bias uncovered by a later astute critic. Nevertheless, it is important to review what is considered to be the present status of scientific knowledge on matters relevant to this study. We have given preference to observed data rather than to the insights and theories of various schools of psychology. To reach any ethical conclusion it is necessary to dialogue with this data, not ignore it. For the rest, we remain fully agreed that the pervasiveness of sin and the often blind urgency of the erotic impulse prohibit the mere frequency of some sexual behavior from becoming an acceptable determinant of sexual ethics. A further comment is apropos: before too long, it is quite possible that some studies reported here will be dated; it is left to the reader to update them.

With these foregoing preliminary remarks, we now come to the central question of this chapter: is there any empirical data available which might support a claim that certain sexual expressions always and everywhere are detrimental to the full development of the human personality? Is there any empirical evidence which would indicate that, independent of cultural influences, some uses of sex are absolutely detrimental to the structure of truly human existence? In other words, are there any culture-free sexual prohibitions?

If any absolutely detrimental sexual behavior could be identified, the finding would be extremely helpful in developing a code of sexual ethics free of relativity. It is obvious that any activity of which one's society disapproves is a potential source of anxiety for one who engages in it. If the cultural values of a society have been internalized by its members and form an integral part of their own meaning system, then behavior contrary to these values would put them at odds with themselves. Conflict with one's society or with oneself impedes the growth of the person. However, if the inconsistency and conflict are simply the result of an historical adoption by a society of one of many possible systems of sexual mores, then the conflict may be resolved by having the society merely modify its system of mores to accommodate the behavior more preferred by a growing number of its members. Until that day arrives, enlightened and well integrated individuals might well free themselves of conflict by simply reflecting on the relativity of their society's sexual ethic and proceed discreetly with their own sexual project.

Our question, therefore, is not what sexual activity happens to create anxiety for individual members of a certain society and results in the cramping of their development. And answer to that question might lead us no further than to identify sexual taboos that may be entirely culturally determined. Such taboos may have no necessary relation to "the very nature of things." The question is rather: is there any identifiable sexual behavior that runs contrary to the very structure of human existence prior to any cultural sanction? Is there any behavior that of itself defeats the growth of a creative and integrated personality?

In pursuing an answer to this question, we will first present a summary overview of the general pattern of scientific findings. We will then give the specific data available.

## OVERVIEW

The first line of approach is to discover if there be any specific behavior that is universally prohibited by all cultures.

This is a variation of the "common consent of mankind" argument familiar to Catholic tradition. Study reveals that every form of sexual human behavior imaginable is sanctioned by one culture or another. There is no universally forbidden behavior. At the same time there is no culture that does not have *some* sexual taboo.

A second approach is inquiry into the sexual behavior of animals. The supporting assumption is that subhuman animals, devoid of freedom to misdirect their sexual impulses, may disclose certain natural absolutes. The findings are that animals at all levels engage in sexual behavior that is not always directed to reproduction but often merely to pleasure. They engage in self-stimulation, homosexuality, and copulation outside the species. Indeed autonomy of sexual play from the reproductive orientation becomes increasingly marked as one proceeds up the evolutionary tree, correlating with development of the cortex. The variety of sexual expression among the primates is strikingly similar to that of man. Thus it is difficult to draw any firm conclusions as to the "naturalness or unnaturalness" of any specific sex behavior from the activity of animals.

The fact that every form of sexual behavior imaginable is indulged in and sanctioned by one culture or another does not yet answer the fundamental question. We still wish to know what effect specific forms of behavior have upon individuals in societies that condone such behavior. Are they harmful to the full flowering of personhood despite their social acceptability? There is insufficient data available even to begin answering that question. Within our own American culture attempts have been made not only to tabulate the frequency of various forms of sexual behavior, but to assess the effect of them on the individual and his relations with others.

All indications are that masturbation is engaged in by almost all of the American male population and two-thirds of the female. It is a practice that continues on into old age. The data suggests to some behavioral scientists that masturbation is not immature or abnormal unless it is the sole method of sexual expression when other methods are readily available. Self-stimulation must be evaluated against the whole context of the individual's life.

Premarital sex and trial marriages are increasing in frequency and social acceptability in our society. There are not enough data to draw firm conclusions, but indications are that young people are experiencing less and less feelings of guilt and anxiety over their sexual indulgence. The effect on subsequent marriage relationships seems to depend on the attitude of the participants in the premarital sexual experiences. Those who felt guilty while engaging in sex prior to marriage found that it had a bad effect upon their eventual marriage. Those who thought their premarital sexual experiences were morally acceptable at the time they indulged in them found that these experiences strengthened the subsequent marriage.

If the pollsters can be believed, more than half of the married men and one fourth of the married women in the United States engage in occasional extramarital intercourse. Mate-swapping is a surprisingly widespread phenomenon. The effect on the individuals concerned and their marriage is not known at this time. No serious study has yet been attempted. What reports there are tend to be anecdotal and partisan.

Homosexuality is the one form of sexual expression whose psychological dimension has received considerable attention in recent years (Weinberg and Bell 1972). Some would say this is the result of increasing political pressure on the part of homosexuals to gain social acceptance and legal protection for their life style (Tripp 1975). Others believe this new visibility and aggressiveness on the part of the homosexual community is the result rather than the cause of increasing research into the personality development of the homosexual. There are research findings which can be interpreted to support the view that personality development among homosexuals as a group is indistinguishable from that of heterosexuals as a group. Some conclude therefore that it is unscientific to view homosexuality as "abnormal" or a form of mental illness. They argue that while statistically homosexuality remains a departure from the norm in our culture, so does left-handedness. Orthodox analysis (Freudian, Adlerian, Jungian) continues to view homosexuality as a form of immaturity and defective personality development rather than simply a statistical deviation. A recent survey (and vote) of the American Psychiatric Association reveals that

American psychiatrists are split on the question.

As to the root cause of homosexual orientation in any individual, the currently prevailing view is that it is neither genetic nor hormonal but environmental. Views differ as to the possibility and desirability of reorienting the homosexual. Research at Johns Hopkins University in recent years indicates that sexual orientation may be fixed and irreversible by two years of age. This despite the dramatic changes in overt behavior sometimes achieved through behavioral modification techniques. Others believe homosexuality can be cured through therapy if the subject truly desires it. This despite the very poor success rate of therapy.

Some philosophical anthropologists question whether any preference should be given to either heterosexual or homosexual orientation. In their view, human beings rise above their biological givens and are free to choose the sexual expression they prefer. They have the potential of integrating any form of expression into their total human project. The only thing "natural" for a person is to embrace life in freedom. Masters and Johnson in their recently published findings on the subject of homosexuality indicated that they are persuaded that homosexuality is an acceptable and satisfying sexual expression.

This is the status of the data on human sexuality. What answer does it suggest for our initial question? It must be said at this time that the behavioral sciences have not identified any sexual expression that can be empirically demonstrated to be, of itself, in a culture-free way detrimental to full human existence. On the other hand, neither have they to date eliminated the possibility that some day such identification and proof may be offered. The theorist, who wishes to hold the view that acts of masturbation, pre- and extramarital sex and homosexuality are absolutely inconsistent with healthy personality development or successful marriage relationships, cannot presently look to empirical data for unambiguous support for his view. On the other hand neither is he irrefutably rebutted on all counts by the same data. Can he at least say firmly that whatever sexual expression is employed by two people must be inspired with love? Is sex without love empty and degrading to the personality? Or can sex be mere fun or mere sensual gratification?

The consensus would seem to be that sex can be for fun in a context of mutual respect and caring. Extramarital sex, however, may not be so innocuous.

While no specific form of sexual expression is universally prohibited, still every culture does have *some* sexual taboo. It would seem that sex is never treated with total neutrality. It appears to have a meaning in human relations that is not totally dependent on the arbitrary choice of the participants.

## THE DATA

### TRANSCULTURAL DATA: IS ANY SPECIFIC SEXUAL BEHAVIOR UNIVERSALLY PROHIBITED?

Evidence for a culture-free maladaptive sexual behavior might be found in some behavior that is universally and transculturally prohibited. Such prohibited behavior, however, has not been found. The closest thing to it is incest (Murdock 1949). However, even incest is merely selectively prohibited: in some societies, for example, a male may be allowed to marry his younger sister, but not his older one (Avebury 1902); in others, only tribal rulers are allowed to marry their daughters, a practice forbidden to subjects (Ford and Beach 1951).

Homosexuality is treated permissively or encouraged in many societies (Tripp 1975). A study of 193 societies revealed that 28% of them gave social acceptance to male homosexuality and 11% accepted female homosexuality as well (Murdock 1934). A study of American Indian tribes found 53% accepting male homosexuality, 17% female homosexuality (Pomeroy 1965, 1966). Homosexuality is sometimes tolerated in childhood but not in adulthood. Some societies, on the other hand, require it of all males along with their heterosexuality. Female homosexuality is widespread in individual societies (Ford and Beach 1951). Nevertheless, homosexuality is never a dominant mode of sexual expression in any society (Ford and Beach 1951).

Masturbation is extremely common among both sexes in almost all societies that have been studied. On the other hand, there is usually some societal disapproval of it for adults. It is widely viewed as immature behavior, appropriate only for children (who are often encouraged to practice it) and for adults who cannot succeed with the opposite sex. However, there are societies that encourage it even among adults (Ford and Beach 1951).

Sexual relations with animals is another form of behavior that is severely punished by some societies and commonly practiced or tolerated by others (Ford and Beach 1951).

The same inconsistency is observed in regard to extramarital intercourse. Some societies strictly forbid it (though it is engaged in surreptitiously) while others are so permissive that they do not even have a word in their language for adultery. A similar wide diversity exists in attitudes toward premarital sex (Ford and Beach 1951). Eskimos exchange mates both as a courtesy to guests and just for fun (Stiller 1961; Freuchen 1956). Such practice seems not to interfere with healthy, harmonious marriages. The extreme physical circumstances surrounding Eskimo existence may prohibit generalizations about the harmlessness of such practices.

No universal consent to the evil of any specific sexual behavior can be found. At the same time there is no culture **that** does not employ some sexual taboo.

## DOES NATURE HAVE A LAW?
## DOES ANIMAL BEHAVIOR DISCLOSE ANY NATURAL ABSOLUTES?

Animal sexual behavior would seem important to the thesis that the freedom of human existence is circumscribed by certain biological determinants. Biological sex differentiation in animals is obviously related to the reproduction and nurturing of offspring. We share animality with the subhuman species. It may be argued that nonhuman animals, bereft of freedom to pervert the intended purposes of their sexuality, will reveal what sexual behavior is consonant with the radical differentiation into male and female. Observations of animal behavior, in fact, indicate that animals engage in a wide range of sexual behavior. Animal behavior is less relevant to those who see sexuality as a radically different phenomenon since it functions within the structure of human subjectivity. However, the following data appear relevant to this point of view as well.

Animals below the primate level respond to internal hormonal control, showing regular and periodic reproductive excitation, males responding to the female estrus. However, if an opposite sex member of the animal's own species is not available, the animal, once aroused, will engage in likesex copulatory behavior and rather ingenious forms of self-stimulation (Ford and Beach 1951). As we proceed up the evolutionary tree, autonomy from internal hormone determinants becomes increasingly evident. As the cortex shows more development and control, there is a gradual separating of the sex drive from mere reproductive functions (Rosenzweig 1973). Thus in the apes, a female may be receptive to sexual advances even when not in estrus. Even when under hormonal excitation she can be selective about the males she encourages. At the peak of estrus she may be unreceptive to any of the males available to her. Male apes, even when excited by estrus, may seek outlets in disinterested females, in other males, or in masturbation. They demonstrate a variety of sex play not related to reproduction (Beach 1958).

While homosexual behavior among animals is common enough, exclusive homosexuality is rare (Ford and Beach 1951) and, according to one researcher, engaged in only by the immature and sexually deprived animal (Pomeroy 1968). As sexual behavior comes more and more under cortical control with resulting independence from hormonal, reproductive dominance, interaction within the animal group becomes an important factor in sexual expression, and behavioral maladjustments become a possibility (Rosenzweig 1973).

This evidence of correlation between cortical development and increasing autonomy of the sex drive from specifically reproductive activity persuades some thinkers that, in humans, bodily presence in the world has transcended the facticity of the male-female dichotomy (Brown 1966; Marcuse 1956; Watts 1958). Some phenomenologists would say that humans with their consciousness so rise above their biochemical and anatomical "givens" that they restructure their sexuality into a highly personal mode, for instance, that of simply "being for the others" (Merleau-Ponty 1962). As such, the sex drive in humans is no longer merely a blind impulse to union of the genders so that the incompleteness of each can be mutually completed as is required biologically for reproduction. Rather it is a drive toward personal encounter, a reaching out from aloneness to "intercoursing" one's life with that of the other. Understood this way, sexuality transcends the male-female differentiation and the notion of complementarity based on gender. In its place is the complementarity of persons, the potential of one bodily existence to respond to the yearning of another for escape from isolation and solipsistic existence (Earle 1961).

Other theorists attempt to leave room for some corporeal, physiological givens and determinants within this general theory (Buytendijk 1954; Jeanniere 1967). Current research here and abroad suggests that, in humans, gender identity may be a phenomenon independent of anatomy and produced by cultural and environmental learning (Hampson and Hampson 1961; Money 1957, 1961, 1972; Rosenzweig 1972; Maccoby and Jacklin 1974). The transcultural studies of Margaret Mead (1949) are somewhat supportive, though she has recently warned against ignoring biological determinants of sexual differentiation (1974). A recent report from Stanford University concludes from all the research reported to date that the only sex difference (other than anatomical and biochemical) which is supported by hard, transcultural data is that males are more aggressive than females. There is no conclusive evidence that tactile sensitivity, competitive spirit, dominance-compliance, activity-passivity, nurturing, "maternal" behavior are traits more typical of one sex than another, when allowances are made for role expectations (Maccoby and Jacklin 1974). An even more recent survey of the discussion points to the wide divergence of opinion on the issue (Lee and Stewart 1976).

Some behavioral scientists protest that all such evidence is being exploited improperly to support an ideological position on homosexuality (cf. Sagarin 1968, who is suspicious of the "politics" of Hooker 1965, Benjamin 1966, Money 1969, and Gannan 1967).

Finally, one respected phenomenologist, who has reflected specifically on the notion of human sexuality in the thought of Husserl and Merleau-Ponty, believes that the human impulse toward the intertwining and intercoursing of lives is inexorably bound up with our need to fathom the mystery of our origins, our birth, and the genesis of the world we inhabit. He is persuaded that the human sexual impulse is oriented to the mystery of creativity and, in particular, to the mystery of procreation. He thus ties heterosexuality and biological facticity into the outward orientation of the genital act, even while emphasizing the intersubjective dimension and its centrality (Paci 1972).

In answer to our original query, then, animal behavior discloses no sexual absolutes. Animals below the primate level are generally responsive to the biological determinants ordered to reproductive behavior. However, in circumstances where heterosexual copulation within the species is not available, aroused animals engage in self-stimulation, homosexuality, and most other forms of sexual expression.

Freedom from hormonal control and reproductive specificity of behavior increases with the development of the cortex. Primates display a wide variety of sexual behavior unrelated to procreation that appears increasingly to be subject to modification by social influences. Whether or not, as some philosophical anthropologists appear to suggest, we arrive in the human species at an ultimate stage of development wherein total freedom from biological givens is possible, is a question that deserves considerably more scrutiny and clarification. This is especially so in view of the fact that there is an overwhelming transcultural predisposition to achieve the "intercoursing" of lives in a heterosexual way.

## "DEVIANT" SEXUAL BEHAVIOR IN THE UNITED STATES: FREQUENCY AND PSYCHOSOCIAL EFFECTS

While every imaginable sexual behavior has been practiced by, and approved of by, some human society, we lack sufficient data to determine finally how these practices have affected the individuals within the given society. Did such practices foster or deter truly human existence within that society? Presently, we do not have any hard data or norms available to assess the quality of human life in these cultures and the contribution to it attributable to its sexual mores. Within our own society some attempts have been made to assess the effects of various forms of sexual behavior on the individual and his relations with others and society. We survey what relevant findings are currently available.

The classical studies of American sexual behavior are, of course, the Kinsey reports (Kinsey 1948, 1953). These have been frequently and severely criticized for bias in the methodology used, especially for the risk of error that may have crept in as result of using volunteers (American Statistical Association Report 1954; Maslow 1952; Mead 1948; Simpson 1955). Despite this weakness and Kinsey's obvious preference for a particular philosophy of sex, the general trend revealed by the studies has been supported on the whole by later limited research. We take note of this as we proceed.

## Masturbation

Studies indicate that 95% of the total male population engages in masturbation at one time or another (Kinsey 1948; Bell, R.R., 1973) and about 70% of the female population (Davis, K.E., 1971). Thirteen percent of both sexes have masturbated by their tenth birthday (Reevey 1961). Adolescent boys are reported to masturbate on an average of twice a week, though 17% may masturbate four or more times weekly. The practice among boys declines in the post-adolescent years but occurs sporadically throughout life (Ford and Beach 1963). Seventy percent of American male college graduates engage in the practice occasionally even after marriage. Twenty-five percent of married men over sixty years of age masturbate from time to time (Kinsey 1948).

Females who masturbate, whether married or unmarried, more characteristically have begun in their late teens; practice increases up to the age of forty-five and then stays at a steady level of occurrence until age seventy. Masturbation is generally the most successful way for women to reach orgasm (Davis, K.E. 1971; Masters and Johnson 1966). For some it is the only way (Sullivan 1969).

In determining whether masturbation is indicative of emotional immaturity, one must keep in mind that half of college educated adults engage in it. A study of sexual fantasies that accompany masturbation persuades one researcher that the practice is not emotionally unhealthy or alienating in itself. It becomes so only if it interferes with actual encounter with the opposite sex (Sullivan 1969). Reflecting on the data presently available, one observer concludes that masturbation would seem to be abnormal only when it is the sole method of sexual outlet when other methods are readily available; or again when it is clearly a part of a psychotic pattern (McCary 1973). Freud was ambivalent about masturbation (1912). The psychoanalytic community today would seem to agree that the adult who engages in masturbation only when an appropriate sexual partner is not available is quite normal (Fenichel 1945; Spitz 1952; Pomeroy 1968). A national sampling of opinion in 1970 indicated that a majority of the American public does not disapprove of masturbation (Levitt 1974).

### Premarital Sex

Kinsey reported that 60% of the women in his sample born after 1900 had engaged in premarital intercourse (1953). More recent studies report 50% of college girls as having engaged in premarital intercourse (Bell, R.R. 1971; Koats 1970; Davis, K.E. 1971). One study made a controlled comparison of co-eds in the classes of 1958 and 1968 at the same large urban university. The finding is that while co-eds in 1958 tended to indulge in intercourse only with those to whom they were engaged, the co-eds of 1968 participated in it to the same extent with young men whom they were simply dating (Bell and Chaskes 1970; Christensen and Gregg 1970). The incidence of co-ed intercourse, however, varies with the location and type of college (Packard 1968). Another study of freshman women at a large state university reports that while in 1967 only 7% were non-virgins, by 1970 the freshman class of women had 15% non-virgins (Walsh 1972).

Of the females in the Kinsey report who had engaged in premarital intercourse, 53% did so with a single partner, 34% with two to five partners, 13% with six or more (Kinsey 1948). Kinsey also reported that 98% of college women born after 1910, whether married or not, had engaged in sexual stimulation of one sort or another with male partners. A third of these had had ten or more partners. A more recent study reports that 90% of the college women included in the study had engaged in genital stimulation with males while unclothed (Davis, K.E. 1971).

There is some evidence to support the widely held opinion that most married couples engage in intercourse with one another prior to marriage (Otto 1971). Another recent study reports that currently 45% of all women who date have sexual intercourse occasionally (Levitt 1974).

Kinsey found in 1948 that premarital intercourse was engaged in by more males with limited education than by the college educated. The percentage of the former was 98%; for the latter 67%. This probably indicated more caution on the part of the college educated than any difference in ethics. Of his college sample, 92% engaged in manipulation of the genitals of the partner to orgasm. This type of petting is engaged in rather promiscuously at present (Bell, R.R. 1971). Moreover, since the advent of the pill there is less need for caution. Yankelovich reportedly found that the sexual attitudes of present-day college and non-college young people are almost indistinguishable (1974).

There is some data on the extent to which religious conviction correlates with attitudes on premarital sex. One study indicated that only 50% of those who attend church weekly disapprove of it under all circumstances (Largey and Taft 1975). Forty-three percent of Catholics approve of it for the engaged (ten years ago only 12% did—National Opinion Research 1975). The majority of the general population approve of it sometimes, at least if there is love present between the participants (Levitt and Klassen 1973).

Little research has been done on the effects of this increasingly liberal sexual behavior. A repeated criticism of the Kinsey reports and other surveys of purported actual behavior of groups is the lack of contextual data that would allow investigators to determine what meaning the interviewees gave to their behavior (Mead 1948; Simpson 1955). It is also noted that the wide notoriety given such reports may have resulted in a self-fulfilling prophecy, leading some to confuse frequency with normalcy and desirability (Berger 1954).

At any rate, one recent study of college students' attitudes reported that anxiety and guilt feelings are decreasing for participants in premarital sex (Bell and Chaskes 1970). The more recent Yankelovich study for the Carnegie Foundation reported that the same permissive ethics formerly associated mainly with college youth is now evident among the non-college blue collar youth (Yankelovich 1974). Attempts have been made to determine the effect of premarital sexual experience on marital adjustment. Present correlations with the endurance of marriages slightly favors premarital chastity (Anderson 1966; Burgess 1953; Reiss 1970; Clatworthy 1976). What has not been determined is whether those who freely engage in premarital sex and trial marriages are not simply a population that can be expected to discontinue the marriage when they come to believe it no longer functions, while those who refrained from premarital sex are simply the same population that would not sever the relationship even though it be at a dead end. In short, we know nothing of the quality of the marriages from such statistics.

In line with the preceding reflection there is the finding that premarital sexual activity does or does not have a significant effect on a subsequent marriage depending on the attitude of the participants at the time of the premarital experiences. Those who felt that such behavior was wrong when they participated in it before the marriage were later more inclined to say that it had a bad effect on their subsequent marriage relationship. Those who saw the behavior as neutral tended to say that the premarital experience strengthened the marriage or at least was not harmful to the marriage relationship (Kirkendall 1971; Burgess and Wallin 1953).

The evidence, then, is that premarital sex is becoming increasingly common among both the educated and less educated. There is some indication that the meaning given to the experiences will determine whether they will have adverse repercussions on the participants. The issue is not thoroughly researched as yet. Another statistic, though, also needs consideration: The Department of Health, Education, and Welfare reports that three out of ten teenage girls who have premarital intercourse, even in this day of the pill, bear a child out of wedlock (1974).

### *Extramarital Sex*

Both early and more recent studies put the incidence of occasional extramarital intercourse by married men in their samplings at between 50% and 75% (Ellis 1972; Kinsey 1948; Terman 1938). Kinsey reported in 1957 that 26% of white American women had an affair by the age of 40. Such adventures outside marriage tend to increase with age among women, most frequently occurring in the late thirties. Men, on the contrary, decrease such behavior with age (Harper 1961). Married women who are unfaithful are as active in pursuing extramarital affairs as are adulterous men (Athanasiou 1970).

Evidence as to the effect of extramarital intercourse on the marriage and family is not conclusive. One third of the divorced couples in the Kinsey study reported adultery to have been the prime factor in the divorce. Of the 26% of married women who admitted to extramarital affairs in the report, 40% believed their husbands knew of the episodes, while an additional 9% believed their husbands were suspicious. Since the women were still married, obviously this knowledge had not resulted in dissolution of the marriage as of the survey. What further effect it had on the relationship was not assessed. Some proponents of the view that extramarital adventures are healthy for the marriage relationship or at least not harmful assume that the Kinsey report passes a final and favorable verdict on this view (see for example Meyers 1973). They offer further anecdotal evidence that some sophisticated couples report that they have profited from such experiences (Meyers and Leggit 1972).

Masters and Johnson are less sanguine; they advise it as a last resort, only to save a marriage if indicated (1974).

Related forms of behavior are "mate-swapping" and group sex among the married. One researcher estimates that one million Americans regularly engage in these practices (Bartell 1970). Catholics apparently participate in the same proportion that they bear to the general population (Smith and Smith 1970).

The effect of such experiences on the participants and the marriage relationships remains unknown. Some researchers report that they found the activity to be "healthy sexual variety" and that no damage was done the relationship (Denfield and Gordon 1970; Rosen 1971). In some cases they report it improved the marriage relationship (Rosen 1971). However, others more cautiously report that "sampling inadequacies have prevented any conclusions to date about relative success or failure of such ventures" (Smith and Smith 1973). Other observers note that no long-range study of the effects of this behavior on the families has been done (Neiger 1971; Bell, R.R. 1971). Masters and Johnson believe that only few can escape damage from the practice (1974). Popular reports of the current status of the phenomenon indicate that many former enthusiasts have begun to revise their views on its long-range effect (e.g. *Time*, Nov. 27, 1974; Denfield 1974). The interest of college students in the practice has hit a plateau (Yankelovich 1974). Rosenzweig suggests that "condoning extramarital sex must await more extensive knowledge as to the individual and social consequences than is presently available" (1973).

## Homosexuality

On December 15, 1973, the trustees of the American Psychiatric Association dropped homosexuality from the list of recognized mental disorders. They suggested, in effect, that homosexuality be no longer considered a mental illness but rather a form of sexual disorientation that requires treatment only when the individual concerned is disturbed by it. They created a new category, namely, "sexual disorientation disturbance."

Portions of the membership of the Association were unhappy with this action of the trustees. They felt it was an unscientific concession to the rising political and social pressure of organized homosexuals. However, the action of the trustees was upheld by vote of the general membership in April 1974. A little over 11,000 of the 17,000 membership participated in the voting on this and other issues. Of these, few less than 6,000 approved of the trustees' action while close to 4,000 disapproved. The remaining voters abstained on this question. Thus the psychiatric community is presently divided on the issue of whether homosexuality should be considered a mental illness per se and thus harmful to personal wholeness or a "disorientation," which may or may not disturb an individual concerned. In either case the Association seems to be saying that homosexuality is not an optimal condition, at least in our society. What else it implies, if anything, is unclear. The results of some research, however, indicate that carefully matched samples of homosexuals and heterosexuals disclose no significant differences on batteries of psychological tests designated to detect personality dysfunction (Hoffman 1969; Hooker 1957, 1958). Attention has already been called to possible ideological bias in this research (Sagarin 1968, 1971).

Freud pointed out long ago the potential for homosexual interest in everyone (1905). Kinsey interpreted his findings as indicating that every individual is somewhere on a continuum between extreme poles of heterosexuality and homosexuality. Some contemporary psychological theorists contend that males generally would develop the fullness of their sexual potential (Freud would speak of "polymorphous perversity"), that is, demonstrate their male/female dimensions, if Western cultural masculine stereotypes would lessen their pressure (Brown 1966; Marcuse 1956; Watts 1958).

A recent study of 20,000 educated higher middle class subjects revealed that more than one-third of all male subjects and one-fifth of the women had had homosexual experiences involving orgasm (Athanasiou 1970). Other estimates of homosexual behavior are that 4% of all American males are exclusively homosexual all their sexual lives; 8% exclusively homosexual for at least three years between the ages of 16 and 55; and 37% of all American males have some homosexual experience after marriage (Cory 1961). Very recently a researcher of the Kinsey Institute reported that the incidence of homosexual contacts is now dramatically declining from what it was at the time of the early Institute studies (Levitt 1975). He suggests that the reason may be the greater opportunity for heterosexual contact in the more liberal atmosphere of today.

While overt female homosexuality is less common than male homosexuality, one study found that 50% of college women experienced intense feelings for other women (David 1929). It is estimated that of women who engage in homosexual activity only a third of them are exclusively homosexual (Bieber 1969; Kaye 1971). The other two-thirds engage in sexual relations with males as well, an instance of so-called bisexuality. The status of the bisexual is unclear as of the present. Some behavioral scientists see them as impoverished personalities incapable of making a commitment of either kind. They see themselves as superior personalities enjoying a richer potential than others. Masters and Johnson found in their hormonal studies that, while homosexuals differed from heterosexuals, bisexuals showed no difference from heterosexuals.

The incidence of active lesbianism among married women in the Kinsey study was 3% (1957).

The exclusivity of male homosexual relationships has also been the topic of recent studies (Sonnenschein 1968). Male homosexuals do not look for steady partners until around thirty years of age. Fifty-one percent of all homosexuals have one or two partners. Twenty-two percent have ten or more. Kinsey reported on the promiscuity of lesbians. He found in his sample that 51% had a single partner, 21% had two partners, and only 4% had ten partners or more. Another rather recent study that inquired into the duration of homosexual relationships found that fully 65% of its sample of homosexuals had sustained a single partnership for as long as nine years (Rubin 1969).

There are presently three basic theories of the causes of homosexual disorientation in the individual: (1) hereditary tendencies, (2) sex hormone imbalance, (3) environmental influences (Coleman 1972; Pomeroy 1966). The theory of hereditary tendencies, of some constitutional determinant, does not receive much support today (Ellis 1963, 1965). The theory of hormone imbalance has alternately gained and lost support over the years. Recently, Masters and Johnson have investigated this theory (1971). The problem with it is that while an imbalance is found in some homosexuals it is not found in most. Moreover, there is the possibility that the hormone imbalance is the result rather than the cause of the psychosocial disorientation. Under conditions which produce anxiety and uncertainty, the same imbalance may be provoked in persons who are otherwise heterosexual.

The theory receiving most support today is that homosexuality develops as the result of environmental factors, with special emphasis on parental influence (Gadpaille 1966; Marmor 1965; Pomeroy 1966; Thorpe 1961). The theory has been especially supported by the recent research at Johns Hopkins University and elsewhere on the different but related issues of sex-role inversion or gender identity. The findings show that some social and psychological influences at work on an individual prior to the age of two years can irreversibly determine his sexual identity (Money 1972; Rosenzweig 1972). Thus, while homosexuality itself is not a confusion as to one's maleness or femaleness but rather a preference in erotic object, the causative factors in sex-role inversion seem to be the same as in homosexuality (Green 1968, 1974; Ferenzi 1950). Margaret Mead's cultural studies also support the cultural modeling of one's sex-role (1949). Tripp (1975) is critical of the emphasis placed on parental influence in the analysis of causes of homosexual preference and gender inversion. Money agrees that the interplay of environmental and hereditary factors is intricate (1957).

Behavior modification studies at Temple University and elsewhere have been successful in altering the sexual behavior of homosexuals at least over a short period. Not everyone agrees that this constitutes an altering of the basic orientation. Psychotherapy has been markedly unsuccessful with homosexuals, though there are those who believe that a true homosexual orientation can be corrected if the homosexual can be brought to desire change sincerely (Bieber 1962, 1968; Ellis 1964). Others believe that the best course of action is to help homosexuals to accept their orientation and socially adapt to it, if it is causing distress (Coleman 1972). Apparently that is the view of a great many members of the American Psychiatric Association and a growing number of the blue-collar population (Yankelovich 1974).

In fine, opinion is divided today as to whether homosexuality is in itself indicative of a personality defect. Orthodox Freudian thought would still view homosexuality as a form of defective sexual development (Bieber 1962 for general psychoanalytic view). The Adlerians understand the logic of sexuality as calling for the individual to participate in the project of building a society. They believe social participation calls the individual to heterosexual relations. The Adlerians view the homosexual as one who is anxious about succeeding socially and, as a result, compulsively escapes into deviant behavior as a form of refusal to participate in the social task (Adler 1917, 1938, 1939; Dreikurs 1946). Jungian thought also views homosexuality as contrary to the structure of complementarity that characterized healthy human existence (Jung 1974). Contrary to these theoretical positions is that of others who view homosexuality as merely a normal variant, such as left-handedness, thus Dr. Lonny Meyers (1973) of the Midwest Population Center, Chicago, and Dr. Allan P. Bell (1976) of the University of Indiana Institute for Sex Research. The same division of viewpoint exists as to whether homosexuality can be successfully treated or whether it is even desirable to change the orientation of the satisfied homosexual.

Public attitude toward homosexuality has been researched extensively. A 1970 study reports that 86% of the general American population disapproves of homosexuality—or did so in 1970 (Levitt and Kassen 1973). One analysis suggested by the researchers is that the general population cannot conceive of love being expressed between homosexuals. The Carnegie Report indicates that by 1973 there was a dramatic increase in young people's tolerance of the homosexual. This was true of both college and non-college youth (Yankelovich 1974). However, three-fourths of the general population that attend church weekly still disapprove of it (Largey and Taft 1975).

## THE ROLE OF LOVE IN SEX

From what has preceded, it is evident that more information is available on the frequency of various forms of sexual behavior than on the effect that such behavior has upon individuals and their relationships. Maslow has observed:

> It would appear that no single sexual act can per se be called abnormal or perverted. It is only abnormal or perverted individuals who can commit abnormal or perverted acts. That is, the dynamic meaning of the act is far more important than the act itself (1966).

The question keeps recurring, however, whether the extreme intimacy of sexual intercourse (if not its procreative potential and social orientation) carries a meaning independent of the intentions of the participants and insinuates that meaning despite those intentions. Can love be separated from sex without robbing human life and relationships of an essential symbolic gesture? Can sex be just "for fun?" Some phenomenologists insist on intrinsic meaning.

> The *logos* is already incarnate in the sexual impulse, as the ingathering principle of unity, which causes two people to come together in eros. . . . It is precisely the strong bond between meaning and body that characterizes genuine sexual life (Smith and Eng 1972).

Maslow believes that it can be for self-actualizing persons "cheerful, humorous and playful" (1954). However, a self-actualizing person is one who acts responsibly toward the other and consequently such sexual behavior occurs in the context of caring (Kirkendall 1971). Even play has its rules and morality (Foote 1954).

Some researchers report that young people have been tending to abandon sex as simple relief from tension and are demanding that it occur in a "meaningful" relationship. A 1973 report out of the University of Indiana Sex Research Institute indicates that while premarital sex is becoming more acceptable to the general public, there is an insistence that it be tied to affection and caring (Levitt and Klassen 1973). Thus one researcher reports college youth are no longer going to prostitutes in the same numbers as formerly (Davis, K.E. 1971) but are engaging in sex with persons with whom they have some on-going relationship. The reason for this change in behavior might well be the pill.

Other researchers have found contradictory data (Benson 1971; Frede 1970). For example, higher social class males apparently continue to exploit lower class females (Ehrman 1961). Teenagers continue to seek sexual release, whether or not there exists any emotional attachment (Kaplan and Sager 1971). College co-eds engage in sex play with people they do not love (Davis, K.E. 1971). There is a growing tendency to make full sexual gratification a part of the general dating pattern (Bell and Chaskes 1970). Even among the "flower children" at Berkeley and the San Francisco area during the late sixties much exploitation of others was found beneath the rhetoric of love and peace (Salisbury and Salisbury 1971). However, the data of these studies may no longer be representative of current attitudes, given the everchanging youth population.

It would seem that sex is in fact very frequently not used as a symbolic gesture of love that desires stable and continuing relationship. And yet abroad there is the conviction that sex has a relationship to some level of commitment. M.S. Calderone suggests that love itself has too many meanings and that the proper emotional context for healthy sex is a mutual desire for intimacy (1971). Another minimal view of humanistic psychology is that sex behavior is merely one aspect of general human behavior, that it has a departmentalized meaning of its own, and that, therefore, it is healthful for the personality and true to human values as long as it is engaged in without intentionally harming the other (Ellis 1971). Masters and Johnson, in their latest attempt to add a humanistic context to their physiological research, see commitment in some form as a necessary ingredient of satisfying sexual encounter (1976). While sensual gratification can readily be obtained from genital activity of whatever kind, the *pleasure* that comes with true sexual intimacy requires a context of commitment. Moreover, should either party feel the need to seek sexual satisfaction with someone else, "the circle of commitment has been broken" (p. 270).

## CONCLUSION

Empirical research to date has provided only inconclusive data on the issues concerning this study. Culture obviously plays a significant role in determining what, to our visceral judgment, shall appear "natural" or "deviant." It is not clear what, if any, evil consequences to the individual or society necessarily follow upon practices thought of as somehow deviant. At the same time, it is not conclusively established that such practices are harmless. As to homosexuality, its causes, the possibility and/or desirability of "curing" it, all remain questions.

Despite this lack of resolution, this excursion into the empirical research has not been without benefit. While no ethical position is compelled by the empirical data, its very inconclusiveness should give pause to one who might otherwise too facilely assume that human experience confirms his moral persuasion. As this study proceeds, an eye will be kept on the research findings.

# IV
# Toward a Theology of Human Sexuality

Recent years have made it increasingly evident, even for those not familiar with the empirical data cited in the foregoing chapter, that there is a growing gap between what the Catholic Church officially teaches in matters sexual and what the faithful have come to believe and practice. One would be shortsighted to believe that the differences are restricted to the debate between the magisterium and theologians regarding the morality of contraception. Repeated surveys, statements, and writings clearly indicate that the differences are more fundamental and pervasive of almost every area of Church teaching on sexuality.

One of the explanations offered for this diversity is the increased awareness of, and respect for, sociological and cultural factors, which always exert a subtle but powerful impact on the sexual mores of people. Another influence that Christians should never lose sight of is the reality of sin and the role it plays in keeping persons from both appreciating and realizing the ideal in their lives. A third factor contributing to this dilemma is an inadequate theology, one which fails to formulate the Christian ideal in a manner faithful to fundamental values yet also responsive to the changing historical, sociological, and cultural conditions in which this ideal must be realized.

Our aim at this point is to address this third factor. Our purpose is to present a theological approach that provides a more adequate orientation and general framework for dealing with particular questions that will follow in the area of human sexuality.

At the outset, three important considerations seem in order. The first concerns moral methodology today. Note should be made of the following admonition given by the Fathers of Vatican II in this regard:

For recent studies and findings of science, history, and philosophy raise new questions which influence life and demand new theological investigations.

Furthermore, while adhering to the methods and requirements proper to theology, theologians are invited to seek continually for more suitable ways of communicating doctrine to the men of their times.

May the faithful, therefore, live in very close union with the men of their time. Let them strive to understand perfectly their way of thinking and feeling, as expressed in their culture. Let them blend modern science and its theories and the understanding of the most recent discoveries with Christian morality and doctrine. Thus their religious practice and morality can keep pace with their scientific knowledge and with an ever advancing technology. Thus too, they will be able to test and interpret all things in a truly Christian spirit.[1]

Moral theology today has the task, therefore, to collaborate with other sciences in the light of our times. Thus we have endeavored to place this study in touch with the empirical data concerning sexuality.

Second, we need to take note of the more dynamic view of human nature expressed at Vatican Council II,[2] for it departs so markedly from the earlier, more static view within our tradition. Concerning human dignity, and significant for our purpose, the same conciliar document states:

God did not create man as a solitary. For from the beginning, "male and female he created them" (Gen 1:17). Their companionship produces the primary form of interpersonal communion. For by his innermost nature man is a social being, and unless he relates himself to others he can neither live nor develop his potential.[3]

The Council Fathers call attention to the idea of human nature as dynamic and relational, and this in accord with our modern self-understanding.

Third, moral theological speculation is necessarily and properly enculturated. This has been demonstrated in our historical survey above, and we see it reaffirmed in the reflections of Vatican II, when it acknowledges that the Church too is an "historical reality." As such, and "with the help of the Holy Spirit, it is the task of the entire people of God, especially pastors and theologians, to hear, distinguish and interpret the many voices of our era, and to judge them in the light of the Divine Word."[4]

Given these considerations, contemporary moral theology is challenged to attempt to articulate a theology of sexuality that is both consistent with Catholic tradition and yet sensitive to modern data.

## PROBLEM

The significant and critical questions raised by recent scientific and theological developments in sexual morality can be reduced to three general areas:

(1) the definition of sexuality,
(2) the principle of integration for the various purposes of sexuality,
(3) the moral evaluation of sexual conduct.

### DEFINITION OF SEXUALITY

Moral textbooks and treatises of the past have generally regarded human sexuality as an experience proper only to married people. The following excerpt from a widely used moral textbook of the 1930s reflects an attitude and approach that has prevailed in moral writings for centuries:

> The rational motive of the virtue of chastity is the reasonableness of controlling sexual appetite in the married and of excluding it in the unmarried, as also of seeking and expressing it in marriage in a rational way, unless the exercise of some higher virtue or more pressing duty justify complete continence, temporary or perpetual, without prejudice to the rights of others. Chastity is a virtue for every state of life. There is a chastity of the married and of the unmarried. Perfect chastity is abstinence from all expressions of the sexual appetite, both in the external act and internal

thought, desire and complacency. This virtue connotes a great victory over an imperious appetite. Few persons of adult age are immune from the incitement and allurement of this appetite. The practice of the virtue is usually arduous, is highly meritorious, gives man a great mastery over himself in this respect, and is pleasing to God. Divines have a good reason, therefore, for assigning a special aureola to virgins, as they do to martyrs and preachers.[5]

According to such a view, children, the severely handicapped, the unmarried, the celibate, the divorced and widowed are not to be sexual beings. The moral ideal for such persons consists in eradicating every sexual impulse and desire. Thus it is not surprising that the same author, together with most of his contemporaries, concludes that "it is grievously sinful in the unmarried deliberately to procure or accept even the smallest degree of true venereal pleasure; secondly, that it is equally sinful to think, say, or do anything with the intention of arousing even the smallest degree of this pleasure."[6]

The reason advanced for these conclusions is that venereal pleasure has no purpose other than to lead to legitimate sexual intercourse and the possibility of procreation. It was argued that to use what was designed for the good of the human race to serve the good of the individual constitutes a substantial inversion of an essential order or relation. Such an approach reflects an understanding of sexuality that is predominantly genital and generative even though it was acknowledged that in the context of married life sexuality could also bring about greater mutual fulfillment of the spouses.

The experience of people today supported by contemporary behavioral and theological sciences understands sexuality much more broadly. Sex is seen as a force that permeates, influences, and affects every act of a person's being at every moment of existence. It is not operative in one restricted area of life but is rather at the core and center of our total life-response. As the recent Vatican *Declaration on Sexual Ethics* maintains: "It is from sex that the human person receives the characteristics which, on the biological, psychological and spiritual levels, make that person a man or a woman, and thereby largely condition his or her progress towards maturity and insertion into society."[7]

Given the wholistic view of person expressed in the documents of Vatican II, a view grounded in the biblical anthropology surveyed above, we suggest that human sexuality must be more broadly understood than it was in much of our earlier tradition. We would, therefore, define human sexuality simply as the way of being in, and relating to, the world as a *male* or *female* person. Men and women, at every moment of life and in every aspect of living, experience themselves, others, and indeed the entire world in a distinctly male or female way. Sexuality then is the mode or manner by which humans experience and express both the incompleteness of their individualities as well as their relatedness to each other as male and female. The book of Genesis reminds us that male and female together reflect the image and likeness of God.[8] To complete this mission, to which every human being is called by the very invitation to life, man must strive to be fully man, a woman to be fully woman, and each must relate to the other. This definition broadens the meaning of sexuality beyond the merely genital and generative and is so to be understood in all that follows.

Human sexuality is the concrete manifestation of the divine call to completion, a call extended to every person in the very act of creation and rooted in the very core of his or her being. From the first moment of existence it summons us incessantly to both intrapersonal and interpersonal growth. Intrapersonally, it propels each person toward the task of creating the male or female each was destined to be. Interpersonally, it calls each to reach out to the other without whom full integration can never be achieved. Thus sexuality like every other aspect of humanness is destined to serve human relationships, not subjugate them. Sexuality is not just an isolated biological or physical phenomenon accidental to human beings but an integral part of their personal self-expression and of their mission of self-communication to others.

From this point of view, sexuality is not elevated into a good in itself nor repressed as somehow tainted with guilt. Sex is rather to be accepted as all other characteristics of humanness and used to facilitate human growth to full maturity. For Christian men and women, this call to full maturity takes on an added dimension inasmuch as we see ourselves as called to growth in Christ, our model. Jesus realized himself fully as a human person and spent his life reaching out to others. His disciples then model their lives after him, "building up the body of Christ, until we all attain to the unity of the faith and of the knowledge of the Son of God, to mature manhood, to the measure of the stature of the fullness of Christ" (Eph 4:12-13). This growth, both intrapersonal and interpersonal, takes place in a sexual person, incomplete in self but reaching toward "fulness" in Christ. It is from this distinctly Christian anthropological perspective that we define and approach the entire question of human sexuality.

PERSONHOOD—THE PRINCIPLE OF INTEGRATION
FOR THE VARIOUS PURPOSES OF SEXUALITY

Sexuality is a pervasive and constitutive factor in the structure of human existence (Chapter III). Implicit in this view is the realization that we *are* our bodies. Our fleshly reality fashions our perception of everything. All levels of consciousness are touched by our embodied presence in the world. The body's way of knowing and tending is there before we reflect upon it. The body asserts its wisdom whether or not we choose to advert to it or even whether we desire to turn from it and deny it.

Within this embodied view of human existence, sexuality is seen as that aspect of our fleshly being-in-the-world whereby we are present and open to that which is not ourselves, to that which is "other." The "other" may be objects or other subjects, persons. Preeminently, it is the mode whereby an isolated subjectivity reaches out to communion with another subject. Embodied subjectivity reaches out to another body-subject in order to banish loneliness and to experience the fullness of being-with-another in the human project. The human being needs another to realize the potential for sharing subjectivity.

Copulation and orgasm are obviously satisfying tension-reducing experiences on all levels of animality. At the level of human existence, an other-directed orientation pervades what otherwise might be considered a blind drive toward biochemical equilibrium. For us humans, the teleology of the pleasure bond is an intercoursing of subjectivities.

Subjectivity is embodied in either a male or a female body. Does this make a difference? The view of human sexuality thus far elucidated gives no reason not to anticipate that intersubjective encounter could be realized as much in the homosexual mode as the heterosexual. The kiss and embrace between close friends of the same biological gender are common enough, at least in some cultures. Moreover, in the view here presented these are indeed sexual expressions. The genital union and that which prepares for it, however, is a different phenomenon—a phenomenon in which the biological difference in gender is significant.

Our understanding of bodily existence requires that the specific structure of one's body colors the manner in which oneself and the world are experienced. A person born with unusually acute hearing or an unusually acute sense of smell perceives the world and himself differently than one differently endowed. A person born with a broad, stubby hand experiences the outside world differently than another born with a small, delicate hand. Anatomy and physiognomy modify the manner in which the world is perceived and form a basis for relationships with that world.

It follows that one who experiences existence in a female body structure perceives reality differently than one born in a male body structure. To what extent anatomical, physiological, and biochemical differences between body structures affect the way in which the genders perceive themselves and the world, independently of cultural manipulation, is currently a much discussed and debated issue. Research thus far reported on the subject is inconclusive for the most part (Chapter III). We are of the opinion that the two sexes experience existence in subtly different ways by reason of their differences in bodily structure.

However that may be, it is apparent that the genital impulse is predisposed in favor of heterosexual union. The incidence of homosexuality remains small. While human sexuality is much more than the impulse to genital union, it hardly excludes this impulse and its urgency. The impulse, biologically tied to procreation and a "given" in each one's existence, assures that the reaching out to a genital encounter will be biased in the direction of heterosexuality. It is in the genital union that the intertwining of subjectivities, of human existences, has the potential for fullest realization.

There exists, then, a sexual atmosphere whenever two human beings meet. This is especially true when the relationship is male-female. The possibility of shared existence, indeed of intimacy and union, emerges on the horizon of movement toward the other. There is a call, an invitation that goes forth from bodily existence to bodily existence. It colors every transaction between the sexes, adding interest and delight, promising mystery and disclosure and delivery from loneliness. At one and the same time it realizes the self and enriches the other.

In view of this understanding of sexuality,[9] it can be said that sexuality serves the development of human persons by calling them to constant creativity, that is, to full openness to being, to the realization of every potential within the personality, to a continued discovery and expression of authentic selfhood. Procreation is one form of this call to creativity but by no means is it the only reason for sexual expression. Sexuality further serves the development of genuine personhood by calling people to a clearer recognition of their relational nature, of their absolute need to reach out and embrace others to achieve personal fulfillment. Sexuality is the Creator's ingenious way of calling people constantly out of themselves into relationship with others.

Throughout much of Catholic history, at least from the patristic period onward, the general thrust of the Church's teaching on sexual morality is fairly accurately summarized in the formulation of Canon Law: "the primary purpose of marriage is the procreation and education of children. The secondary purpose is mutual support and a remedy for concupiscence."[10] Vatican II took a major step forward when it deliberately rejected this priority of the procreative over the unitive end of marriage.[11] It insisted on the inseparable connection between these two purposes of sexuality and suggested the consideration of the human person as the integrating principle that could harmonize them.[12] It also recognized the tremendous role conjugal love plays in calling marriage partners to continuing personal and mutual growth. The 1975 Vatican Declaration on sexual ethics further extended this development by identifying human sexuality even in the unmarried as the source of a person's most fundamental characteristics and as a crucial element leading to personal maturity and integration into society.[13] We think it appropriate, therefore, to broaden the traditional formulation of the purpose of sexuality from *procreative and unitive* to *creative and integrative.*

Wholesome human sexuality is that which fosters a *creative growth toward integration.* Destructive sexuality results in personal frustration and interpersonal alienation. In the light of this deeper insight into the meaning of human sexuality, it is our conviction that creativity and integration or, more precisely, "creative growth toward integration" better expresses the basic finality of sexuality. We further believe that this formulation while being essentially rooted in the traditional expression of the procreative and unitive purposes of sexuality moves beyond the limitations inherent in this formula. Without excluding the former purposes, creative growth toward integration helps to unfold the fuller dimensions implied in asserting that "the nature of the human person and his acts" constitutes the harmonizing principle of human sexuality. As such, it represents a development of, rather than a departure from, the traditional formulation. We maintain that this newer terminology better expresses the purpose of sexuality for the following reasons:

(1) It is faithful to the essential insights of the biblical understanding of human nature (Chapter I); consistent with the fundamental values upheld throughout the Christian tradition (Chapter II); and more compatible with the data provided by the empirical sciences (Chapter III).

(2) It better articulates the modern insight into what makes life truly human, enhances human dignity and thereby constitutes our moral task. This view of the purpose of sexuality is consistent with the proposition that whatever humanizes people is commensurate with their vocation to be and become the image of God. We maintain that creative growth toward integration—intrapersonally and interpersonally—is

the essence of the human and Christian vocation.[14]

(3) Given today's insight into the fact that sexuality is at the core of each person's being, we further suggest that this view of the purpose of sexuality is more properly addressed to modern men and women in terms of "their way of thinking and feeling as expressed in their culture." It blends "modern science and its theories and the understanding of most recent discoveries with Christian morality and doctrine," as called for by Vatican II.[15]

(4) Finally, this terminology seems to reflect more accurately the profound and radical understanding of human sexuality expressed in the Church's more recent documents. Vatican II's dynamic concept of personhood, springing as it does from a renewed and de-stoicized Christian anthropology, provides the basis for this new approach further extended in the 1975 *Declaration on Sexual Ethics*. Creative growth and integration, grounded in this more dynamic vision of human nature, provide a more total and inclusive way of expressing the whole finality of human sexuality. Given this new concept of Christian personhood and proclaiming "the nature of the human person and his acts" as the harmonizing principle, it is our contention that the older expression of procreative and unitive is too static and limiting to be of value in guiding the development of a theology of human sexuality. Such a formulation too narrowly restricts the meaning of sexuality to the context of marriage as has been the case throughout much of our tradition.

In appreciating human sexuality as a call to creative and integrative growth, Christians will be further helped in their understanding by keeping in mind the example and command of Jesus: "Love one another as I have loved you" (Jn 15:12). Jesus' demand, illustrated by his selfless life and death, calls for a level of concern for others ("unto death on the cross") that has perhaps been realized only seldom in Christian history, although it remains an ideal for all. The extent of concern for the other, demanded and exemplified by this fundamental Christian law, provides a basis for human living that is at the core of the Gospel message and at the same time at the apex of the Christian ideal for the fullness of growth and integration "in Christ." True, sexuality is temporal and passing. But when caught up in this Christian motivation, it transcends the temporal and becomes sacramental. The Gospel invitation to celibacy "for the sake of the Kingdom" and to fidelity in a tragic marital situation "for the sake of the Kingdom" are important reminders that transcendent values must influence a Christian evaluation of the meaning of human sexuality.

## THE MORAL EVALUATION OF SEXUAL CONDUCT

Catholic tradition in evaluating moral behavior, has placed a heavy emphasis in recent centuries on the objective moral nature of the given act itself. Particularly with regard to sexuality, it was believed that there is a meaning intrinsic to the very nature of the act itself—a meaning that is absolutely unchangeable and in no way modifiable by extenuating circumstances or special context. Thus, masturbation, any premarital sexual pleasure, adultery, fornication, homosexuality, sodomy, and bestiality were considered intrinsically evil acts, seriously immoral, and under no circumstances justifiable. This approach was influenced to a great extent by an oversimplification of the natural law theory of St. Thomas, the negative sin-oriented approach of the moral manuals, and a strong desire for clear, precise absolute norms to govern moral conduct.

Biblical, historical, and empirical evidence raises serious questions regarding such an approach. Both the Old and New Testament are far more person-oriented than act-oriented in their evaluation of human sexuality. The multiple moral distinctions with regard to the same physical expression of sexuality found in the medieval penitentials indicate a similar appreciation that there is more to the evaluation of human sexual behavior than the act itself. In the empirical data, acts of masturbation are found to be helpful, indifferent, or harmful to the growth and development of the person as a result of circumstances apart from the act itself. Current studies have likewise revealed a significant difference in the human value of sexual activity occurring in a context of caring commitment and that same activity occurring in a casual or loveless context.

It is not surprising then that recent developments in moral theology have called into serious doubt the impersonalism, legalism, and minimalism that often result from such an act-oriented approach. Focusing on the isolated act and assigning it an inviolable moral value in the abstract left little room for consideration of the personal and interpersonal values that are central to genuine morality. Modern trends, returning to some of the emphases observed in Sacred Scripture, in the Middle Ages, and in the theology of St. Thomas, prefer to give greater importance to attitude over act, to pattern or habit over the isolated instance, and to the intersubjective and social over the abstract and individual.[16]

The process of moral evaluation becomes especially difficult in actions that involve both good and evil effects. In the past these decisions were usually made on the principle of double effect interpreted with a "narrowly behavioral or physical understanding of human activity."[17] Contemporary theologians are once again insisting that any attempt to evaluate the moral object of an action apart from motive and circumstances is necessarily incomplete and inadequate. It is the whole action including circumstances and intention that constitutes the basis for ethical judgment. This is not to say that the concrete act is not an important consideration. It is simply to insist that the genuine moral meaning of particular individual acts is most accurately discerned not solely from an abstract analysis of the biology of the act but necessarily including the circumstances as well as intention that surround the action.[18]

Vatican II called for a renewal of moral theology in which morality is seen as a vocation, a way of life, a total response to God's invitation lived out from the depths of a person's being. Morality must never allow itself to be reduced to a simple external conformity to prejudged and prespecified patterns of behavior. For this reason, we find it woefully inadequate to return to a method of evaluating human sexual behavior based on an abstract absolute predetermination of any sexual expressions as intrinsically evil and always immoral.

One alternative to this exaggerated objective approach to moral evaluation is the position that there is no intrinsic objective significance at all to sexual behavior. All sexual behavior draws its meaning and significance from the intention or motive of the person or persons involved. To be sure, the motive must be directed by Christ's command of love, which is regarded as the one and only ultimate norm of morality, but there are no prescriptive rules or norms that necessarily must guide such a response.[19]

To our mind, such a view of sexual morality falls into the danger of being completely subjective, totally relative, and easily mutable according to individual tastes, preferences, and dispositions. Moral rules in such an approach reflect nothing more than the collective choices of different human individuals and societies.

Although we recognize the personal element as indispensable to any moral evaluation, we regard this latter position as too narrow in its restriction of morality to love-motivation, particularly for its neglect of the social and communal implications of sexual behavior. Therefore, we view approaches along these lines to the moral evaluation of sexual behavior as inadequate.

A sound approach to the moral evaluation of sexual behavior must do justice to several extremely complex factors:

(1) It must recognize both the objective and the subjective aspects of human behavior as indispensable to any genuine moral judgment. To ignore either aspect results either in a rigid moral externalism or self-serving moral subjectivism.

(2) It must acknowledge the radical complexity and unity of the human person's sexual nature and avoid any attempt to establish a hierarchy of creativity over integration or vice-versa.

(3) It must demand a constant awareness of the delicate, interpersonal dimension of this experience which constitutes an integral part of any moral standard or judgment.

In view of these considerations we heartily endorse the recommendation of Vatican II that "the nature of the human person and his acts" provides a basic principle from which to evaluate the morality of sexual behavior. A broader definition of human sexuality has led us to suggest that the traditional "procreative and unitive" purposes of sexuality may be more aptly and accurately described as "creative and integrative." It is in the very nature of the human person that these quite distinct dimensions (intrapersonal and interpersonal) are harmonized and integrated.

Traditionally the question of evaluating the morality of sexual behavior has been approached by asking the simple, direct question: "Is this act moral or immoral?" Such **an** approach is flawed in two highly significant ways.

First, it does a disservice to the complexity of the human moral enterprise. It implies that morality can occur apart from personal intention and human decision and that moral evaluation can be made of specific acts viewed in this isolated way. Morality, however, is a reality that involves not only the specific objective act but also relevant circumstances and the mystery of human intention. Therefore, from the point of view of ethical methodology, the question should be formulated: Is this act, in and of itself, predictably an appropriate and productive means of expressing human sexuality? Can it constitute, from a perspective that is broadly humanistic and deeply influenced by the Gospel, an objective value or disvalue?

But even in this more precise expression, the above question remains flawed. For, in the second place, it implies a greatly oversimplified understanding of sexuality. That any specific act can be measured and evaluated in a way totally adequate to the intricate manifold of human experience is dubious at best. Human sexuality is simply too complex, too mysterious, too sacred a human experience for such categorization. Tentativity is inevitable in the attempt to discern the objective significance of such a mysterious and many-splendored reality.

Yet the human spirit must ask such questions. It is a human inevitability. It is also a clear moral challenge flowing from the Gospel call to authentic and genuine living. Hence we suggest that it is both possible and quite necessary to articulate some of the values which sexuality ought to preserve and promote, to indicate some of the functions which sexuality serves in the human Christian community, and thereby to sketch, at least in a tentative way, a series of criteria in terms of which the great variety of sexual behavior may be honestly evaluated.

In short, we maintain that it is appropriate to ask whether specific sexual behavior realizes certain values that are conducive to creative growth and integration of the human person. Among these values we would single out the following as particularly significant:

(1) *Self-liberating:* Human sexuality flows freely and spontaneously from the depth of a person's being. It is neither fearful nor anxious but rather genuinely expressive of one's authentic self. It begets self-assurance, thereby enhancing the full development of a person's potential for growth and self-expression. There is a legitimate self-interest and self-fulfillment that sexual expression is meant to serve and satisfy. To deny this is unrealistic and a contradiction of universal human experience. Too frequently in theological literature sexual union is seen as a sign and expression of the total gift of self to another. Little attention is given to the element of wholesome self-interest that must be part of authentic human sexual expression. This characteristic underscores the importance of sexuality as a source and means of personal growth toward maturity and rejects as unacceptable sexual expression that is self-enslaving. For this reason, it is a serious distortion to speak of the sexual relationship exclusively in terms of expressing a totally altruistic giving of self to another.[20]

(2) *Other-enriching:* Human sexuality gives expression to a generous interest and concern for the well-being of the other. It is sensitive, considerate, thoughtful, compassionate, understanding, and supportive. It forgives and heals and constantly calls forth the best from the other without being demeaning or domineering. This quality calls for more than mere non-manipulation or non-exploitation of others against their will. It insists that wholesome sexuality must contribute positively to the growth process of the other.[21]

(3) *Honest:* Human sexuality expresses openly and candidly and as truthfully as possible the depth of the relationship that exists between people. It avoids pre-

tense, evasion, and deception in every form as a betrayal of the mutual trust that any sexual expression should imply if it is truly creative and integrative. Many writers call attention to the difficulty in maintaining honesty in a sexual relationship. The force of passion, the psychological differences in the male and female natures, and the diversity in cultural background, education, and personal sensitivities all tend to make this a very difficult quality to maintain. The prudent counsel and advice given in this area deserves special hearing.[22]

(4) *Faithful:* Human sexuality is characterized by a consistent pattern of interest and concern that can grow ever deeper and richer. Fidelity facilitates the development of stable relationships, strengthening them against threatening challenges. In marriage, this fidelity is called to a perfection unmatched at any other level and establishing a very special, distinct, and particular relationship. Even this unique relationship, however, should not be understood as totally isolating a spouse from all other relationships thereby opening the way to jealousy, distrust, and crippling possessiveness.[23]

(5) *Socially responsible:* Wholesome human sexuality gives expression not only to individual relationships but in a way also reflects the relationship and responsibility of the individuals to the larger community (family, nation, world). Since human beings are by nature social beings, it is only fitting that the creative and integrative force of human sexuality be exercised in the best interest of the larger community as well. The precise implications of this responsibility may vary considerably with time, place, and culture, but a genuinely responsible exercise of human sexuality cannot ignore this dimension. Both the historical and empirical data indicate that every society has found it necessary to give direction and impose restrictions on the expression of human sexuality in the interests of the common good. This characteristic, however, goes

far beyond what is required for the good order of society. One may observe the law of a given society and still be far from leading a moral life. Law cannot be expected to legislate personal morality. What is required here is that people use their sexuality in a way that reveals an awareness of the societal implications of their behavior and in a manner that truly builds the human community. At times, this may mean a willingness to forego personal benefit and growth in order to preserve or promote the greater good of society.[24]

(6) *Life-serving:* Every expression of human sexuality must respect the intimate relationship between the "creative" and "integrative" aspects.[25] And every life style provides means for giving expression to this life-serving quality. For the celibate and the unmarried, human sexuality may find expression in a life of dedicated service to people through church or society. For the married, this life-serving purpose will generally be expressed through the loving procreation and education of children.

Persons giving themselves totally to each other should realize that, from the beginning, the Creator has chosen the complete intimate union of man and woman to be both a special sign of their commitment to one another and the normal means of transmitting life for the continuation of the human race. Precisely in this total giving of themselves to one another are they able to express their sexual creativity and to move toward their personal integration. A genuine openness and sincere readiness to become responsible "interpreters of God's will"[26] in this regard should underlie such total expressions of human sexuality. In most cases, this openness and readiness will lead marriage partners to become generous cooperators with God in the task of responsibly transmitting life. In some instances, however, this value could mean that a responsible interpretation of God's will leads to a life-serving decision not to beget children. In both instances, the "creative" and "integrative" aspects of human sexuality will be harmonized in the overriding life-serving orientation of the sexual expression. Full sexual expression with an accompanying abortive intent should procreation ensue would be a clear contradiction of this life-serving quality of human sexuality.[27]

(7) *Joyous:* Wholesome sexual expression should give witness to exuberant appreciation of the gift of life and mystery of love. It must never become a mere passive submission to duty or a heartless conformity to expectation. The importance of the erotic element, that is, instinctual desire for pleasure and gratification deserves to be affirmed and encouraged. Human sexual expression is meant to be enjoyed without feelings of guilt or remorse.[28] It should reflect the passionate celebration of life, which it calls forth.

Where such qualities prevail, one can be reasonably sure that the sexual behavior that has brought them forth is wholesome and moral. On the contrary, where sexual conduct becomes personally frustrating and self-destructive, manipulative and enslaving of others, deceitful and dishonest, inconsistent and unstable, indiscriminate and promiscuous, irresponsible and non-life-serving, burdensome and repugnant, ungenerous and un-Christlike, it is clear that God's ingenious gift for calling us to creative and integrative growth has been seriously abused. By focusing on the many-splendored values of wholesome sexuality and avoiding absolute categorizations of isolated, individual sexual actions, one can arrive at a much more sensitive and responsible method of evaluating the morality of sexual patterns and expressions.

Again let it be recalled that all of these values must be enlightened and permeated by the core principle of Christian conduct, the Gospel law of love. It is in the light of the life of the Lord that each of these values or qualities is illuminated by a unique Christian dimension or motivation. In the light of the life of the Lord the Christian has the potential to take each of these values and transcend the temporal to contribute thereby to the coming of the kingdom to give to human living a Christic dimension.

Sexuality then can be elevated to its potential sacramental meaning. The Old Testament saw sexuality as symbolic of the covenant reality of the love of God for his people. St. Paul spoke of it in marriage as the sign of the union of Christ and his Church. Only when it has been humanized and Christianized by the law of love can sex reach this full potential of significance in the lives of those men and women who would use it according to the example of the Lord as a source of their fullest growth and integration as Christian people of God.

At this point, it might be helpful to recall several levels of moral evaluation as one moves from abstract principle to concrete decision. The first level is that of universal principle. We have accepted Vatican II's recommendation that the nature of the person and his acts be the fundamental criterion for evaluating wholesome sexual behavior.[29] The implications of this basic evaluative norm for the area of human sexuality are brought out more explicitly by expressing it in terms of creativity and integration. This principle of creative growth toward integration, which encompasses the Christian meaning of person, reflects an unfolding of Christ's ultimate commandment of love into the sphere of human sexuality. It expresses in a very general but fundamental manner the way in which sexuality is to serve the human person and be consonant with human dignity. In its abstract formulation as a principle, it is absolute and universal providing an overall direction or thrust toward which all wholesome sexual activity ought to tend.

At a second level, the identification of the more particular values associated with human sexuality—self-liberation, other-enrichment, honesty, fidelity, service to life, social responsibility, joy—serves to further unfold the meaning of the basic principle of creative growth toward integration. Note that these values are not expressed in terms of concrete, physical actions. Nor is it likely that each of these values will be equally served or protected in any specific sexual expression. They are not meant to serve as a check-list, the full and complete presence of which will guarantee wholesome sexual expression. This would be an unreal expectation and contradictory to human experience. Humans are finite beings who cannot possibly realize all human values fully at every moment of their existence.

In applying these values to reach a moral decision regarding specific sexual behavior, one must beware not to lose sight of the fundamental principle of creative growth toward integration. This principle provides a framework in the light of which the significance and interrelatedness of these various individual values are to be appreciated and interpreted. Though each value may not be equally served in any particular sexual expression, the substantial violation of any of these values should raise serious questions about the ability of that sexual expression to enhance creative and integrative growth of the human person.

The third level of moral evaluation consists of more concrete norms, rules, precepts, or guidelines. These formulations attempt to distill from the experience of the Christian community the most practical and effective way that the desired values may be realized. They serve to enlighten the Christian conscience as to which particular patterns or forms of sexual behavior have proven generally to be conducive to or destructive of creativity and integration. To the extent that they refer to concrete, physical actions (e.g., masturbation, sterilization, contraception, premarital sex) without specifying particular circumstances or intention, to that extent they cannot be regarded as universal and absolute moral norms.

These norms indicate what Christian experience has proven to occur generally (*ut in pluribus*). If the formulation is adequate, it constitutes a presumption that is usually valid and serves as a helpful guide in reaching a responsible moral decision, especially in doubtful situations. Exceptions may occur, but in these instances the burden of the proof that departure from the norm will nonetheless be creative and integrative not only for the individuals involved but for the larger community as well rests with those who choose to make the exception. Because such norms are not universal moral absolutes, we have chosen to refer to these more concrete formulations as "guidelines." The following chapter entitled "Pastoral Guidelines for Human Sexuality" will deal with these formulations in detail. It is hoped that this terminology will caution against an oversimplistic and absolute application of such criteria in forming moral judgments. The direction of contemporary moral theology (Janssens, Fuchs, Knauer, Schuller, et al)[30] and the aspirations of the Christian conscience seem to require this.

The final level of moral evaluation is the individual concrete decision. It is here that personal conscience finds its sphere of competence and must be respected. Christian moral life may not be looked upon solely from the viewpoint of conformity to predetermined rules or standards. Such an approach would deny that God-given freedom of response essential to human dignity and lying at the core of Christian moraliry.

The well-formed Christian conscience will be well aware of the fundamental principle of creative growth toward integration that ought to guide all sexual activity. It will be open and responsive to the complexity of values involved in this many-splendored gift of human sexual expression. It will be attentive to the more concrete guidelines which reflect the wisdom of the Christian experience and which surface considerations that should be part of every serious moral decision. But it knows that such guidelines must be read and understood not as commands imposed from without but as demands of the inner dynamism of human and Christian life. Their application to a particular decision will usually entail a great deal of prudence and wisdom. This is the place where personal conscience must exercise its responsibility.

In the last analysis, guidelines will serve to enlighten the judgment of conscience; they cannot replace it.[31] The well-formed individual conscience responsive to principles, values, and guidelines remains the ultimate subjective source for evaluating the morality of particular sexual expressions.

# V

# Pastoral Guidelines for Human Sexuality

## INTRODUCTION

### SEXUALITY AND PERSONHOOD

As understood in this study, sexuality is a pervasive and constitutive factor in human existence (Chapter III). The principles and values that govern the evaluation of this human characteristic are grounded in the dynamic view of person emerging from the documents of Vatican II (Chapter IV).

Pastoral implications are present in these reflections. It is our sexuality that makes possible the openness to being that must characterize the human person. As males or females, Christians should be schooled to anticipate that the presence of the other will stimulate interest. Their bodies will pre-reflexively know what possibilities the other holds for them. Far from being disconcerted by this attraction, they should be encouraged to delight in this receptivity. They should be advised of the risk that they run in denying to consciousness this sexual interest and allurement. The movement toward the other, especially and peculiarly toward one of another gender, is *there*, implicit in their bodily existence. Should they choose to banish it from consciousness, they cannot banish it from their existence. If they fail to integrate it into their conscious encounter with the world and with the other, it may pursue its objective in a furtive, dissociated way. The more they deafen themselves to the call of bodily existence, the more they delimit the possibilities of Christian growth. Christians must therefore be encouraged to embrace their sexuality joyfully and in full consciousness.

99

At the same time, Christians must integrate their sexuality into their total life project. The other's bodily presence suggests a possibility and radiates an invitation. Persons already committed to another or to a choice that excludes genital encounter, do not by that fact disengage their sexuality when they encounter another. The call of being is not banished by an act of will. What response is appropriate in such situations will be discussed in the following pages. But married or celibate Christians must be encouraged to remain open to and conscious of their continuing sexual interest in all bodily existences. They blind themselves to it at their own peril and to their own impoverishment. If not acknowledged and integrated into a dialogue with the whole of one's being, the sexual reaching out may pursue a direction independent of and tangential to one's life project.

## THE VIRTUE OF CHASTITY

In the recent past, most moral treatises on human sexuality opened with a definition of chastity as the virtue that regulates sexual passion. Typical of such definitions is the following: "Chastity is the moral virtue that controls in the married and altogether excludes in the unmarried all voluntary expression of the sensitive appetite for venereal pleasure."[1] The latter was often referred to as "perfect chastity" and consisted of "abstinence from all expression of the sensual appetite both in the external act and internal thought, desire, and complacency."[2]

Such an understanding of chastity makes a virtue of the denial, repression, and submersion of all human sexuality outside the context of marriage and procreation. This approach is reasonable if the purpose of human sexuality is seen as primarily procreative. Vatican II, however, officially and explicitly rejected such a view as incomplete, and with good reason. It cannot serve as an adequate basis for a theology of human sexuality. The 1975 Vatican *Declaration on Sexual Ethics* accentuates the positive role of chastity.

The virtue of chastity, however, is in no way confined solely to avoiding the faults already listed. It is aimed at attaining higher and more positive goals. It is a virtue which concerns the whole personality, as regards both interior and outward behavior.[3]

To give expression to the fuller understanding of human sexuality as reflected in this study, it is necessary to define the virtue of chastity in broader and more positive terms. Chastity may be defined, therefore, as that virtue which enables a person to transform the power of human sexuality into a creative and integrative force in his or her life. It facilitates the fullest realization of one's being as male or female and encourages the integration of self with others in the human community. Chastity makes possible both intrapersonal and interpersonal development calling for an active response to the possibilities that human sexuality offers. The repression, submersion, or **denial** of these possibilities is as much a deviation from virtue as **is the** mindless pursuit of sensual pleasure as the ultimate goal of **life.** "Insensitivity is as unspiritual as is promiscuity."[4] The task of developing one's sexuality into a creative and integrative force in life makes the acquisition of the virtue of chastity a constant challenge. Some of the conditions conducive to the fostering of chastity would include the following:

    (1) a clear and accurate knowledge of the basic facts and meaning of human sexuality;

    (2) a positive acceptance of one's sexuality as God-given and fundamentally good; this implies a rejection of views that regard human sexuality as tainted, the source of sin, beneath human's dignity, or a less honorable aspect of being human;

    (3) a proper respect and reverence for human sexuality as a means of interpersonal communication and not merely a biological, physical, genital, or emotional reality;

    (4) a recognition that the pursuit of chastity calls one to a life-long process of openness to the challenges and risks that human sexuality involves; thus, patience and

perseverance are important allies, if chastity is to be pursued;

(5) a Christian appreciation of the fact that God's grace underlies every thrust toward fulfillment and perfection; hence, the recognition that a deeply spiritual life will prove a source of much needed strength and motivation for the pursuit of the virtue of chastity;

(6) the creative integration of human sexuality is not accomplished without struggle; a healthy dose of asceticism and self-discipline must necessarily accompany the effort to be sexually sensitive and responsive, especially in moments calling for restraint and non-expression as the most effective means of achieving creativity and integration.

Chastity calls one to a generous pursuit of that creative growth toward integration that is the purpose of human sexuality. This remains true for any way of life, that is, for the married, unmarried, celibate, or homosexual. Different states of life may call for a different expression of this basic gift of human sexuality, but in no way of life is it to be dismissed as non-existent or unimportant. The task remains of discovering the most effective way to utilize the force of human sexuality in each state of life so as to bring about a creative growth toward integration.

The pastoral considerations that follow approach the phenomenon of human sexuality fundamentally as a way of life. Only in the context of one's state of life can the expression of human sexuality be evaluated properly. This approach bespeaks the conviction that, morally speaking, attitudes, patterns, and habits that reflect a continuing life-style are far more significant than individual, isolated acts.

## MARITAL SEXUALITY

### CALL TO RESPONSIBLE PARTNERSHIP

*Scripture*

"It is not good that the man should be alone. I will make him a helpmate" (Gen 2:18).

The expressions used in the Genesis account of Eve's creation—"helpmate," "bone of my bones and flesh of my flesh," "two in one flesh"—summarize eloquently the biblical vision of marriage as a complete and total sharing by the spouses of their life in common.[5] It is not merely a defense of Eve as a being identical in nature and truly equal to man that this passage underscores, but rather a recognition of marriage as a free and full commitment of partners to share in the mutual task of building the future.

To see here a confirmation of the full modern understanding of personal relationship in marriage may be an exaggeration, but the Bible clearly points to a community of life between man and woman based on equality, total sharing, mutual respect, and support.

Other passages in the Old Testament highlight even more explicitly the personal dimensions of the husband-wife relationship. The touching biblical accounts of the love between Abraham and Sara, Elkanah and Hanna (1 Sam 1:1ff), Tobias and Anna, Tobias and Sara, and David and Bathsheba give ample evidence of the Israelite appreciation of this aspect of human sexuality. Further illustrations can be found in the earthy but eloquent description of love expressed in the Canticle of Canticles as well as in the legal provision that allowed a newly married Israelite a full year of freedom from military and business obligation "to be happy at home with his wife whom he has taken" (Dt 24:5; 20:7).

In the New Testament, Jesus' scathing attack on the easy divorce practice of his time can be best understood in the light of this image of a covenant relationship. This image calls for dedication and life-commitment that ought to be reflected in the fidelity of marriage partners to one another. The possibility of easy divorce made mockery of personal love and fidelity and encouraged Jewish men to regard women, even their wives, as inferior beings to be used at will and discarded as they saw fit. Jesus' denunciation of adultery, even in internal thought and desire indicates how radical and complete the love commitment among his followers is expected to be. Other than this basic command to mutual love and fidelity, the gospels do not present any more specific norms for guiding the conduct of married partners.

St. Paul, however, is more concrete, when he acknowledges the need for wholesome sexual expression between husband and wife and cautions against periods of prolonged abstinence (2 Cor 7). He emphasizes the equality of husband and
wife in their marital relationship and warns against any manipulative or exploitative behavior. On the one hand, Paul reflects
the understanding of his time when he describes the husband-
wife sexual relationship in terms of rendering a mutual debt
and as a remedy against temptation. This fails to do justice to
the role of sexuality in fostering mutual love and growth. On
the other hand, he reveals the depth of the commitment that is
to exist between husband and wife when he dares to compare
the husband and wife relationship to the faithful love that
Christ lavishes upon the Church. Significantly, although children are always seen as a blessing, nowhere does the New Testament single out the procreative responsibility of husband and
wife as deserving special attention. This is simply taken for
granted.

Paul does not counsel asceticism of self-denial out of contempt for the body; he is no Gnostic nor Hellenistic dualist.
His advice on marriage is very much influenced by his imminent expectation of the Parousia: "The appointed time had
grown very short. . . . The form of this world is passing away"
(1 Cor 7:29, 31). In the light of Corinth's notorious reputation
for sexual excesses, Paul's counsel appears to be a realistic and
practical attempt to obviate difficulties that could create a
serious threat to marital fidelity.

In short, the Bible clearly places the greatest emphasis on
the responsibility of spouses to love one another in mutual and
lasting fidelity. It is far more concerned with this overall thrust
and direction than with moralizing about specific forms of sexual behavior. Marital sexuality is viewed in the context of its
ability to serve and enrich the mutual relationship of the
spouses.

### Tradition

The historical section of this study details how, quite in
contrast to the New Testament, dominant emphasis came to
be given to the procreative rather than the personal aspect of

sexuality in the historical development of Church teaching and attitudes. This emphasis on the procreative dimension led eventually to the evaluation of marital sexuality primarily in terms of openness to procreation and only secondarily in terms of mutual love and support. The unitive aspect of sexuality in marriage was never denied or excluded but rather subordinated to the procreative task.

The moral manuals of the recent past reflected this emphasis in their development of an elaborate theology of marital sexuality that gave the overriding priority to the procreative purpose. Any sexual expression that frustrated procreation, e.g., contraception, masturbation, or sodomy was regarded as intrinsically evil and a serious violation of moral law.[6] As long as procreative integrity was secured, all other sexual expressions between marriage partners, including oral sex, were not regarded as seriously sinful.[7] Any reasonable cause, e.g., fostering of love or relief of concupiscence justified such expressions and rendered them moral and virtuous. Pure pleasure-seeking was not considered a justifying reason in itself, but even if sensual gratification were the only motive, such activity was never regarded as more than venially sinful.

An interesting difference of opinion seems to have existed as to whether orgasm in the female apart from procreation could be said to constitute pollution in the same sense as seminal emission in the male; female secretions in orgasm were not viewed as essential for procreation in the same way that male semen was required.[8] Such precise and intricate distinctions indicate the seriousness with which most theologians of the past considered the procreative purpose of human sexuality normative. Their careful statements regarding sexual pleasure in the context of married life reveal some appreciation of the importance of this aspect of human sexuality, but it was seen most often as a remedy against concupiscence or a means of preserving fidelity. Thus, they concluded, a spouse whose partner was in danger of incontinence could not morally refuse the marriage debt even for fear that the children might be born defective or stillborn, or that the family might be forced to live a life of abject poverty.[9] This conviction was supported with the theological argument that even if the fetus were stillborn or aborted and died in original sin without the opportunity for heaven, this condition would be better than not to have existed at all.[10]

Instances of a more positive view of sexual intercourse as a means of fostering love, enhancing mutual growth, and deepening commitment are decidedly rare in moral theological writings of the past and they are always subordinated to the primary concern for ensuring procreative integrity. Procreation constituted the primary purpose of human sexuality and allowed no compromise. It is not surprising that in such a context birth control came commonly to be regarded as the most frequent violation of marital chastity. It was recognized that one could sin by refusing to render the "marriage debt," but this was less often confessed as serious sin because of various "justifying" circumstances.

### Growth and Integration through Intimacy

The beginnings of the 20th century witnessed a return to the biblical appreciation and emphasis on the interpersonal dimension of human sexuality in the context of marriage. Pius XI reflected this developing trend in his encyclical on Christian Marriage when he stated that:

> This mutual inward molding of a husband and wife, this determined effort to perfect each other can, in a very real sense, be said to be the chief reason and purpose of matrimony, provided matrimony be looked at not in the restricted sense as instituted for the proper conception and education of the child, but more widely as the blending of life as a whole and the mutual interchange and sharing thereof.[11]

He was able to make such a statement even though speaking still out of a context in which the procreative purpose remained primary.

It remained for Vatican II, however, to culminate this movement by giving official Church recognition to the personal dimension of human sexuality as being of no less importance than the procreative. The implications of this decision can hardly be overestimated. The Council's deliberate rejection of the centuries-long tradition that regarded the procreative end as supreme, necessitates a thorough rewriting of the theology of marital sexuality found in the moral manuals. The chapter on marriage in Vatican II's *Constitution on the Church in the Modern World* provides the basis for a contemporary Catholic theology of marital sexuality. One of the fundamental principles of this renewed theology of marital sexuality is the recognition that the very essence of marriage as enunciated by the Council calls for a mutual commitment to *responsible partnership:*

> The intimate partnership of married life and love has been established by the Creator and qualified by His laws. It is rooted in the conjugal covenant of irrevocable personal consent. Hence, by that human act whereby spouses mutually bestow and accept each other, a relationship arises which by divine will and in the eyes of society too, is a lasting one.[12]

Characteristic of this responsible partnership is a commitment to continuing mutual growth, as Vatican II abundantly makes clear:

> Thus, a man and a woman, who by the marriage covenant of conjugal love "are no longer two but one flesh" (Mt 19:6), render mutual help and service to each other through an intimate union of their persons and of their actions. Through this union they experience the meaning of their oneness and attain to it with growing perfection day by day. As a mutual gift of two persons, this intimate union, as well as the good of the children, imposes total fidelity on the spouses and argues for an unbreakable oneness between them.[13]

The role of sexuality in realizing this vision of marriage is briefly but beautifully described in the Council's reflections on conjugal love. The importance and uniqueness of the spouses' sexual expression of their mutual love is strongly emphasized:

> The biblical Word of God several times urges the betrothed and the married to nourish and develop their wed-

lock by pure conjugal love and undivided affection. Many men of our own age also highly regard true love between husband and wife as it manifests itself in a variety of ways depending on the worthy customs of various peoples and times.[14]

In decidedly positive terms the Council affirmed that sexual intimacy properly integrated into the whole life of a married couple is the very means through which the commitment to responsible partnership is realized:

> This love is an eminently human one since it is directed from one person to another through an affection of the will. It involves the good of the whole person. Therefore it can enrich the expressions of body and mind with a unique dignity, ennobling these expressions as special ingredients and signs of the friendship distinctive of marriage. This love the Lord has judged worthy of special gifts, healing, perfecting, and exalting gifts of grace and of charity.
>
> Such love, merging the human with the divine, leads the spouses to a free and mutual gift of themselves, a gift proving itself by gentle affection and by deed. Such love pervades the whole of their lives. Indeed, by its generous activity it grows better and grows greater. Therefore it far excels mere erotic inclination, which selfishly pursued, soon enough fades wretchedly away.[15]

In a special way Vatican II singled out intercourse between husband and wife as particularly expressive and effective in fostering this responsible partnership. It is worth noting that the Council describes the marital act as both sign and cause of intimate partnership ("expressed and perfected," "signifies and promotes"), the same way as the Church has traditionally described the nature of the sacraments:

> This love is uniquely expressed and perfected through the marital act. The actions within marriage by which the couple are united intimately and chastely are noble and worthy ones. Expressed in a manner which is truly human, these actions signify and promote that mutual self-giving by which spouses enrich each other with a joyful and a thankful will.[16]

Finally, reminiscent of St. Paul, the Council Fathers cautioned against the consequences that could result in marriages where sexual expression of love is absent:

> But where the intimacy of married life is broken off, it is not rare for its faithfulness to be imperiled and its quality of fruitfulness ruined. For then the upbringing of the children and the courage to accept new ones are both endangered.[17]

Serious reflection on this theology of responsible partnership indicates that much more attention must be given to this personal dimension in any evaluation of what constitutes wholesome sexual behavior for the married.

## Pastoral Reflections

In light of the foregoing, we offer the following pastoral reflections on the role of sexuality with regard to building responsible partnership:

(1) Marriage, in recent Church documents, is defined as an "intimate partnership," a "community of love," a "conjugal covenant," a "mutual gift of two persons." The fundamental task of marriage is described as "the determined effort to perfect each other" through the mutual interchange and sharing of life as a whole. Thus, sexuality in marriage is human and moral to the extent and degree that it serves and promotes this fundamental task of marriage. Pastoral leaders should take special care to make married couples aware that this is an ongoing task that ought to embrace and pervade every aspect of their lives. Since the completeness of mutual self-giving is a mutual life-giving process, within the abilities of the couple, it follows that responsible partnership cannot be achieved without a serious mutual consideration as well of the obligation to responsible parenthood.

(2) The fact that the majority of American marriages suffer from a significant degree of frigidity and lack of sexual communication, seriously hampering the build-

ing of responsible partnership, indicates that education and sensitization in this area are an urgent pastoral need and responsibility of our time. Through educational programs, individual and group counseling, sermons and specialized instruction, married people deserve to be supported in their efforts to develop better communication and deeper intimacy. Until the lack of marital communication and mutual support to growth is regarded as a serious neglect of marital responsibility (far more pervasive and devastating than contraception), pastoral leaders in the Church fail deplorably in their task as moral educators of the married.

(3) Moral evaluation of sexual intimacies in marriage requires that they be measured in terms of their ability to foster creative and integrative growth and not in terms of their physical nature. No physical expression of sexuality, including oral sex, provided it be mutually sensitive and acceptable, should be prejudged as morally wrong or perverse. Empirical studies indicate that background, culture, education, formation, and personal disposition, as well as other factors, account for the widespread diversity of sexual expressions which can be conducive to growth. Mutual sensitivity to this diversity must play an important role in determining what is morally acceptable in a particular marriage relationship. The ability of these actions to foster the values of self-liberation, other-enrichment, honesty, fidelity, life-service, social responsibility, and joyousness will provide the objective framework for moral judgment.

(4) Complete sexual union expresses and perfects mutual sharing in a singularly effective and unique manner. The sexual act itself, however, is enriched in meaning and takes its full human significance only from the total commitment of the marriage partners in every other aspect of their lives. It is not enough, therefore, to be concerned simply or primarily about the biological integrity of the genital expression of sexuality. The

sexual behavior of married couples must be measured according to the values of responsible partnership as well as responsible parenthood. Such questions as the following may be helpful in assisting couples to evaluate better their sexual intimacy from this perspective:

Does your sexual expression deepen your love and respect for each other? Does it reflect sensitivity, thoughtfulness, and concern for the other? Or is it more an imposition of self upon the other with an almost exclusive concern for sensual gratification? Is it exploitative and manipulative of the other? Does it enhance or restrict mutual respect, trust, and growth?

### CALL TO RESPONSIBLE PARENTHOOD

*Scripture*
"Increase, multiply and fill the earth" (Gen 1:28). From the opening pages of Genesis the biblical call to parenthood is clear and explicit. The high regard with which the Israelites viewed their procreative mission is evidenced throughout the biblical literature in their attitudes toward family and children. Children were a sign of God's providence and blessing (Ps 128:4). Childlessness and sterility were among the more serious curses that could be visited on anyone (Jgs 11:37). Celibacy and virginity were simply incomprehensible life-styles for the Old Testament Israelite. The social and economic benefits that children brought to the household as well as conviction that the deceased live on in their progeny all contributed to the desire to have numerous children (Gen 12:1-2).

These values together with a fundamental commitment to the welfare of the chosen people guided much of Old Testament morality in the area of marriage. Thus, in special circumstances, the begetting of children through a maid servant (Gen 16) was approved. The law of levirate marriage even obliged an incestuous relationship in order that the family line might be preserved (Gen 38; Dt 25:5-10). Polygamy likewise was tolerated and seems to have been a common practice in the earliest centuries.

The New Testament is much less explicit. It simply takes

for granted that children are a blessing and that parents share in God's continuing work of creation. The New Testament focuses rather on the mutual responsibilities between children and parents. Responsible parenthood, according to St. Paul, involves not only begetting children but the far more difficult ongoing task of forming them in the image and likeness of their Maker (Eph 6:3-4; Tit 2:5). The parental responsibilities of loving, guiding, forming, and caring for children are repeatedly emphasized.

The Scriptures, though they clearly call spouses to responsible parenthood, have nothing specific to say about the morality of contraception or sterilization. Past attempts to read into the account of Onan a biblical condemnation of contraception are widely rejected as untenable by contemporary Scripture scholars.[18] Likewise, the use of passages prohibiting mutilation in general as proof of a biblical condemnation of sterilization is regarded as exegetically and theologically simplistic.[19] Guidance for the determination of the morality of such behavior must be sought from sources other than the Bible.

### Church Teaching

In the historical section of this study (Chapter II) we traced the origin of the Church's insistence on the primacy of the procreative over the personal to Stoic sources rather than to Scripture. For centuries, this Stoic influence, supported by other factors (high infant mortality rate, low longevity, the economic advantage of having many children, fear of war, plague, famine—all events that could threaten the very survival of the human race) resulted in a submersion and subordination of personalist values to the procreative task of continuing the human race. In rejecting this hierarchical ordering of the ends of marriage, Vatican II opened the way to a fuller recognition of the unitive aspect of human sexuality. The Council's recommendation that the tension between the procreative and unitive (creative and integrative) aspects of sexuality be harmonized in fidelity to the "nature of the human person and his acts," has far-reaching implications for the realization of responsible parenthood in marriage.

Vatican Council II required of spouses the realization that through the powers of procreation they are called to be "co-operators with the love of God" and "interpreters of that love."[20] This call implies a generous openness and willingness to accept the task of parenthood. At the same time it imposes on parents a sober realization that as "interpreters of that love" they must assume personal responsibility for determining the manner and extent of this procreative response.

Vatican II was clearly aware of the need and sometimes even the serious obligation to limit procreation:

> This Council realizes that certain modern conditions often keep couples from arranging their married lives harmoniously, and that they find themselves in circumstances where at least temporarily the size of their families should not be increased.[21]

The attitude, therefore, of "leaving it all in the hands of God and accepting whatever he sends" is both simplistic and morally irresponsible. Responsible parenthood demands readiness to acknowledge that there are situations and conditions where it would be irresponsible and hence immoral to beget children.

Responsible parenthood requires that spouses do not shirk this difficult decision by insisting that the Church, a priest, or a doctor make their decision. In no uncertain terms, Vatican II clearly states: "The parents themselves, and no one else, should ultimately make this judgment in the sight of God."[22] The role of the priest or counselor is not to make a decision for others but rather to assist them in reaching a prudent, responsible decision and to support them in its implementation.

In view of the broader understanding of the meaning of marriage and of human sexuality, it is apparent that this decision must be based on a wide spectrum of considerations. Vatican II summarizes the major areas of consideration when it writes:

> They will thoughtfully take into account both their own welfare and that of their children, those already born and those which may be foreseen. For this accounting they will reckon with both the material and the spiritual conditions of the times as well as of their state in life. Finally, they will

consult the interests of the family group, of temporal society, and of the Church herself.[23]

The physical, emotional, and psychological well-being of both wife and husband must be an important consideration in this decision. The welfare of other members of the family particularly where there may be need for special attention or care cannot be overlooked either. The Council openly suggested that parents take a long-range view of their responsibilities sensitive to the added demands that new children may bring. Together with the economic situation of the individual family, the conditions of society likewise must not be overlooked. Concern for overpopulation as well as underpopulation must be faced honestly and realistically. In a word, the call to responsible parenthood means that the decision regarding family size must reflect a concern not only for the desires and possibilities of the individual parents and family but for the well-being of society as a whole.

The reasons for deciding that it would be responsible to limit one's family are many and complex. At times, one or another of these considerations may not be sufficiently strong of itself, but taken together these factors may well provide the basis for a responsible moral conviction that the family should be limited. Although husband and wife together must ultimately accept the responsibility for their judgment, the complexity of such a decision warrants the advice and support of a prudent and sensitive priest or counselor.

### Contraception

Once a responsible decision has been reached regarding family limitation, there remains the further decision regarding the method for achieving it. There is a great variety of methods available for contraception today, and parents need to give serious consideration to their medical, psychological, economic, personal, and moral implications.

Among the methods employed for contraceptive purposes are: (1) complete abstinence, (2) rhythm, (3) the birth control pill, (4) ovulation, (5) the progesterone pill, (6) intrauterine devices, (7) diaphragms, (8) condoms, (9) basal temperature, (10) spermicides, (11) withdrawal, (12) the DES morning-after pill, (13) sterilization.

As a general principle to guide parents in the moral evaluation of the various available methods, Vatican II suggests the following norm:

> Therefore when there is question of harmonizing conjugal love with the responsible transmission of life, the moral aspect of any procedure does not depend solely on sincere intentions or on an evaluation of motives. It must be determined by objective standards. These, *based on the nature of the human person and his acts*, preserve the full sense of mutual self-giving and human procreation in the context of true love. Such a goal cannot be achieved unless the virtue of conjugal chastity is sincerely practiced.[24]

The insistence that the total nature of the human person and his actions constitute the norm for evaluating the morality of the method to be employed marks a significant development from earlier teachings of the Church which focused this judgment solely on the nature of the act. If one is to be true to this teaching of Vatican II, approved by the Holy Father and by bishops throughout the world, one cannot judge methods of contraception as immoral or unacceptable solely for physical or biological reasons that flow from the nature of the act itself. Moral judgment must always reflect a concern for the total well-being of the person. It must be made in terms of the value conflicts and realistic possibilities that confront people in their concrete life situation. Conscience must play a crucial role in honestly assessing the objective considerations on which the decision is to be based. The decision should not be purely subjective, relying on a false sincerity that refuses to face the objective evidence. Parents need to consider honestly and carefully the medical, psychological, economic, and religious implications of each method in regard to their total well-being before reaching a decision.

Such an interpretation of the teaching of Vatican II on marriage recognizes that there are times when the decision to use artificial methods of contraception is both morally responsible and justified. In such instances, special consideration should be given to the particular effects a given method may have on the overall nature and well-being of the persons involved. Among such considerations the following are particularly important:

### (1) *Medical Considerations*

In choosing among the various methods of contraception one should be well informed regarding the nature of the contraceptive method, its manner of operation, its relative effectiveness as well as its immediate and long-range consequences (see Chart, Appendix 1). Variations do occur and the effects indicated may be further complicated by the particular state of health of the persons involved. Consequently, decisions regarding the use of any method should only be made in consultation with and upon recommendation of a competent physician or medical expert. It is not the task of the priest or religious counselor to recommend or approve any specific method of contraception.

### (2) *Psychological Considerations*

If the nature of the whole human person is the criterion by which various methods of family limitation are to be evaluated, then the possible psychological implications of any particular method for the peace of mind and general psychological well-being of the couple cannot be overlooked. Individual differences are subject to an even greater variety than the medical factors. In some instances, it is simply a matter of aesthetics that determines which method is personally acceptable or unacceptable. More frequently, the degree of effectiveness of a particular method plays a considerable role in determining the impact of a particular means on the psychological well-being of the couple. At times, other factors more difficult to discern, but nonetheless genuine, can cause a psychological block to certain methods of contraception.

Some questions that could be helpful in reaching a responsible moral decision would include the following: How important is it to avoid pregnancy? What would be the consequences to child, mother, other members of family, society? What is the risk of pregnancy with the particular method under consideration? If the method is not fully effective, would the fear of pregnancy diminish peace of mind and affect the capacity for interrelationship? Does the method itself introduce stress and tension into the marital relationship? Is the method psychologically and aesthetically acceptable? Will the use of the method affect either party's emotional response to life and to the marriage relationship?

### (3) *Personal Considerations*

Other factors beyond the medical and psychological may also enter into the picture in determining the method most suitable to serving the needs of the whole person. For instance, is the method relatively simple and easy to use in terms of the individual's intellectual and emotional capacities? Or does it require the kind of involvement and maturity that is beyond the capacity of its users? Is the method within the financial means of the couple, or will its use create an intolerable economic hardship?

### (4) *Religious Considerations*

The mature Catholic acknowledges a responsibility to take into consideration the official teaching of the Church when forming his or her conscience on moral matters. For many Catholics the major argument against the use of any artificial methods of contraception is the repeated explicit condemnation of such means by Pius XI, Pius XII, and Paul VI. Paul VI in his encyclical *Humanae Vitae* insists that "each and every marriage act must remain open to the transmission of life." In accordance with this teaching as elaborated in the encyclical, abstinence or rhythm would be the only morally licit means of exercising responsible parenthood. It is important to note the reasons that the Holy Father advances for his judgment:

> That teaching, often set forth by the magisterium, is founded upon the inseparable connection, willed by God and unable to be broken by man on his own initiative, between the two meanings of the conjugal act: the unitive meaning and the procreative meaning. Indeed, by its intimate structure, the conjugal act, while most closely uniting husband and wife, capacitates them for the generation of new lives, according to laws inscribed in the very being of man and woman. By safeguarding both these essential aspects, the unitive and the procreative, the conjugal act preserves in its fullness the sense of true mutual love and its ordination toward man's most high calling to parenthood.[25]
>
> To use this divine gift destroying, even if only partially its meaning and its purpose is to contradict the nature both of man and of woman and of their most intimate relationship, and therefore it is to contradict also the plan of God and his will.[26]

The encyclical's rejection of all artificial means of contraception is based primarily on the inseparable connection it sees between the unitive and procreative meanings of the conjugal act. The fact that the encyclical approves of rhythm, however, suggests that a deliberate intention not to propagate life does not disrupt the relationship between the procreative and unitive. "The openness to the transmission of life" that the encyclical calls for does not require a "readiness to transmit life" but rather a respect for the "laws of the generative process" or a faithful observance of biological "laws and rhythms."[27] According to this view, the unifying factor of these two aspects is a willingness not to interfere with the biological process of generation.

Even theologians who accept in principle an inseparable connection between the procreative and unitive elements of sexuality regard the explanation given in the encyclical as too heavily biological. It flows from an understanding of natural law that is more physical than moral. It seems, in their opinion, to attach an overriding importance to respect for the biological aspects of human nature above all other considerations. They prefer to explain the connection between the procreative and unitive aspects of sexuality on other grounds.

Vatican II, as we have pointed out, suggests the "human person and his acts" provides a more appropriate principle for integrating these two elements.

> Therefore when there is question of harmonizing conjugal love with the responsible transmission of life, the moral aspect of any procedure does not depend solely on sincere intentions or an evaluation of motives. It must be determined by objective standards. These based on the nature of the human person and his acts, preserve the full sense of mutual self-giving and human procreation in the context of true love. Such a goal cannot be achieved unless the virtue of conugal chastity is sincerely practiced.[28]

Bernard Haring, who deserves credit for authoring much of the Vatican II statement, explains the way in which the "human person and his acts" can be the integrating element:

> It can be positively said that when a couple strives in the best possible way to grow in mutual affection, to promote the unity and stability of the marriage so as to better fulfill the parental vocation as regards good education and readiness to desire as many children as they can responsibly accept, then they preserve the human connection between the two meanings. Total continence can undermine a whole marriage. . . . The close relationship between the procreative and the unitive good of marriage and of the conjugal act must be explained at a much higher, more demanding and less frustrating level than that of an absolute respect for biological "laws and rhythm" which are anything but absolute.[29]

The Majority Report of the Papal Commission appointed to study the problem of human sexuality reflected a similar person-oriented approach:

> A right ordering toward the good of the child within the conjugal and familial community pertains to the essence of human sexuality. Therefore the morality of sexual acts between married people takes its meaning first of all and spe-

cifically from the ordering of their actions in a fruitful married life, that is, one which is practiced with responsible, generous and prudent parenthood. It does not depend upon the direct fecundity of each and every particular act. . . . So the Church, particularly through the teaching of Pius XII, has come to realize more fully that marriage has another meaning and another end besides that of procreation alone, even though it remains wholly and definitely ordered to procreation, though not always immediately.

What has been condemned in the past and remains so today is the unjustified refusal of life, arbitrary human intervention for the sake of moments of egotistic pleasure; in short, the rejection of procreation as a specific task of marriage. In the past, the Church could not speak other than she did, because the problem of birth control did not confront human consciousness in the same way. Today, having clearly recognized the legitimacy and even the duty of regulating births, she recognizes too that human intervention in the process of the marriage act for reasons drawn from the finality of marriage itself should not always be excluded, provided that the criteria of morality are always safeguarded.

If an arbitrarily contraceptive mentality is to be condemned as has always been the Church's view, an intervention to regulate conception in a spirit of true, reasonable and generous charity does not deserve to be, because if it were, other goods of marriage might be endangered. So what is always to be condemned is not the regulation of conception, but an egotistic married life, refusing a creative opening-out of the family circle, and so refusing a truly human—and therefore truly Christian—married love. This is the anti-conception that is against the Christian ideal of marriage.

As for the means that husband and wife can legitimately employ, it is their task to decide these together, without drifting into arbitrary decisions but always taking into account the objective criteria of morality. These criteria are in the first place those that relate to the totality of married life and sexuality.[30]

Charles Curran offers still another explanation of this relationship:

What about the relationship between sexuality and procreation? In the past, Catholic theology seems to have erred by seeing a connection between every act of sexual intercourse and procreation. Those who would argue for extramarital or premarital sex would naturally deny any necessary connection between sexuality and procreation. It is obvious that there is some connection between sexuality and procreation. The creation story in Genesis bears witness to this relationship. But even the approval of rhythm, to say nothing of the widespread rejection of the ethical conclusion of *Humanae Vitae*, indicates that not every act of sexual intercourse has to be open to procreation. Catholic theologians generally speak now of a connection between procreation and sexuality to the extent that sexual intercourse has meaning only within a realm of procreative acts or with a person with whom one is joined in procreative union; in other words, in marriage. Sexuality as an expression of love also calls for some real connection with an openness to procreation. Love itself is creative. The covenanted love of husband and wife tends to procreation just as the covenant of Yahweh with his people and Christ with his Church is a life-giving covenant to love. A problem arises in some cases in which even a married couple should not have children (e.g., because of a genetic problem or even societal reasons), for even their marital sexuality should not be procreative. Paul Ramsey answers this objection by saying that such married partners would still be saying that if either has a child it would come about only through their one flesh unity.[31]

This diversity of views within the Church in no way contests the fundamental fact that there is a connection between the procreative and unitive aspects of the conjugal act that needs to be respected. The way that one interprets this relationship, however, can lead to quite different conclusions regarding the acceptability of artificial forms of contraception.

More dialogue and reflection are clearly needed to arrive at a better understanding and formulation of the relationship between the procreative and unitive aspects of sexual intercourse. The explanations, however, which set this relationship within the total context of the person are far more congruent with the findings of this study than those which rely exclusively on a non-interference with the biological processes as the integrating element.

Another argument that the encyclical advances to support its judgment regarding the objective evil of contraception is the conviction that this practice inevitably results in a "general lowering of morality," "conjugal infidelity," "loss of respect for the woman," and abusing one's marriage partner as a "mere instrument of selfish enjoyment." Thus the encyclical states:

> Upright men can even better convince themselves of the solid grounds on which the teaching of the Church in this field is based, if they care to reflect upon the consequences of methods of artificial birth control. Let them consider, first of all, how wide and easy a road would thus be opened up toward conjugal infidelity and the general lowering of morality. Not much experience is needed in order to know human weakness, and to understand that men—especially the young, who are so vulnerable on this point—have need of encouragement to be faithful to the moral law, so that they must not be offered some easy means of eluding its observance. It is also to be feared that the man, growing used to the employment of anticonceptive practices, may finally lose respect for the woman, and no longer caring for her physical and psychological equilibrium, may come to the point of considering her as a mere instrument of selfish enjoyment, and no longer as his respected and beloved companion.[32]

Where such consequences are foreseen to follow as a result of the introduction of artificial means of contraception, no one will contest that their use is immoral. Many sincere, respected, and experienced people, however, find it difficult to accept these effects as inevitable consequences. Quite the contrary, they contend that the use of such means can at times serve to preserve marital fidelity, deepen the mutual love and respect of the spouses, bring peace and healing, and raise the whole level of moral responsibility of the marriage partners. The overwhelming number and authority of those who have expressed such conviction as well as the intrinsic reasons that they offer to support their position are more than sufficient to render this divergent opinion as theologically solidly probable. The intrinsic evidence for theological probability consists of the positive reasons or arguments that are presented to explain or define a position.

Those who view contraception or sterilization as morally licit in certain instances offer a number of positive reasons to support their opinion. Principal among these are:

## (1) *The Person-Centered Approach to Moral Judgments*

Paragraph No. 51 of the *Constitution on the Church in the Modern World* indicates that the moral evaluation of any procedure attempting to harmonize conjugal love with the responsible transmission of life must be "based on the nature of the human person and his acts." Fidelity to this criterion implies that the moral evaluation of contraception and sterilization must be made in the light of the total welfare of the person. Theologians instrumental in preparing this paragraph support such an interpretation of this principle.[33] In practice, this principle would permit contraception in those instances where it would contribute to the total well-being of the person.

## (2) *Biblical Exegesis and Teaching on Moral Matters*

Catholic biblical scholarship in recent years has come to recognize that the biblical passages cited in the past as prohibiting contraception have been seriously misinterpreted. Careful study of the moral teachings and demands of the New Testament, however, lends strong support to greater emphasis being placed on the total person and his relationship, rather than on an analysis of the physical act as the locus of moral judgment. Worthy of note, *Humanae Vitae* did not point to any scriptural evidence in support of the position advanced therein.

## (3) *Renewed Understanding of Natural Law*

Recent years have seen considerable discussion and reflection brought to bear on the meaning and role of natural law in reaching moral judgments. There has been a widespread and general consensus among moralists in moving away from a static, predominantly biological, understanding of natural law to a more dynamic interpretation of it as our rational participation in God's plan. From this point of view, the basis for moral judgment lies not in acts predetermined as intrinsically evil, but rather in a person's response to God's call in the concrete realities of existence.

## (4) *Scientific and Medical Advances regarding the Reproductive Process*

Medical research knowledge and technology have given rise to new understanding and insight regarding human procreative powers. These advances have increased both our ability and responsibility to become "cooperators" and "interpreters" of the love of God in the task of transmitting life. As long as a husband was unaware of the dangers involved in a new pregnancy for his wife or of the high probability that the child would be born seriously defective, he was justified in not feeling concerned about a future pregnancy. Today, however, to ignore such knowledge when it is available would be highly irresponsible. Thus, contemporary theology has come to approach the moral aspects of intervention differently. As one author writes:

> Any arbitrary destruction or mutilation of human fertility must definitely be denied. Scientific doubts concern only those cases where the health of the entire person calls for an operation. . . . There are extreme cases where expert interpretation of the situation clearly arrives at the conclusion that, on the level of natural law—that is to say, a rational evaluation of the facts and of human responsibility— any further fertility must be eliminated for good. An operation performed with these realizations in mind (in order to save a life or a marriage) would, then, in a moral sense, not be sterilization properly so called, since it is not a destruction of responsible human fertility; responsible reasoning would exclude it anyhow.[34]

(5) *New Insights from the Behavioral and Psychological
Sciences*

Social and economic conditions of past centuries placed
heavy emphasis on people's procreative responsibility to ensure
the survival of the human race. High infant mortality, the constant threat of decimating plagues or natural calamities, and
the short average life span placed this responsibility in an altogether different perspective than that which we experience
today. Survival of the human race is viewed by many scientists
today as threatened not by underpopulation but rather overpopulation. Vatican II and Pope Paul VI have recognized that
this concern ought not to go unheeded, even though the means
chosen to resolve the problem must be considered carefully.
Rapidly changing social and economic conditions in recent decades, greater sensitivity to the world population explosion,
growing concern for improved standard of living for all have
brought many entirely new elements to bear on the decision of
what constitutes responsible procreation. These concerns have
led moralists to formulate an approach that would place all the
elements in better balance.

(6) *Renewed Appreciation of the Relation between Conjugal
Love and Procreation in Married Life*

The deliberate refusal of the Council Fathers at Vatican II
to retain the traditional hierarchy of primary and secondary
ends of marriage has opened the Catholic Church to a new and
deeper understanding of the meaning and value of conjugal
love. The bishops' explicit recognition of the dangers that can
result when the intimacy of married life is broken off has fos-
tered a new appreciation of the beauty, power, and importance
of the marital relationship. This deeper insight and emphasis
on the centrality of conjugal love in marriage has rendered less
than adequate approaches that still consider the procreative
aspect as primary and supreme. Current approaches attempt to
reflect a better harmony and integration of the procreative and

unitive aspects in rendering moral judgments regarding contraception.

These foregoing considerations, which are to be found in current moral evaluations of contraception, show clearly that the approach adopted by this study is based on more than negative arguments. Rather we can appeal to serious, positive reasons, demonstrating genuine concern about the realization of God's plan for the welfare of the total person.

Finally, the diversity of views and arguments presented here indicate that the question of artificial contraception has not yet found a definitive resolution in the Church or a satisfying formulation. This fact alone should caution against any rash and absolute judgments on the matter. The Church's long tradition of respect for the role of conscience and its recognition of the right to follow solidly probable opinion in moral matters would seem to point the way to the individual's resolution of the dilemma. Certainly, one must regard as morally responsible the thoughtful decision of a couple to use artificial birth control as the most effective way of harmonizing procreative and unitive values in their conjugal life, as they pursue creative growth toward integration.

*Pastoral Reflections*

1. Pastors and counselors need to emphasize the *basic consensus* that exists in the Church on the fundamental meaning and most important values regarding responsible parenthood. Pope, bishops, theologians, priests, and the sense of the faithful agree that:
   (a) The procreative mission must be carried out responsibly.
   (b) At times this demands family limitation.
   (c) Parents themselves are the ultimate decision makers in this matter.
   (d) This decision must involve medical, psychological, personal, familial, societal, and religious considerations.
   (e) The method chosen to carry out responsible family

limitation must respect the total nature of the human person and his acts.

2. Regarding methods of contraception, the legitimate diversity of opinion that exists in the present state of the question should be recognized and admitted. Confessors and counselors may not impose any position in an absolutely binding way. Their principal task is not to impose a position but to assist people in arriving at a responsible decision.

3. The position of *Humanae Vitae* regarding the objective evil of artificial contraception and its consequences should be clearly stated by the confessor or counselor. Then the arguments of those who deny the inevitability of these consequences and see artificial contraception in some circumstances as fostering positive values should also be carefully considered. The final decision and verification as to whether the use of contraceptive means is morally disruptive or preservative of greater values ought then to be left to the consciences of the individuals concerned.

4. The mere fact that a couple is using artificial means of birth control cannot provide a sufficient basis to make a judgment about the morality or immorality of their married life and sexual expression. Where the decision to limit their family is morally sound, pastoral concern should be directed to assisting couples to see in their sexuality a means of realizing those values that build a community of love, an intimate partnership, a sharing and blending of their lives as a whole. If their sexuality serves this purpose by making them more sensitive, thoughtful, understanding, considerate, and loving of one another, then it is wholesome and moral. If, on the contrary, contraception leads to greater self-centeredness, preoccupation with pleasure, the manipulation or exploitation of the other, a breakdown of moral character and infidelity, then it is obviously immoral.

5. Recent developments in natural family planning techniques as well as improved ways of educating and supporting couples in the use of these methods have increased the effectiveness and reliability of this approach. Growing fears about the long-range side-effects of chemical and mechanical contraceptives have further enhanced the acceptability of this

method. Natural family planning deserves serious consideration among the alternatives for exercising responsible parenthood. The Church would render a considerable service by supporting clinics and organizations where accurate and up-to-date information could be available to interested couples.[35]

6. Special caution and reserve need to be expressed with regard to the "intra-uterine device" and the "morning after pill" since it is not established whether their mode of operation is contraceptive or abortifacient. Arguments for either position at the present time are inconclusive. It simply is not known whether they achieve their effect by diverting or destroying the sperm (contraceptive) or by affecting the uterine wall in a way that prevents implantation of the fertilized ovum (possibly abortive). A further doubt arises as to whether or not a human being is present prior to implantation. Arguments, here too, for either position are inconclusive. A responsible decision must honestly face these considerations; at the same time the very doubts that exist caution against any certain and absolute judgments of abortion in the event that such methods are employed.

7. Catholic health care institutions, especially those that provide maternal health services, have a special opportunity to witness to Christian values concerning responsible parenthood. Educational programs and counseling services that provide not only reliable medical data but also moral awareness of the values involved ought to be made available to patients in need.

### Sterilization

Sterilization may be defined, for our purposes, as the irreversible termination of the capacity for reproduction. The following medical procedures accomplish this effect:

(a) salpingectomy—the ligation of the fallopian tubes in the female
(b) vasectomy     —ligation of the vasa deferentia in the male
(c) oophorectomy—removal of the ovaries
(d) orchidectomy —removal of the testes
(e) hysterectomy —removal of the uterus

Sterilization as a method of family limitation was totally unknown during biblical times. It would be vain therefore to search the Scriptures for any direct or explicit references to the morality of such a procedure. Moralists in the past have applied to the sterilization question Scripture passages relating to respect for bodily integrity and mutilation. Though such an extension of Scripture may, in some instances, be legitimate, it would be incorrect to conclude that the Bible supports any absolute or general condemnation of sterilization as such.

In recent times, the Church's magisterium has spoken out on various occasions on the issue of sterilization:

(1) On December 31, 1930, Pius XI in his encyclical letter on *Christian Marriage* explicitly condemned eugenic sterilization:

> Private individuals have no other power over the members of their bodies than that which pertains to their natural ends, and they are not free to destroy or mutilate their members, or in any way render themselves unfit for their natural functions, except when no other provision can be made for the good of the whole person.[36]

(2) On March 21, 1931, the following question was addressed to the Holy Office:

> What is to be thought of the so-called "Eugenic theory," whether "positive" or "negative" and of the means which it proposes for the improvement of human progeny, in disregard of laws, natural, divine, or ecclesiastical, pertaining to marriage and the rights of individuals?[37]

The reply of the Holy Office given with the approval of Pope Pius XI was:

> That theory is to be absolutely disapproved, held as false and condemned as declared in the Encyclical on Christian Marriage, *Casti Connubii* of Dec. 31, 1930.[38]

(3) On February 24, 1940, another question was directed to the Holy Office:

Whether the direct sterilization of man or woman, whether perpetual or temporary, is licit?

*Reply:* In the negative; it is forbidden by the law of nature, and as regards eugenic sterilization, it has already been condemned by the decree of the Sacred Congregation of March 21, 1931.[39]

This response extended the Church's earlier condemnation of eugenic sterilization to all forms of direct sterilization and indicated that such procedures were contrary to natural law.

(4) On October 29, 1951, in his address to Catholic Midwives Pius XII reemphasized this teaching when he declared:

Direct sterilization, that which aims at making procreation impossible as both means and end, is a grave violation of the moral law, and therefore illicit. Even public authority has no right to permit it under the pretext of any "indication" whatsoever, and still less to prescribe it or to have it carried out to the harm of the innocent. This principle has been already stated in the Encyclical of Pius XI which We have quoted. Therefore, ten years ago, when sterilization came to be more widely applied, the Holy See found itself in need of stating expressly and publicly that direct sterilization, either permanent or temporary, of man or of woman, is illegal by virtue of the natural law from which, as you are aware, the Church has no power to dispense.[40]

(5) In 1953 Pius XII indicated that the principle of totality did not justify the removal of healthy fallopian tubes when pregnancy might be dangerous by reason of diseases of the heart, lungs, kidneys, etc.

In this case, the danger that threatens the mother does not arise, either directly or indirectly, from the presence of the normal functioning of the tubes, nor from their influence on the diseased organs—kidneys, lungs, heart. The danger would arise only if free sexual activity would start a pregnancy that would threaten the aforesaid weak or sick organs. The conditions that would allow the disposal of one part for the good of the whole by reason of the principle of totality are lacking. It is therefore not morally permitted to interfere with healthy tubes.[41]

(6) In July 1968 Pope Paul VI in his encyclical *Humanae Vitae* reaffirmed the position taken by his immediate predecessors:

> Equally to be excluded, as the teaching authority of the Church has frequently declared, is direct sterilization, whether perpetual or temporary, whether of the man or of the woman.[42]

(7) In November 1972 the American Bishops approved the *Ethical and Religious Directives for Catholic Health Care Facilities,* containing the following directive on sterilization:

> Procedures that induce sterility, whether permanent or temporary, are permitted when: (a) they are immediately directed to the cure, diminution, or prevention of a serious pathological condition and are not directly contraceptive (that is, contraception is not the purpose); and (b) a simpler treatment is not reasonably available. Hence, for example, oophorectomy or irradiation of the ovaries may be allowed in treating carcinoma of the breast and metastasis therefrom; and orchidectomy is permitted in the treatment of carcinoma of the prostate.[43]

(8) On April 14, 1975, in response to the question whether the above directive would permit direct sterilization for the total good of the patient, for instance, because of a heart or kidney ailment which might be aggravated by a future pregnancy, Archbishop Bernardin in the name of the Executive Committee of the National Conference of Catholic Bishops responded as follows:

> The question was referred to the Committee on Health Affairs, which presented it to its Advisory Committee on Medical-Moral Questions. The matter was examined at length, including consultation with the Holy See. With the concurrence of the Executive Committee, I am writing to

give assurance that the 1971 guideline stands as written, and that direct sterilization is not to be considered as justified by the common good, the principle of totality, the existence of contrary opinion, or any other argument. This means that Catholic hospitals, as a matter of institutional policy may not authorize sterilization procedures for reasons other than those contained in the guidelines. If questions of material cooperation arise, the traditional norms of moral theology are to be applied.[44]

This statement was an attempt to summarize a lengthier and more carefully nuanced confidential response on the matter issued by the Sacred Congregation for the Doctrine of the Faith to the American hierarchy on March 13, 1975 (see Appendix 2). It should be noted that the Roman document addresses itself primarily to the question of institutional policy rather than personal morality and does acknowledge that situations may arise where such procedures may need to be tolerated on the principle of material cooperation in order to avoid greater evil. The implications of this principle and its application to specific situations would need to be worked out by individual institutions on the local level.

Archbishop Bernardin's summary certainly clarified any ambiguity regarding the intent or meaning of the directive. Its sweeping elimination, however, of any other approaches to the problem including the long-accepted principle of probabilism tends to impose morality by authority and goes far beyond the statement from the Roman Congregation.

While the official teaching of the Church on sterilization has become increasingly restrictive over recent years, it cannot be said that medical moral theological development has fully supported this trend. In March 1955 Gerald Kelly in commenting on Pius XII's statement of 1953 expressed some reservations:

Whatever be the ultimate explanation, it is clear enough from the papal teaching that the principle of totality cannot be invoked to justify direct sterilization. This is certainly the per se rule. But one may legitimately ask whether by reason of entirely special circumstances, an individual might acquire the right to destroy his procreative power or to consent to its destruction. For instance, there is the case discussed by Fr. Connery concerning the individual who can avoid unjust detention in a state institution only by consenting to a sterilization. I would agree with Fr. Connery that the individual may probably give consent.[45]

In July 1966 the Majority Report of the Papal Commission appointed to study the whole issue of family limitation issued a far more cautious and carefully nuanced statement than the official teaching: "Sterilization, since it is a drastic and irreversible intervention in a matter of great importance, is generally to be excluded as a means of responsibly avoiding conception."[46]

A recent *Policy Manual*[47] compiled for St. Joseph's Hospital in London, Ontario, and issued with the approval of the local Ordinary provides very specific medical, obstetrical, and psychiatric indications for sterilization that are consistent with the principle of Vatican II but constitute a departure from the norms of *Humanae Vitae.*

Many serious and respected theologians applying the criterion of Vatican II, that is, "the nature of the person and his acts," to the question of sterilization have also reached quite different conclusions. Bernard Haring indicates that the traditional approach distinguishing between direct and indirect sterilization is much too narrow. In his judgment:

Wherever the direct preoccupation is responsible care for the health of persons or for saving a marriage (which also affects the total health of all persons involved) sterilization can then receive its justification from valid medical reasons. If, therefore, a competent physician can determine, in full agreement with his patient, that in this particular situation a new pregnancy must be excluded now and forever because it would be thoroughly irresponsible, and if from a medical point of view sterilization is the best possible solution, it cannot be against the principles of medical ethics, nor is it against "natural law."[48]

Thomas Wassmer reaches a similar conclusion when he writes:

It would seem that the wider horizon that has been given to the meaning of marriage and the empirical evidence in cases similar to the one we have been considering would suggest that the classical arguments for the prohibition of every *direct contraceptive sterilization* are not compelling. The conclusion is not that the prohibition should not stand but that the prohibition is not one that "the light of human reason makes most clear." The universality of the prohibition is in the light of the continuous and evolving theology of marriage difficult to establish and the empirical verifiable evidence is not on the side of universality. While it is clear to us that it cannot always be shown to be wrong that a person in certain concrete circumstances would decide in favor of a *direct contraceptive sterilization*, the resolution of the ethical problem for the individual conscience would be the result of the tension that exists between the two ethics of conviction and responsibility. The individual conscience would have to assure itself that the totality of marriage is being damaged by the serious ethical choice of a direct contraceptive sterilization. To make this option the person has to call upon the best resources of the ethic of responsibility and the ethic of conviction and to resolve satisfactorily the tension between the two. Difficult, yes: but it is the only authentic contemporary ethical way to exist.[49]

A clear and decisive majority of contemporary theologians writing on the subject finds it difficult to support the restrictive conclusions of official Church teaching; they prefer instead to develop their conclusions in harmony with Vatican II's principle based on the nature of the person and his acts. The existence of such diversity should make confessors and counselors aware that the matter of sterilization, like that of contraception, is still far from a universally acceptable and definitive resolution in the Church. There is need, therefore, to respect the legitimate diversity of existing opinion and to avoid the imposition of moral threats or sanctions which violate a person's right to a free and informed conscience. Rather in such situations, there is need to promote, as Vatican II suggests, honest discussion, mutual respect, and, above all, a concern for the common good.[50]

*Pastoral Reflections*

1. Sterilization, whether in the form of tubal ligation for a woman or vasectomy for a man, is in the present state of medical science generally irreversible and therefore to be considered as a permanent means of contraception. Morally, it differs from other methods of contraception in that it permanently and irreversibly deprives one of the freedom to respond to a call to responsible procreation. The crucial moral question with regard to sterilization is to determine whether one can with sufficient certitude decide that responsible procreation will never again be a possibility for this person. To terminate the potential for procreation when it is certain that this power could never again be used responsibly, removes the major moral objection to sterilization. It is presumed, of course, that in reaching this judgment the same factors will have been considered as recommended for evaluating the morality of contraception.

2. Pastorally, the following considerations might provide a convenient schema for reaching a sound decision regarding the morality of a sterilization procedure:

(a) *Age:* The closer one approaches menopause, the easier it is to reach a decision that one's procreative responsibility is definitely completed. It is far easier to make this projection for five years than it is for twenty-five.

b) *Medical Indications:* A serious pathological condition (e.g., severe hypertension, heart disease, renal disease, diabetes, thrombophlebitis) that would render any future pregnancy a serious threat to the life or well-being of the mother could provide a proportionately justifiable basis for sterilization.

(c) *Obstetrical Indications:* Serious risk to the life or well-being of mother or fetus resulting from obstetrical indications could also provide a suitable basis for sterilization (e.g. severe Rh sensitization, the probability of serious genetic disease, weakened uterine wall from repeated Caesarian sections, severe, recurrent hypertensive disorder of pregnancy).

(d) *Psychiatric Indications:* Clinical evidence indicating that future pregnancy would lead to severe emotional regression and possibly irreversible damage to the personality of the mother could also justify sterilization. Although it is difficult to establish reliable criteria to render such a judgment, and caution needs to be exercised, the possibility of such evidence cannot be ruled out.

(e) *Socio-economic Indications:* Socio-economic factors by themselves seldom provide sufficient basis for a responsible judgment regarding sterilization. A surgical procedure is not the normal solution to a socio-economic problem. It is a category that deserves consideration as part of the total set of values that serve as a basis for decisions regarding responsible parenthood.

(f) *Personal Attitudinal Considerations:* Past fears that sterilization procedures often resulted in severe emotional difficulties, interfered with one's sexual potency, and produced grave guilt feelings have proved to be without foundation. Such consequences will occur only if the person enters upon such a procedure with emotional difficulties, guilt feelings, and a sense of sexual inadequacy. In a word, although the procedure does not ordinarily create new problems, it may aggravate previously existing ones. Pastors and counselors share an important responsibility in preventing such consequences by dispelling any false guilt and by supporting people in their efforts to reach a sound decision.

3. The fact that vasectomy for the male is a much simpler procedure than tubal ligation for the female should not ordinarily be the decisive factor in determining which spouse is to be sterilized. The procedure ordinarily should be performed on the partner whose medical, obstetrical, or psychological condition renders that person incapable of further responsible procreation.

4. Catholic hospitals and health care institutions need to study how effectively their current institutional policy regarding sterilization serves the total good of the patient. Likewise careful consultation needs to be taken regarding the implications of the principle of material cooperation and their institutional policy on sterilization. Varying circumstances and conditions in different hospitals preclude any simple generalizations on this matter.

*Artificial Insemination*

Artificial insemination consists in the placing of male semen into the female reproductive tract, not by sexual intercourse, but through the use of an instrument, usually a syringe.

The purpose of such insemination is to make a marriage fruitful when, because of some physical condition in husband or wife, it is not possible to conceive children through normal intercourse. For legal and moral reasons authors distinguish two kinds of artificial insemination:

(1) homologous artificial insemination (AIH), which involves the use of semen derived from the husband of the woman inseminated;

(2) heterologous artificial insemination (AID), which involves the use of semen derived from a donor who is not the husband of the woman inseminated.

The official position of the magisterium on artificial insemination is contained in two allocutions of Pope Pius XII. In the first address to the Fourth International Convention of Catholic Physicians in October 1949 Pius XII stated:

(1) Artificial insemination outside marriage is to be condemned purely and simply as immoral.

(2) Artificial insemination in marriage, with the use of an active element from a third person, is equally immoral and as such to be rejected summarily.

(3) With regard to the lawfulness of artificial insemination, in marriage . . . . it must be rejected entirely. With such a pronouncement one does not necessarily proscribe the use of certain artificial methods intended simply either to facilitate the natural act or to enable the natural act, effected in a normal manner, to attain its end.

Two years later on November 26, 1951, in an address to the Congress of the Italian Catholic Union of Midwives, Pius XII elaborated on the reasons for his position:

To reduce cohabitation and the conjugal act to a simple organic function for the transmission of seed would be converting the home, the sanctuary of the family, into a mere biological laboratory. In our address of September 29, 1949, to the International Congress of Catholic Doctors, we formally excluded artificial insemination from marriage. In its natural structure, the conjugal act is a personal action, a simultaneous and immediate cooperation on the part of the husband and wife which by the very nature of the agents and the propriety of the act is the expression of the mutual gift which according to Holy Scripture brings about "union in one flesh only." This is something much more than the union of two seeds, which may be brought about even artificially, without the natural action of husband and wife. The conjugal act, ordained and willed by nature, is a personal act of cooperation, the right to which husband and wife give each other when they marry.

Developments in medicine and theology over the past two decades have added significant new dimensions to the question of artificial insemination. Since there have been no additional magisterial pronouncements in this area, our search for moral norms must look to the reflections of theologians for guidance.

The discussions of the last decade on artificial insemination by the husband's sperm indicate an increasing openness to its acceptability. The principal moral concern that "the child should be the fruit of love" does not seem to be threatened in any way by the biological modification in the process of insemination. The former concern regarding the manner of obtaining semen, which seemed to underlie much of Pius XII's objection to this procedure, is no longer regarded by most moralists as a serious obstacle to this procedure. When the sperm comes from the husband and the whole marriage is lived in a climate of love, it is easy to affirm a strong moral unity between the act of love and the child who results from artificial insemination. Pastoral counselors should feel free to support childless couples who turn to this method in their desire to become parents and to realize their procreative mission. The technical details should be left to the doctor and the couple to be worked out in a way most keeping with the dignity and sensitivities of the parties concerned.

With regard to heterologous artificial insemination, that

is, through a donor, there is considerably less agreement. For some, this represents an intrusion into the exclusivity and intimacy of the conjugal bond that is hard to reconcile with the Christian understanding of the nature of conjugal love. A further difficulty arises from the potential threat that the donor-conceived child represents to the husband. The child might well come to be regarded by the husband as a painful reminder of his impotency, the fruit of an adulterous union on the part of his wife, an unwanted intruder into the intimacy of their married life. Such possibilities create a risk and threat to the marriage itself if both partners are not mature and fully open to the idea. There is contrary evidence, however, that many couples have been able successfully to surmount these obstacles and beget children through heterologous artificial insemination and to enrich their personal and marital lives immensely. This should caution one against closing off this possibility altogether. Adoption is suggested by many authors as an alternative to artificial insemination. But where there exists a strong mutual desire on the part of husband and wife and sufficient stability in the marital life to offset the risks indicated, the difficulties raised do not seem strong enough to justify prohibiting such a decision.

A relatively new question medical and technological advances place before us is the phenomenon of "in vitro fertilization." Experimentation in this area holds forth great promise for contributing to increased knowledge and understanding of the whole birth-and-life process. This in turn could lead to the prevention or elimination of many hazards to early fetal life and the general improvement of conditions surrounding the early life growth process.

The present state of science leaves many serious questions unanswered. What are the risks, biologically and psychologically, for this pre-fabricated person? How can this be reconciled with our Christian understanding that the child is to be the product of mutual parental love? What will the impact be on the family unit and society? Those who are firmly convinced that zygotes are not fully human before implantation would see lesser difficulties than those who consider the product of artificial fertilization as already a human being in the full sense.

There is, however, a rather strong consensus among moralists that the unanswered questions are too many and too serious to lend approval or encouragement to such experimentation at the present time. The moratorium on such experimentation called for by the American Medical Association until the ethical, moral, religious, and social implications can be further clarified and resolved seems a wise and sound moral stance for the present.

### Child-Free Marriage

Child-free marriage is the licensed union of two individuals of the opposite sex for life, with no anticipation of divorce or separation, but with definite plans for no children, either their own or adopted. It is a marriage that is childless by choice. Census figures and sociological studies indicate that this form of marriage has increased dramatically on the American scene during the past twenty years. The exact extent of the increase is difficult to measure because of the difficulty of distinguishing child-free marriages from childless marriages, since the latter can also include those who intended to have children but could not. (Undoubtedly, there are also instances of those who intended a child-free marriage, but failed in this intent!) Perhaps more significant than the actual incidence of child-free marriages is the growing indication in sociological studies that a majority of people do not disapprove of this state, at least for others, and this even in largely Catholic samplings.[51]

The reasons for the increase of child-free marriage are many and varied. The following would be some of the more important. First, there is a growing and real concern, particularly among people of higher educational levels, for the problems of overpopulation and overcrowding. A given couple might genuinely feel that it would be wrong to add to this problem, and determine to live their marriage child-free as a personal effort to address this very real human concern. Second, a highly motivated couple might feel that the pursuit of their professional careers is of greater importance than the personal raising of a family. It is not difficult to find examples of such a decision in cases of couples who do in point of fact accomplish a great deal of good for the entire community through their important and productive careers, e.g., in the areas of research, medicine, social work, and education. Further, child-free couples with careers often spend a greater proportion of their extra time and money supporting important social works of charity.

A third possibility of child-free motivation could be genetic. A given couple might have scientific knowledge of genetic dangers that would make the propagation of offspring unwise. A fourth possibility would be economic, given the high cost of both the procreation and the education of children in today's society. A fifth motive could spring from age. Here would be included those for whom childbearing is no longer possible, as well as those who, having married later in life, find childbearing possible but unwise for health and emotional reasons.

A sixth reason could be the knowledge that a couple simply would not make good parents, given today's greater insight into the physical, psychological, and emotional demands of parenthood. It is a curious inconsistency that our society, which demands years of training for so many professions, assumes that practically everyone has the native ability to be a responsible parent. It should be noted as significant at this point that Pope Pius XII in his *Address to Italian Midwives* (1951) spoke of "indications," be they "medical, eugenic, economic, and social," which might provide "serious motives" for using rhythm, even for prolonged periods of time and even for the entire duration of the marriage.[52] Finally, and quite obviously, a given couple may be motivated by purely self-serving reasons, preferring a more luxurious and affluent life-style than would be possible if rearing children. In this case one can only suggest that given their values such individuals would make less than ideal parents.

In discussing the moral and ethical ramifications of child-free marriage, it should be acknowledged at the outset that we are aware that a positive act of the will excluding the good of children (*contra bonum prolis*) is considered by the *Code of Canon Law* to be an invalidating intention or condition.[53] According to the strict interpretation of this law, no couple could validly marry if they had an explicit and absolute intention (not open to reevaluation) not to have children. The law, however, does admit of exceptions, as in the case of the sterile, the aged, and those who wish to enter a virginal marriage (modeled after the example of Mary and Joseph).[54] Pope Pius XII further broadened these legal exceptions with his discussion of the serious "medical, eugenic, economic, and social" reasons cited above.[55]

In view of the sociological incidence of this growing phenomenon, as well as the "indications" proposed by Pope Pius XII, a number of questions seem to be in order. The critical question is whether or not a couple in a child-free situation is attempting to uphold the principles that would make their marriage a truly creative Christian marriage, one productive of interpersonal and intrapersonal growth toward integration.

Given this criterion, it is not difficult to see how in particular cases, a couple might live out its marriage commitment in a truly Christian way, contributing to its own growth and that of the community at large, without necessarily including child-bearing in that process. This approach can be applied to married couples in a variety of circumstances: those who can have children but for higher reasons do not want to do so, those who can have children but for reasons of health or eugenics should not do so, those who cannot have children and yet make their marriage productive of true personal growth toward integration, interpersonal and intrapersonal, with each other and the entire community. In all cases, if the relationship is to be Christian, the quality of being a life-serving marriage must be upheld. In child-free marriages, then, as in other situations, the principle of creative growth toward integration provides a theological base upon which to judge the moral or ethical aspects of human sexuality.[56]

We are dealing here with a variant form of marriage, one which will not be lived out by most. For the majority of married couples, human creativity in sexual relations will be life-serving in the sense of procreation of offspring. However, given the variety of reasons for child-free marriage in our society today, sociological trends suggest that this form of marriage will become increasingly more common.

It remains for those concerned with counseling couples to consider more carefully the reasons advanced, the "indicators" that might suggest child-free marriage and, most importantly, the way in which the life-serving quality of Christian marriage is to be upheld. When these situations are creative and integrative, in a responsible and Christian way, child-free marriages should rightly become more acceptable.

## VARIANT PATTERNS

Traditional monogamous marriage is under attack today in American society from a variety of fronts. A primary result of this attack is the establishment, in practice if not in theory, of what has been termed "consecutive monogamy" or "monogyny," that is, the process of one monogamous marriage after another, or consecutive pair bonding. There exists today the statistical likelihood of one in every three marriages ending in divorce; in some parts of the country the divorce rate has risen as high as 70%. Concomitant with this phenomenon there has developed a variety of methods of providing married individuals with "secondary" sexual relationships beyond the primary pair bond, often with the agreement and cooperation of the marriage partner. Such relationships, which in the past were grouped along with more covert activity under the general category of adultery, are perhaps better considered today as different phenomena.

The causes of these pressures on monogamous marriage are many and varied. Some of the key factors in these newer trends can be identified as the following. First, the simple fact of extended human longevity has made the likelihood of marriage "until death do us part" a much more difficult reality. The fact that most marriages entered into in the late teens or early twenties have an expectancy of fifty or more years before the death of one of the partners obviously raises the possibility of infidelity from the sheer weight of time. Second, ours is a highly eroticized and permissive environment, in which opportunity for extramarital activity is highly available on all levels. Third, prosperity and mobility have made possible covert activity, which, in previous years, was beyond the financial and practical means of many. Fourth, the complete control of conception has made extramarital activity practically safe and secure for men and women alike. Fifth, the emergence of women into all walks of business and culture has made more numerous contacts between men and women a part and parcel of daily activity in all walks of life. Finally, the social (if not the moral) acceptance of premarital sex with one or more partners, has led to a lowering of the sense of responsibility to one partner in marriage. As a result of these and other factors, a variety of variant forms of sexual expression has been proposed and to some degree practiced in American society today.

As indicated earlier (Chapter II), the attitude of the Old Testament toward extramarital sexuality was somewhat mixed. As long as there was no violation of the wife, betrothed, or daughter of a fellow Israelite, a man was not forbidden extramarital relations. In the New Testament, Jesus, in his radical concern for the oppressed, grounded moral precepts on the law of love. The woman taken in adultery is told to go and sin no more, rather than being subjected to the stoning required by the Jewish law. Jesus' radical concern for the oppressed is in evidence here, as well as his attitude toward forgiveness. The absence of the man involved in this incident reflects the double standard of the day.

Concerned with the moral degeneration of his contemporaries in the Greco-Roman world, St. Paul attacked the license and prostitution of his age, symptomatic of the unredeemed state. Paul's teaching on marital fidelity in 1 Corinthians 7 was heavily influenced by his expectation of the second coming of Jesus and argued for maintaining the status quo. However, this was not to interfere with Christian freedom; those who wished to marry were free to do so. Fundamental to Paul's teaching is the idea that the Christian is called to fidelity to God and to the good of the community of believers.

Early Christian tradition identified three goods of marriage: children, fidelity, and the sacrament. Under the influence of a variety of forces, the early Church sharply focused its teaching on human sexuality on the procreation of offspring and the alleviation of concupiscence. Pleasure, especially sexual pleasure, was suspect; virtue was to be found in ordination to a proper end, excess was always indicative of sin. Given the objectivity of moral discourse, anything that could be defined as outside of the three goods of marriage was thereby sinful. This attitude coupled with that era's understanding of the complexity of human relations, sexual and otherwise, led to an equally oversimplistic categorization of sexual sins. In too many instances, the complexity of today's life has resulted in the breakdown of these simple categories in the lives of many. An effort will be made to reexamine some of the current situations in which extramarital sexual relations are practiced, and to assess them in the light of current data and the theological principles developed within this study.

## Common Law Marriage

Marriage, with all its deep interpersonal meaning, has always been a matter of social and community significance as well. Thus, those forms of common law living which represent a total rejection of social values are morally objectionable. Equally to be deplored, however, are the laws and social structures that make such activity necessary. It is a matter of fact that the highest incidence of common law living is to be found not among the young, but among the elderly. Retirees in the United States today are often forced to this recourse in order to avoid adverse and even impossible economic hardship resulting from current social welfare legislation. In such cases, one can only conclude that such relationships, which can be truly creative and integrative for the individuals involved, can also be morally acceptable, at least until such time as the civil restrictions to legal marriage are removed. It would seem that each case must be judged on its own merits and not by any overriding absolute, civil or religious. Those engaged in counseling need to take careful note of the motives and reasons for this extraordinary form of marriage in each case.

## Communal Living

The term "communal living" seems to mean a variety of things to different people. For some, it refers to a form of commune in which a group of people of both sexes live together in something of a protest against society and its values, with sexual liaison between any and all members of the opposite sex commonly practiced. Illustrative of this form would be the communes of the American counter-culture.

For others, the term refers to that form of common life in which a group of people of both sexes share their lives together, highly motivated by religious values, common goals, or background; each contributes to the good of the community according to his or her ability and draws upon the resources of the community according to his or her needs. An example of this form would be the early Christian community in Jerusalem described in the Acts of Apostles. Given the high degree of variety of forms that this way of life can take, communal living cannot simply be dismissed as repugnant to Christian values.

In general, communal living may be defined as a familial state of life in which a variety of people, married or unmarried, lay or religious—but usually not related to each other—live a community life together and work collectively for the common good. Usually such people are bound together by some common goal or objective in life, often by some religious bond. Some communes have developed as a rejection by the young of the too common form of consecutive monogamy common in American society. Others have developed among groups of former religious, as a sort of halfway house between the religious and lay state. Often this form is more transitional than permanent, although it can be quite enduring. Communal living has also developed among groups of people, often happily married, who simply seek a better form of genuine human interrelatedness.

Throughout history, there have been those who looked upon communal living arrangements as destructive of Christian values. Even among groups motivated by religious values, including that of consecrated virginity, such living arrangements when they involved members of both sexes were considered suspect. History at times warranted the suspicion; even among those who seemed motivated by the highest of ideals, the ideal and the real were seldom in harmony, and human destruction and alienation were often the result.

Working within the principles formulated above, it would seem that the possibility of living out such a communal relationship, while preserving the desired characteristics of being other-enriching and honest, faithful and self-liberating, is unlikely for most persons, if not for all. Indeed, it should be acknowledged that some individuals enter into such relationships motivated more by a fear of a truly other-enriching relationship with another particular individual, losing themselves as it were in the larger group. However, we cannot rule out the possibility that some truly charismatic group might be able to offer a new model of Christian living that would be deeply religious and a source of renewed vitality to the community at large. Such a possibility should not, however, preclude the careful weighing out of the indicators of true human creative growth and personal integration by those interested in such a life-style and those who are their counselors. In sum, the risk of interpersonal harm and alienation should be steadfastly avoided.

### Swinging

Under the comprehensive title of "swinging," free sex has become a somewhat popular pastime for many single, divorced, widowed, and married people. It has become particularly popular among the middle-aged rather than the young. The question is: can such activity be truly creative or integrative, especially since it appears to lack the characteristics of being "other-centered" or "other-enriching." Swinging, by its very definition, seems to be a radical contradiction of the value of "fidelity." Too often it is exposed as a thinly veiled form of self-gratification, offensive to true Christian interpersonalism and devoid of the joy that characterizes good sexual relations. Recent studies indicate that such activity proves superficial in the long run and too often results in alienation for those involved. While remaining open to the results of further research, we find that, given the qualities of wholesome sexuality discussed above, swinging seems destructive and alienating and therefore generally dehumanizing.

## Adultery

Adultery includes a variety of extramarital relations, which admit of separate discussion. By definition, the term "adultery" refers to illicit intercourse between a married person and someone other than the marriage partner. Covert and/or commercial sexual relations are the most obvious forms. Empirical studies indicate (Chapter III) a high incidence of "cheating" during marriage on the American scene today. The evidence, however, is inconclusive as to the effects of such behavior on the individuals involved and on their marriages.

The moral assessment of adultery must necessarily consider the effects on at least three people: the marriage partners and the third party, with attention given to the "creative growth" and the "human integration" of each person and with especial consideration of the effects upon the already existing marriage of the bonded pair. In general, it seems difficult to imagine a situation where such activity would be considered to be good for all involved. Traditional moral teaching condemns all adultery as contrary to the purpose of marriage. The principle of "creative growth toward integration" needs to be applied in all of these cases. The characteristics of other-enriching, honest, and faithful are of special concern in cases of covert and commercial sexual relations. Further, counselors might take special note of patterns that may develop in such cases, mindful that patterns of behavior are more important than individual acts and that the meaning of an act merits more consideration than the act itself.

Two other forms of extramarital activity that may be placed under the traditional category of adultery are those of "co-marital" (threesome) sexual relations and "mate swapping" (a foursome, or two couples). The terms are applied to those situations that involve sexual activity with one or more persons beyond the primary pair bond, with the consent and often encouragement of the marriage partner. Much is being written about this dimension of sexual experience today. Some authors have advocated this form of human interrelatedness as a truly Christian response to the problems and needs of particular groups in society, such as the elderly and the "unhappily single." Often in these groups there is a disproportionate imbalance between the number of males and females.[57]

As suggested previously, the empirical data does not as yet warrant any solid conclusions on the effects of such behavior, particularly from the long-range point of view. Traditional Catholic teaching considers all such cases unjustifiable, as contrary to the nature and purpose of marriage. Others would acknowledge at least the theoretical possibility that such an arrangement could uphold the principles of true human growth and full integration.[58] In practice, however, such relationships would seem to contradict many of the characteristics of wholesome sexual interrelatedness, and, above all, to compromise the "covenant fidelity" presented by Scripture as an ideal. Thus, while remaining open to further evidence from the empirical sciences, we would urge the greatest caution in all such matters, lest they compromise the growth and integration so necessary in all human activity.

*Current Approaches to the Morality*
*of Variant Marriage Patterns*

In attempting to make moral judgments about variant marriage patterns, at least three principal approaches seem evident:

(1) All variant marriage patterns are evil, regardless of circumstances. According to this position, each of the above variant patterns is evil, because it rejects some essential characteristic of marriage. The strength of this approach lies in its fidelity to a carefully developed legal understanding of marriage. Its weakness lies in its assumption that such activity is always destructive of human personhood, without due regard for any

empirical evidence that might support or repudiate such an assumption. This position does not appear convincing to many people of good will today.

(2) Variant marriage patterns depart to one degree or another from the Christian ideal of what marriage ought to be. Therefore, they are not to be tolerated at least in most cases. This approach is most interested in ideals, such as fidelity, honesty, other-centeredness. It is sensitive to the effects of the various deviations or variations from traditional marriage on both the people involved and on the rest of society. Social ramifications of such variant patterns are critically important in this approach, for it recognizes that the welfare of the social order makes objective demands upon the decision-making process of all members of society. The weakness of this approach lies in its inability to make universal application of its demands; its strength lies in its demand for high ideals while being open to possible exceptions in particular cases.

(3) Variant marriage patterns are largely private matters, dependent upon the mature consent of the participants, and therefore perfectly acceptable as long as no one else gets hurt. This approach is strong in its appeal to personal freedom and self-determination. It fails, however, to take due note of the social dimension of marriage, and its unique Christian dimension insofar as it has been made a part of the sacramental system of the Church of Jesus Christ.

In light of the principles and values developed above, we find the second moral approach most compatible with our own.

### Pastoral Reflections

(1) Today more and more men and women find themselves dealing with each other on an ever expanding variety of levels and with an ever increasing amount of deep interpersonal involvement. More opportunity exists for increasing interpersonal and intrapersonal growth in the reality of one's unique maleness or femaleness. This can lead to greater personal integration and to fuller Christian fellowship. At the same time, there is greater danger in the possibilities for developing de-

structive and alienating relationships. What is called for is not a restriction on involvement or an emphasis on the possible dangers, but rather an exhortation to the ideals of Christian living as fully sexual human beings, called to live out their personhood in fellowship with others.

(2) Rather than deal with absolute prohibitions, enlightened pastoral guidance requires a careful study of the aspects of each human interpersonal encounter, taking due note of all the effects of the given activity, short and long-range. The pastor or counselor should always keep in mind the ideal of growth toward full integration.[59]

(3) In order to avoid pure subjectivism, three key factors must be kept in mind: (a) gospel principles, particularly the principle of selfless love, (b) the actual experience of Christian people, open to both the working of the Spirit and the shared experience of the whole people,[60] and (c) the data of the empirical sciences, relating to the effects of variant behavior and the development of new forms of human living. A purely act-centered objective judgment of complex human interpersonal activity should be avoided.

(4) What is permissible is not always prudent. The possibility of exception does not preclude the danger inherent in deviation. To those who counsel others, we would suggest that they study each situation carefully in the light of the experience of the whole community, past, present as well as in the light of the facts of the individual case. On the one hand, to determine the morality of a case *a prioristically* is to fail to give due respect to individual dignity. On the other hand, to fail to suggest caution where there is deviation is to fail to respect human experience.

In short, an overall assessment of the variant forms of extramarital relationships leads us to counsel extreme caution. Such relationships generally fail in their ability to be "other-enriching."[61] To one degree or another, they offend against the quality of fidelity.[62] Further, moral judgments about such relationships should not be made solely on the basis of the individuals involved; human relationships must also be socially responsible.[63] These facts, however, do not rule out the possibility that there may occasionally arise exceptions, where such relationships can truly be "creative" and "integrative" for all involved, and therefore morally acceptable.[64] Extreme caution is imperative in arriving at such a conclusion in particular cases. Great care should be exerted in any pastoral situation to uphold the principles and ideals of wholesome sexuality.

## NON-MARITAL SEXUALITY

### SEX RELATIONS OUTSIDE OF MARRIAGE

No society has ever been completely indifferent to the sexual behavior of its members. Never has sex been viewed as a purely private affair between two individuals. In every known culture, sexual activity has been regulated at least to some extent.[65] This fact of experience is explained by the radically social nature of human existence, particularly the social dimension of sexuality. Sexual behavior has implications and significance for society. The universal means by which societies have legitimated, regulated, and institutionalized the sexual relations of their members are marriage and the family.

*Scripture*

From the very beginning, Christian tradition has seen the sexual union of a man and woman achieving its full and proper significance as a sign of the deeper, more encompassing union of their lives. It is a fundamental principle, therefore, of Catholic moral theology that there exists an essential relationship between sex and marriage.

This relationship between sex and marriage has not always been recognized as absolute, however. As the foregoing historical survey (Chapter I) has indicated, polygamy and prostitution, so long as they were not idolatrous, were both countenanced in the Old Testament.[66] Marriage was originally a family event rather than a religious or civil affair. Certain values lay behind the Old Testament sexual mores, however, and these evolved from concern for property rights to personal rights.[67] The basic value of human dignity was foremost in Jesus' teaching, exemplified in his stand on marital fidelity and divorce.[68] He rejected the treatment of women as chattel. Jesus' personalism was continued by St. Paul's emphatic condemnation of prostitution, which was representative of every form of depersonalized and depersonalizing sexual activity.[69] Immanuel Kant's maxim is closer in spirit to Christian morality and piety than to rationalist ethics: So act as to treat humanity, whether in your own person or in that of any other, always at the same time as an end, and never merely as a means.[70]

*Tradition*

The social dimension of sexuality, the values of fidelity and love within sexual relationships, the significance of sexuality to life, the dignity of the human person—all have been matters of grave moral concern within Christian tradition. Catholic moral theology has consistently refused to treat human sexuality as trivial or sexual behavior as indifferent or unimportant. It has consistently condemned promiscuity as injurious and immoral. This attitude has found expression in the long-standing tradition in Catholic theology of seeing all forms of premarital sexual intercourse as fornication, as little different from prostitution, and always as gravely sinful.

Fornication has customarily been defined by Catholic moralists as sexual intercourse with mutual consent between an unmarried man and an unmarried woman.[71] In the tradition of St. Thomas Aquinas, fornication was listed among the sins against chastity, which are not also against nature, in that they are not also contraceptive.[72] Although Catholic moralists have traditionally made distinctions regarding premarital intercourse on the grounds whether or not it was procreative, no specific distinction was drawn between fornication and prostitution, or fornication and concubinage.[73] No distinctions were drawn either regarding premarital intercourse between couples engaged to be married and those enjoying a casual liaison, between adults and adolescents, between people in love and those for whom sexual intercourse was simply a matter of sexual gratification.

Catholic moral theology has traditionally judged all forms of premarital intercourse as fornication and, as such, intrinsically and gravely sinful.[74] Not only premarital sexual intercourse, but if directly willed, all touches, embraces, and kisses of a passionate nature between the unmarried were regarded as serious sins. All deliberate enjoyment of sexual pleasure outside of marriage was regarded as mortal sin.

To evaluate properly the tradition that has come down to us regarding premarital sexuality, care must be taken to place it within its historical context. Simply accepting it uncritically without a deeper appreciation of the arguments posited in its support would be a one-sided abstraction and ultimately a misunderstanding of the tradition. The unanimous conviction of the malice of all premarital sexual relations was not without good reasons.[75]

Until most recently, Catholic moral theologians were of the common opinion that all premarital sex was forbidden by the Bible. St. Alphonsus taught that all forms of unchastity were at least implicitly prohibited by the sixth and ninth commandments.[76] He did not have at his disposal the tools or findings of today's critical historical biblical scholarship. He was not aware of the distinction the Old Testament made between secular intercourse and idolatrous, cultic intercourse. He was not aware that the *porneia* condemned by St. Paul referred not simply to premarital intercourse but to the promiscuity typified by intercourse with prostitutes. Understandably, therefore, St. Alphonsus, and Catholic moralists after him, taught that all premarital intercourse was expressly forbidden in the Bible by divine positive law, as found in Lev 19:29; Dt 23:17; 1 Cor 6:9.

Arthur Vermeersch (1858-1936) was the first Catholic moral theologian to recognize that the Old Testament does not contain a prohibition against premarital intercourse as such.[77] With regard to the New Testament, Vermeersch also realized that the *porneia* condemned by St. Paul referred to involvement with prostitutes and cannot be simply identified with those engaging in premarital intercourse. One or two acts of premarital intercourse do not constitute prostitution. Yet, neither was it clear to Vermeersch how merely the greater plurality of instances of premarital sex could constitute its sinfulness. His conclusion was that the Bible prohibited premarital intercourse only indirectly. The real argument for such prohibition must be derived from natural law, known by natural human reason.[78] In the same vein, Joseph Fuchs also admits that the New Testament cannot simply be cited as prohibiting all forms of premarital intercourse.[79]

Catholic moralists today recognize that the condemnation of *porneia* in the New Testament refers variously to adultery, incest, and the depersonalization and promiscuity exemplified by prostitution. There is no prohibition of all premarital intercourse as such. What is certain, however, is that the New Testament explicitly condemns completely unhampered sexual intercourse. At the time the New Testament was composed, premarital intercourse was understood differently from today —only as completely unhampered sexual intercourse, i.e., relations with prostitutes.[80] The New Testament can be said to condemn "loveless unhampered sexual intercourse, especially with a prostitute."[81] It does not address the question of loving, responsible sexual intercourse of a couple engaged to be married.

Catholic moralists censured premarital intercourse not merely because of the Bible. They viewed fornication as gravely contrary to natural law as well.[82] To appreciate the argumentation from reason, however, it must be remembered that the teaching of Catholic moralists was influenced by the anthropology of the patristic era. The Fathers were in turn influenced by Hellenistic philosophy and the view that sexual intercourse and the pleasure connected with it are morally reprehensible in themselves. Sex was not viewed in terms of love but of lust, and lust was directly opposed to holiness. It was very much a basic assumption of Catholic moral tradition that sexual intercourse is of itself an evil that can be "excused" only on the basis of the benefits accruing to marriage, the first and foremost of those benefits being the procreation of children.[83] Thus, St. Alphonsus takes it completely for granted that sex is ordered toward procreation, and that any sexual activity that is not procreative is sinful.[84] Given the presumption that sexual intercourse is ordered primarily toward procreation, it is clear why premarital sexual activity would be deemed as gravely sinful: nature demands not only the procreation but also the proper education of children. Only within the context of marriage and the family is there the guarantee that children would be provided for and raised properly. St. Thomas Aquinas argued that premarital intercourse is injurious to the life of a child born of such a union; a child "requires not only the mother's care for his nourishment, but much more the care of his father."[85] St. Thomas maintained, as did St. Alphonsus after him, that the prohibition by natural law holds true even when sufficient provision is made for the proper upbringing of a child; moral precepts look to what happens in general and not to particular exceptions.[86]

From the time of St. Alphonsus to our own, Catholic moralists have consistently argued that premarital intercourse is seriously sinful, in virtue of the natural law, which requires that children be brought up properly within marriage and a family. Difficulties with the argument, however, have not gone without notice. If premarital intercourse is sinful because it endangers the infant that may be born, why is it sinful when there is no hope or possibility of conception? Or is it? Are there other natural reasons besides conception out of wedlock that would forbid premarital intercourse? If so, what are they? When confronted with these difficulties, Vermeersch was compelled to agree with Tamburini and Palmieri before him and confess that Catholic moral theology was not able to produce clear and cogent *a priori* reasons for regarding premarital intercourse as always intrinsically and gravely sinful.[87]

Even when Catholic moralists did not see the weakness or difficulties of the traditional argumentation, they gave a variety of other reasons why premarital intercourse is always gravely sinful. These arguments vary both in their cogency and perspective.[88] Some arguments look to the individuals involved and see premarital intercourse as endangering physical health or psychic well-being; for example, it may raise the incidence of venereal disease. Others argued that people need marriage and the assistance of external social structures to integrate and control their sex drives.

Moralists also looked to social considerations. Even when there is no danger of conception, they held that no individual exceptions can be made to the general norm; there is always the danger of bad example to others. Premarital intercourse was also seen as detrimental to the dignity and security of women, as posing a danger to already existing marriages, and thereby threatening the good order of society. Incredible from our point of view today is the frequent argument that, if sexual pleasure were permissible outside of wedlock, people in many instances would not marry. There would be no reason for them to assume the burdens of marriage and family.

More recently, claims have been raised that premarital sexual activity damages subsequent marriages, jeopardizing the mutual trust and fidelity of the married couple. No evidence however has yet been produced to substantiate such claims empirically.[89] Furthermore, recognizing that the New Testament does not explicitly forbid all premarital intercourse, attempts have been made to maintain the tradition on the basis of the Christian view of love, particularly with respect to the dignity of persons.[90] It is argued that sexual relations to be meaningful require a mutual, total, and exclusive self-giving for life, such as is found only in marriage. Physical self-giving is but the expression of a life-long, total, personal self-giving. How or why sexual relations always make these exacting requirements has not been made altogether clear. That intercourse makes these demands in every case has yet to be fully demonstrated.[91]

Consideration of the argumentation against premarital sexual activity of any kind is important in the light of a basic principle of Catholic moral theology to the effect that laws exist to protect values. Law exists for a purpose. If a law loses its purpose, it loses its force and no longer binds. This was the teaching both of St. Thomas Aquinas[92] and of St. Alphonsus, and pertains not only to human laws but to natural law as well. An act is not evil if it can be stripped of its evil aspects.[93]

Certainly the arguments presented by moral theology upholding the reservation of sexual intercourse to marriage merit respect and consideration for the values they represent. Even a friendly critic, however, cannot help but be uncomfortable with the weaknesses of claims to absolute and exclusive validity raised on their behalf. The traditional argument against all premarital intercourse was convincing at a time when procreation could not be avoided with certainty, at a time when, under the shadow of Augustinian pessimism regarding sex, moralists saw sexuality as something to be controlled, permitted only for procreation. Over the last several decades, a more positive valuation of sexual intercourse has developed within Catholic theology, recognizing sexual relations as an experience and expression of love. No longer is intercourse viewed as excusable only if procreative. At the same time, modern methods of contraception serve to mitigate the danger of bearing children out of wedlock. As a result, the traditional argument against premarital intercourse is no longer as convincing as it once was in the past.

So too with the other arguments from natural law and the dangers they represent. None of these dangers, whether to the individuals involved or to society, are universal or such that they cannot be obviated. Their principal weakness lies in their proponents' lack of familiarity with the empirical data and their inability to present evidence to substantiate their claims. Examination of the argumentation, therefore, would seem to warrant the conclusion that "moral theologians have not yet succeeded in producing convincing proof as to why in *every* case sexual intercourse must be reserved to marriage."[94] Their difficulties in doing so do not constitute a license for promiscuity, however. Rather, they give us reason to pause and consider each case more carefully, no longer ready to regard every exception to the norm as immoral.

*Current Approaches to the Morality of*
*Premarital Sexuality*

In current literature, one can discern a variety of approaches to the morality of premarital expression.

(1) *All directly voluntary sexual pleasure outside wedlock is grievously sinful.*

This traditional position in most of the moral manuals of the recent past is defined rather typically by Henry Davis in his *Moral and Pastoral Theology:*

> It is contrary to nature's purpose, and seriously so, if this pleasure is sought or accepted outside legitimate sexual intercourse, for the pleasure is annexed to an act that must be employed socially in legitimate wedlock, and not for the individual's gratification outside wedlock, since the obvious and only purpose in nature's, that is, God's, intention is that this pleasure should be experienced in, and should attract to,

that mutual act between man and wife, designed by nature for the propagation of the race, whether or not the effect ensue. No other purpose for this pleasure can be rationally assigned, and therefore no use of it outside wedlock can be rational.

Even the smallest degree of incomplete venereal pleasure has reference by its very nature to legitimate sexual intercourse and to that alone. No other purpose can be rationally assigned to it. If, then, such pleasure be procured or accepted with no reference to its only purpose, a serious perversion of nature has taken place.

It is grievously sinful in the unmarried deliberately to procure or to accept even the smallest degree of true venereal pleasure; secondly, it is equally sinful to think, say, or do anything with intention of arousing even the smallest degree of this pleasure.[95]

The reasoning advanced for this position is that even the smallest amount of this pleasure is an inducement to indulgence in the fullest amount of it and this would be fatal to the human race.

The heavily, almost exclusively, procreative concept of human sexuality underlying this position has been replaced in more recent Church statements by a broader and more balanced understanding. Both Vatican II and the 1975 Vatican Declaration on Sexual Ethics make it abundantly clear that sexuality serves other purposes than merely procreation. Likewise, it seems an exaggeration to hold that even the smallest degree of incomplete venereal pleasure involves necessarily a complete inversion of the purpose of sexuality and would be catastrophic for the human race. Davis maintained in 1936 that all Catholic moralists hold this position and "for the moral theologian the discussion is now closed." On the contrary, one would have to admit that few moralists hold so rigid a position today. The topic itself is very much a matter of discussion.

(2) *Every genital act outside the context of marriage is immoral.*

The recent Vatican Declaration on Sexual Ethics seems to favor such a position:

Today there are many who vindicate the rights to sexual union before marriage, at least in those cases where a firm intention to marry and an affection which is already in some way conjugal in the psychology of the subjects require this completion, which they judge to be connatural. This is especially the case when the celebration of marriage is impeded by circumstances or when this intimate relationship seems necessary in order for love to be preserved.

This opinion is contrary to Christian doctrine which states that every genital act must be within the framework of marriage.[96]

The reason advanced for this stance is that sexual intercourse finds its full meaning only in a stable marriage sustained by a conjugal contract guaranteed by society. This position reflects a genuine concern for the societal implications involved in human sexual expression, and certainly these should not be lightly dismissed. Its insistence, however, that a valid marriage contract ultimately legitimates sexual intercourse tends to identify and confuse the moral and legal orders. Although this formulation may reflect what should exist in the ideal order, it does not do full justice to the imperfect ambiguous real world in which we live. The conjugal contract and civil recognition do not always guarantee a genuine mutual commitment.

(3) *Premarital intercourse is wrong but preceremonial intercourse may be moral.*

This approach attempts to draw a sharper distinction between the inner mutual consent that constitutes the existential bond of marriage and the external manifestation of this commitment before society. It contends that these two moments for various reasons do not always coincide and may result in a situation where the expression of sexual intimacy can be more properly termed preceremonial rather than premarital.[97] Others carry this line of reasoning a bit further suggesting that since marriage is a process, there may be a point at which sexual intercourse becomes an appropriate commitment of the partners' intent, even prior to the formal exchange of vows.

Like most of life's decisions, becoming married is not an instantaneous action, but a process that takes time. At a certain point in the process coitus becomes an appropriate expression of the love that exists and of the will to place all that one is in the service of the other. How is this point to be determined? The couple must judge for themselves. The criteria mentioned above should be taken into account. As a general rule of thumb, however, it might be suggested that the couple should have manifested to others their sincere intention to marry, and that the ceremony itself is not too far distant.[98]

This would be especially true regarding couples engaged to be married or those who, although mature enough to marry and desiring to do so, are prevented from marrying because of external reasons, such as prolonged courses of study, need to care for one's family, or financial considerations.

Advocates of this position would certainly uphold the restriction of intercourse to marriage as the ideal. They would regard a norm to this effect as describing the ideal toward which every engaged couple should strive. The careful nuancing of their position seems to be an attempt to reflect more accurately the multi-faceted, complex process of seeking a lifemate.

This process requires the reaching out of two people toward one another, a mutual searching, revealing, and coming to know each other. It is a process with many stages, and the forms of intimacy and expressions of affection appropriate to the relationship vary according to the stages of the process.

Some of the objections raised against this approach are:

(a) It too easily identifies the intention to marry with the existential marriage bond itself, which is not always indicative of total commitment.

(b) By exaggerating the importance of sexual intimacy in the growth of their relationship, it interferes with the principal task of the engaged parties, namely, to get to know each other's strengths, weaknesses, and interests.

(c) It creates a threat to society as a whole by naively supposing that the concessions will be claimed only by engaged couples. The British Council of Churches stated in its report: "To weaken the rule may well encourage free sexual intercourse between the unmarried, and ultimately increase the incidence of promiscuity and of adultery."[99]

(4) *Sexual intimacy may be an appropriate expression of*

> *the quality and depth of a relationship, whether marriage is intended or not.*

Exponents of this position argue generally that the unitive and procreative aspects of sexuality are not inseparably united, and either purpose may justify sexual expression provided it is not destructive of individuals or community. They view moral norms as relative and strongly defend the freedom of mature individuals to set aside the rule and act in accordance with their own judgment for the best interest of the parties involved and of society. *The Study Document on Sexuality and the Human Community* presented to the United Presbyterian Church in the United States of America seems to reflect this position when it states:

> In place of the simple, but ineffective and widely disregarded standard of premarital virginity, we would prefer to hear our Church speak in favor of the more significant standard of responsibly appropriate behavior. Responsibly appropriate behavior might be defined as sexual expression which is proportional to the depth and maturity of the relationship and to the degree to which it approaches the permanence of the marriage covenant.[100]

In its attempt to offer guidance for single adult persons, the study further states:

> Sexual expression with the goal of developing a caring relationship is an important aspect of personal existence and cannot be confined to the married and about-to-be married.[101]

The principle objections against such a thesis are the following:

(a) It assigns undue importance to motivation as a determinant of morality favoring the subjective criteria over the objective.

(b) It is vague and unclear in the guidelines it offers regarding what constitutes the depth and quality of a relationship. This decision left to the judgment of the involved individuals, who are least capable of such a decision, can easily deteriorate into a mutually destructive emotional exploitation of one another.

(c) Its understanding of sexuality too easily separates the procreative from the unitive, and thus lacks a wholistic vision.

(d) It claims an exaggerated role for the freedom of individuals, which is incompatible with a responsible attitude to society at large. Others would argue that general moral norms are meant to prescribe what is normally good for society as a whole and ought to be observed even at some sacrifice of personal liberty.

(5) *Sexual experience including intercourse is a natural human function which serves functions other than procreation or expression of intimacy.*

This position maintains that sexual expression is an important and healthy human experience because it provides enjoyment, enrichment, and a release of tension. Even apart from any expression of intimacy or intent to procreate, physical pleasure is an important part of human experience. According to this humanist approach, "The satisfaction of intimate body responsiveness is the right of everyone throughout life."[102] Some would maintain that intercourse is the healthiest and most beneficial expression of human existence and "the individual should seek to have healthy orgasms in accord with his needs."[103]

One advocate of this position offers the following guidance for enjoying sex at an early age:

> If intercourse is to be practicable at all for these young adults, they must be able to guarantee the following conditions:
> (1) that they will not conceive an unwanted child;
> (2) that, should they fail in their use of birth control methods, they will be able to handle the problem of an unplanned pregnancy;
> (3) that they can provide an aesthetically satisfying environment for the flowering of their sexual love, such as a safe place for lovemaking without fear of interruptions or police intervention;
> (4) that they must be free from feelings of guilt. In other words, they must be able to tell themselves, with convic-

> tion, that what they are doing is in accord with what
> they believe to be right; otherwise, the sexual experience
> itself can be overshadowed by their fears.[104]

The principal objection to such a view is that it robs
human sexuality of its deepest and richest meaning as an expression of intimacy and love. To justify intercourse for even brief,
casual encounters, as long as mutual consent is freely given, is
to reduce human sexuality to a purely biological function and
the human person to a physical pleasure machine. This radical
separation of sexuality from its deeper intrapersonal and interpersonal meaning is rejected by Christian moralists in general
and regarded as dehumanizing and depersonalizing both for the
individual and for society.

The sheer variety of contemporary approaches attempting
to provide guidance and direction for the evaluation of non-
marital and premarital sexuality makes clear the complexity
and delicacy of the task. It would be rash to presume that a
clear and unambiguous norm will provide a simple resolution
of the problem, so that nothing more need be said. Such statements have hardly been effective in guiding and influencing the
moral values and behavior of Christians today. If genuine
moral behavior is to be a response from internal conviction
rather than a mere imposition of norms, we must continue to
ask the difficult questions, to reject unfounded assumptions
and unsatisfying answers, and to articulate more clearly and
convincingly the values in which we Christians believe.

In the light of our understanding of human sexuality presented above (Chapter IV), it seems clear that the extreme
positions (1 and 5), which reject every deliberate experience of
sexual pleasure outside the marriage context or which exalt
sexual experience purely in terms of physical enjoyment and
release of tension, simply do not do justice to the rich and
profound meaning of human sexuality. It also seems abundantly clear that one cannot simplistically categorize every act of
intercourse as equally immoral regardless of circumstances or
relationship. There is a vast difference between the deliberate
exploitation of others, as in prostitution, and an act of sexual
intercourse that expresses a growing commitment of persons to

one another, as among the engaged. The characteristic values for wholesome human sexuality advanced in this study can provide helpful guidelines for individuals to discern what is appropriate sexual behavior in their life.

The second approach outlined here, requiring a valid societal contract as a necessary condition for justifying sexual intimacy, seems too extrinsic and legal to serve as a moral norm for an expression that is primarily, though not exclusively, internal and personal. Such a principle may express the absolute ideal, but in a real world in which personal and societal values often cannot be fully harmonized, the bias in favor of the societal over the individual and interpersonal does not seem well founded in every instance.

The fourth approach on the other hand, justifying full sexual intimacy in terms of developing a caring relationship, casts its bias in favor of the individual and of interpersonal values over the societal ones. This approach in our judgment, does not show sufficient concern for the vagaries of human interrelationships, nor does it value sufficiently the importance of fidelity as an indispensable quality for a caring relationship. The consequences for society would also discourage our acceptance of such a general norm.

The third approach that calls for the serious and growing commitment of partners toward each other as a condition for justifying sexual intimacy seems to be most consistent with the vision of human sexuality expressed in this study. The characteristic values advanced herein for gauging wholesome human sexuality can provide more specific guidelines toward balancing individual and societal interests for those unmarried individuals who are seeking to discern what is appropriate sexual behavior in their lives. The following pastoral reflections may provide further cautions and counsels both for them and for those guiding others toward a mature personal decision in this delicate area.

*Pastoral Reflections*

Without being able to sustain its position with apodictic arguments, traditional Catholic ethics said "No" to all instances of intercourse before marriage and with it to all intimacies conducive to venereal pleasure, whether "necking," "petting," or "prolonged passionate kissing." Today's youth, needless to say, finds this global "No" of the traditional code to be dubious, inadequate, and unrealistic. Pastors and chaplains ministering to young people do not need sociological surveys to inform them of the high incidence of premarital sexual activity. Whether it is higher, however, than in previous generations is questionable. Kinsey saw no appreciable difference between generations with respect to premarital sexual activity as a whole (1948). An examination of the marriage and baptismal records, precisely of Catholic countries, has indicated a tradition in certain locales of ensuring an heir by waiting to marry until a child was expected.[105]

Previous generations were characterized by fear of unwanted pregnancy and anxiety about the sinfulness of premarital sex. Young people today do not feel the same fear or measure of anxiety.[106] Traditional norms have become questionable, and social pressures to ensure adherence have decreased considerably. This is not to say that young people are more promiscuous. On the contrary, a young man's first sexual encounter fifty years ago was likely to have been with a prostitute; today it is likely to be with a girl with whom he can have a loving relationship.[107]

Studies indicate that sexual behavior patterns are changing. More college students, particularly college girls, engage in premarital intercourse than their counterparts did twenty years ago. But indiscriminate sexual activity has not increased. Even though marriage is not commonly considered a prerequisite for sexual intercourse, there seems to be a strong emphasis on a loving relationship and some measure of mutual commitment before sexual involvement.

If there ever was a time when the "thou shalt not" approach to premarital sexual morality was successful, that day is over. The blanket condemnation of all premarital sexual intimacy is simply no longer taken seriously by a majority of Catholics in the United States today. As of 1973, only 45% of American Catholics believe premarital sex is wrong.[108] Sexual intercourse between an engaged couple is approved by 43% of

American Catholics.[109] And even among the clergy, support for the traditional absolutes is eroding. While 80% of the priests in this country still regard premarital sex as immoral, 25% of those thirty-five and under and 19% of those between the ages of thirty-six and forty-five do not object to premarital intercourse in certain instances.[110]

There can be no doubt but that the traditional moral code regarding premarital sex is inadequate, particularly in its lack of distinction between the ages, attitudes, and intentions of the people involved. The alternative, however, is not simply moral relativism or the surrender of human values, Christian ideals, or ethical norms. Fidelity, fairness, and respect for the dignity of persons are fundamental and enduring aspects of the Christian ethical response to the revelation of God's love in Jesus Christ.

(1) Sexual behavior for a Christian must be guided by the same values and norms as all other human behavior. Sexual morality for a Christian is but one part of a moral stance that encompasses all facets of human life. Pastors or counselors can appeal not only to the New Testament and Christian tradition but also to empirical sciences, human experience, and personalist idealism in warning against promiscuity, irresponsibility, and the manipulative use of persons as mere instruments for sexual gratification.

(2) Even though pastoral ministers and counselors are in no position to dispense a catalogue of apodictic don't's, they can offer much important guidance to the unmarried by pointing out that sexual intercourse calls for durability in a relationship. Sexuality is not simply physical or biological. Sexual intercourse is an expression of a person's whole being, the deepest core of one's personality. The introduction of sexual intercourse into a relationship alters that relationship radically in that it calls for repetition. Intercourse, therefore, to be honest, requires a commitment to a relationship and frequent physical presence with one's partner. The intensity of the emotional involvement resulting from repeated acts of sexual intercourse is such that it invariably leads either to exclusiveness and eventually marriage or to superficiality and promiscuity.[111]

A casual attitude toward sexual intercourse, requiring no

commitment either to exclusiveness or durability, sustains only a superficial relationship and leads logically to promiscuity. Sexual relations—that do not represent the whole person, that do not have the possibility of a lasting relationship, that do not express the reality of two people being there in an exclusive way for one another—are simply forms of exploitation, at best a matter of casual play unworthy of the seriousness of sex. Such exploitation certainly falls short of the command of love enjoined by Jesus Christ upon his followers.

(3) Certainly it is both superficial and unrealistic to say that any passionate kiss before marriage is always sinful, even for the engaged. Honest forms of intimacy must be determined by the age and maturity of the individuals and the seriousness of their relationship regarding the possibilities of marriage. At what point in a relationship sexual intimacies are responsible and morally justifiable cannot be easily or precisely defined. Boundaries do exist, however, the transgression of which cannot be morally justified. There are intimacies that are not signs of affection but simply a stimulation of sexual gratification. There are clearly cases of casual sexual intimacies in which the partner is not seen as a person but an object of conquest or exploitation, a source of personal sexual satisfaction. There are clearly instances in which sexual intimacies are both depersonalized and depersonalizing.

Premarital sexual morality is largely a matter of drawing honest and appropriate lines. To this end, the characteristics of wholesome human sexual behavior outlined above (Chapter IV) can serve as useful criteria for judging what kind of intimacy is honest and appropriate to a given relationship. Is it self-liberating, other-enriching, honest, faithful, life-serving, and joyous? To what extent, if any, is there selfishness, dishonesty, disrespect, promiscuity, the danger of scandal or of hurting or shaming family and loved ones? Young people in particular should be challenged to question themselves as to whether they are not simply using each other to prove their respective masculinity, femininity, sexual attractiveness or prowess. To this should be added for young and old alike the question of willingness to accept a child if one is conceived. No contraceptive device thus far invented is altogether foolproof.

Dishonesty is certainly involved when a man engages in sexual intercourse with a woman with whom he would not want to have a child.[112]

(4) The line between moral and immoral sexual behavior for the unmarried was certainly more clearly drawn in the traditional moral code than can be provided by the criteria offered here for judging the characteristic of wholesome sexual behavior. The human condition and the fallibility of human judgment when applying norms to concrete situations cannot remove the reality of risk from a decision of conscience. Distorted vision and self-deception is an ever present possibility that can never be eliminated with the security of absolute certitude.

In helping the unmarried to find moral certitude about the honesty and appropriateness of their sexual behavior, pastors and counselors can lead them to look at their entire lives, their relationship with God, and their moral stance toward all life situations. Selfishness and dishonesty in other areas indicates a likelihood of the same in the sexual sphere of life. Unselfishness, honesty, and the desire to lead a truly Christian life with respect to other relations and dimensions can safely indicate similar qualities in a couple's sexual behavior. In dealing with unmarried Catholics, the moral seriousness and quality of a relationship can also be gauged by the place given to prayer and participation together in the Church's sacraments, especially the eucharist.

It bears repeating: there exists an essential relationship between sex and marriage. Even in the wake of a sexual revolution, it can be maintained and substantiated that marriage is the ideal context for the full human realization and self-communication that is involved in the sexual expression of love. Among the characteristics of wholesome human sexuality, fidelity is not among the least. One would be well advised not to trust oneself to be trustworthy, much less ask another to trust him or her, without assuming the commitments of marriage.[113] It is the human capacity for responsibility and fidelity to the being and well-being of another that makes marriage possible; it is the human inclination to irresponsibility and infidelity that makes marriage necessary.

DATING AND COURTSHIP

*Scripture*

For the most part, custom and human convention regulated the mores surrounding courtship and marriage in biblical times. Usually, the parents or an elder member of the family played a major role in choosing a marriage partner (Gen 21:21, 24; Sir 7:23-25; 1 Cor 7:36-38). But instances of young people meeting by chance, falling in love and marrying are not foreign to the Bible (Gen 24; Ex 2:16-21). Virginity in women before marriage was, of course, highly prized, and societal customs and law tried to ensure the realization of this ideal. Detailed rules, however, regarding the conduct appropriate for those remotely or proximately preparing for marriage are simply not to be found either in the Old or New Testament.

In the Old Testament the highest ethical norm for people's dealings with one another, including, therefore, sexual relations was the law: "Love your neighbor as yourself." Respect for the other as a person was a fundamental principle governing all human relations including the sexual. In the Old Testament account of Tamar and Amnon (2 Sam 13:1-19), we read Tamar's rebuke, "No, my brother, for this wrong in sending me away is greater than the other which you did to me." This passage clearly underscores the real sin in this incident to be not the physical intercourse, but the abuse of person, the treating of another as an object that can be taken up and thrown away as one pleases.[114]

The New Testament supports this Old Testament formulation and reinforces it with the ideals of Christ's own example of perfect love. "Love one another as I have loved you" (Jn 15:12). Jesus Christ, who succeeded in being entirely himself and at the same time entirely for others, became the ultimate norm for the behavior of his followers. Such an ideal, properly understood, is far more demanding than any detailed ethical code.

No set of concrete rules or laws can be as all encompassing as the principle of Christ-like love. That is why rules and laws that exist in Christianity can never represent its essence. Questions like: "How far can I go?" or "Is French kissing a mortal sin?" reflect a mentality at odds with Christian origins. A Christian is one who belongs to Christ in every thought and action, one who like Christ sees the fundamental morality or immorality of any sexual act or expression not in an abstract analysis of the act but in the respect or disrespect it shows the other person. This basic truth needs to be kept in mind especially as one reads through St. Paul's list of sins that exclude from the Kingdom of God. The fundamental disrespect and violation of a person is the essence of sin. The particular form this disrespect takes is, morally speaking, neither the heart of the matter nor the principal focus of the condemnation.

### Tradition

Tradition reflects various widely divergent attempts on the part of Christian thinkers to formulate concrete and specific norms regarding the appropriate sexual behavior of the unmarried. These range from St. Jerome's strong condemnation of the use of cosmetics to the fascinating distinctions of the penitentials (a simple kiss—six special fasts; a licentious kiss without pollution—eight special fasts; a licentious kiss with pollution or embrace—ten special fasts)[115] to the elaborate arrangements regarding chaperones whenever young lovers were together lest something immoral occur. The principle underlying much of this is that even the smallest degree of sexual pleasure is directed by nature toward complete sexual intercourse and serves no other purpose. As one author expressed it:

> All venereal pleasure that is sought outside marriage destroys that relation and transfers to the good (i.e., the pleasure) of the individual what is designed for the good (i.e., the perpetuation) of the race. This violation of that necessary relation to the race is intrinsically and seriously evil, precisely because it is the inversion of an essential order or relation.[116]

Father Gerald Kelly in a widely used booklet entitled *Modern Youth and Chastity* reduced the whole of sexual ethics for the unmarried to the following practical moral principles:

1. Every directly venereal action is against the law of God and a serious sin of impurity.

2. Any action is a serious sin against chastity when it is performed with intention of stimulating or promoting venereal pleasure.
3. It is a mortal sin for one to expose oneself freely and knowingly to the proximate danger of performing a directly venereal action or of consenting to venereal pleasure.
4. It is venial sin to perform an indirectly venereal action without a relatively sufficient reason.
5. Indirectly venereal actions are not sinful if one has a good and sufficient reason for beginning or continuing such actions.[117]

This summary reflects substantially what has been the approach of the vast majority of Catholic writers and theologians until recently.

## Pastoral Reflections

The onset of dating, that is, the occasional sharing of another's company for reasons of mutual enjoyment and enrichment without any commitment either to exclusivity or marriage, marks an important step in the gradual unfolding, development, and integration of a person's social and sexual life. The fascination and attraction by which people find themselves drawn to each other may well be seen as part of God's ingenious plan to call persons forth to fuller realization of self and fuller relationship with others. There is no doubt that this experience offers considerable challenge to those embarking upon it. To the unprepared it can easily lead to an obsession with the pursuit of pleasure, using others for one's own self-gratification. For the maturing it offers a wondrous opportunity to move dramatically forward toward that creative integration that is the goal of human sexuality.

To facilitate this growth process, we recommend the following pastoral considerations:

1. Parents, educators, and priests should be conscious of their moral responsibility to take seriously the repeated recommendations of the official Church magisterium to provide for

the education and formation of the young with adequate sexual information and positive attitudinal orientation.

2. The noticeable trend in North America toward earlier and steadier dating results often enough in premature teen-age marriages. This is not particularly conducive to a gradual and orderly integration of sexuality. The rising importance of peer pressure, a dominant force in forming a young person's attitudinal and behavioral patterns regarding sexuality, is a further phenomenon to be reckoned with. It signals the end of an era in which it was felt that moral values could be imparted by parental command or ecclesiastical pronouncement. This means that a much more patient, persistent, and personal effort needs to be made to help youngsters discern the fundamental moral values at stake and to assist them in the difficult task of internalizing these values into personal moral convictions.

3. The natural goodness and sacredness of human sexuality as a creative and integrative force needs to be accentuated. Expressions and approaches that are fear-dominated, consequence-oriented, and sin-centered should be avoided.

4. The moral approach of the past that regarded every willful enjoyment of pleasure before marriage as a serious deordination of one's relational life and consequently mortal sin needs to be re-examined. Is the premise valid which states that all sexual pleasure, even the slightest, is directed by nature toward the complete act of intercourse? Is there no other purpose that sexual pleasure can legitimately and wholesomely serve? Is the fear well-founded that if pleasure is allowed before marriage, many will be dissuaded from entering the married state, thereby endangering the continuation of the human race? Should physical pleasure be the dominant moral factor in evaluating the sexual behavior of the unmarried? Empirical evidence, history, and current theological reflection are raising some serious questions regarding the validity of these fundamental presuppositions.

There is reason to cast serious doubt about the adequacy of evaluating the sexual behavior of the unmarried in terms of the negative principle of illicit venereal pleasure. Greater justice can be done then by a more positive approach based on the principle of creative integration and evaluated in terms of the many values that human sexuality involves.

5. In applying the principle of creative integration to sexual expression among the unmarried, it becomes immediately apparent that categorical "yes" and "no" answers cannot be given to such direct and concrete questions as: "Is kissing a sin?" "What about French kissing," "petting," "necking"? The very phrasing of the question in this manner should alert the prudent counselor to the fact that the questioner's greatest moral need is not a direct answer but a better understanding of the nature and complexity of moral values, particularly as they relate to sexuality. It is a far more demanding and formidable task for the counselor to lead his counselee to a deeper appreciation and internalization of the interpersonal and intrapersonal values that human sexuality involves. Yet this responsibility cannot be avoided if the counselor is to be faithful to his task of forming morally sensitive and mature people.

No single question will suffice to determine the morality of any sexual behavior. To ask simply, as some suggest, "Do you love each other?" is woefully inadequate. Depending on a person's understanding of love, the question itself is loaded with too many ambiguities to provide an acceptable basis for moral evaluation. Rather, a series of questions corresponding to the many-faceted values involved in any sexual expression will need to be raised to permit a more adequate moral evaluation of the given behavior. Some questions that may be raised in this respect include the following:

Are you personally comfortable with what you are doing? Upon reflection are you morally convinced that it is right and proper? Does it express genuine respect for the other? Are you using or exploiting one another? Do you consider it an honest and fitting expression of the degree and depth of your relationship? Is this conviction shared mutually? Is it socially responsible? Does it show respect for legitimate family and community expectations? Does it lead to greater mutual trust, support, and fidelity? Does it reflect an awareness and sensitivity to the life-serving function of human sexuality? Does it result in genuine peace, joy, and happiness without regrets or misgivings?

This method of evaluating the morality of human sexual conduct may prove frustrating and difficult to apply for those who have not grasped the deeper meaning and purpose of human sexuality. It promises, however, to provide a far more reliable and accurate means for discerning whether any given sexual behavior is truly creative and integrative of the human person or destructive and divisive.

## THE SINGLE STATE

Given the agrarian culture from which they arose, it is not surprising that both Scripture and Christian tradition have little to say about the single state. Yet, in American society today, there are in excess of forty-one million single adults. About five million of these are divorced or widowed, and many of the remainder will one day marry. However, statistics indicate that there is a growing number of people remaining single for a variety of reasons:

(1) More women are finding it possible to find fulfilling careers and professions, which often preclude the possibility of marriage, in practice if not in principle. What was once tolerated by society in only a few cases, for example that of the single dedicated teacher is rapidly becoming more acceptable.[118]

(2) The high divorce rate in America, with its attendant psychological, emotional, and financial shock is coming to be viewed more critically by the young. They are less likely today to enter marriage hastily. This is particularly true of young collegians who generally can be somewhat independent and self-supporting. Often such individuals find the single life-style quite satisfactory and postpone marriage indefinitely and perhaps even permanently. (This observation does not mean to deny the very real problem of too many young people—generally not the college-educated group—seeking early marriage.)

(3) Gradually the social stigma attached to being "eligible but unmarried" is passing; with it there is developing an acceptance of the single person in general society. Further, there is also a growing tendency to provide social outlets for singles only, particularly in the large cities.

(4) The high degree of mobility required by American business of its work force is making family ties less desirable to many men and women. (In 1971 the average American air passenger spent 55 days away from home; by 1976 this is projected to be as high as 96 days.)

(5) Many young people today are sincerely concerned with population projections that forecast dire consequences unless continued growth in population is curtailed. Some feel that marriage would frustrate their strong feelings on this problem. (Recent indications of progress toward a more stable population growth may in time alleviate these negative feelings on the part of the young. As of now, many still suggest these concerns as their reason for postponing marriage, at least temporarily.)[119]

(6) The practical control of conception has made sexual relations with an acquaintance relatively safe from undesired consequences.[120] Singles can satisfy sexual desires without the consequences of marriage and the responsibility demanded by parenthood.

Unfortunately, insufficient emphasis has been placed in the past on responsible living in the single state. Traditional discussions of vocations have for the most part emphasized the married and religious state. Beyond these categories there has sometimes been rather guarded discussion of the "dedicated single state" as a third way. Usually such discussion centers on two points, namely, that such a state requires: (1) heroic virtue to observe sexual abstinence without the benefits of clerical or community living; and (2) some sort of dedication to a particular work or vocation lest the single life become an occasion for living solely for self. That such a limited discussion of the single state was ever adequate is open to debate. That it is inadequate today is self-evident, given our insights into the central role of sexuality in one's growth and development as a person.

Individuals who bury themselves in their work while maintaining a superficial web of casual relationships with family, acquaintances, and business associates are too often less than fully integrated human beings. Too often they are motivated by fear of entering into a close personal relationship with another person, whether of the same or opposite sex. This fear of personal involvement is often less than virtuous, less than "other-enriching" and integrating. According to today's insights and experiences and as exemplified by the life of Jesus Christ, involvement in the Christian community demands more.

In current discussions on the single state, three radically different approaches are discernible:

(1) Those living in the single state must live their lives without entering into any kind of interpersonal relationship that might result in the arousing of physical "venereal pleasure." According to this view, emphasis must be laid on the "occasions" within which such pleasure might be aroused, and all such occasions must be reasonably avoided. The advantage of such a view is that it clearly avoids any situation in which the possibility of sinful activity might occur. Its weakness lies in its failure in far too many cases, to provide for the kind of healthy personal interrelationships that are essential to full human development.[121]

(2) Those living in the single state must live their lives in a manner that will contribute to their own growth and integration as well as that of others. According to this view, the emphasis lies on interpersonal growth and development, regardless of the state of life of the people involved while at the same time respecting that state. The advantage of such a view is that it is essentially the same for all people, married, single, or religious. Its weakness lies in the fact that it involves a certain amount of risk and responsibility in entering into personal involvements with others, who ought to be enriched by the encounter and not exploited.[122]

(3) Those living in the single state are free to live their lives in any manner they see fit, as long as the individuals with whom they interrelate are in agreement on the nature and limits of the activity engaged in. Such a view provides a minimum of individual restrictions. It fails in most cases to give adequate protection to the rights of others, particularly the rights of society at large in a responsible way. It tends toward excessive permissiveness.

We find the second approach more in accord with the principles and values developed in this study. When considering this question, four kinds of persons are to be kept in mind:

(1) Voluntary singles—those who never married and for a variety of reasons will probably never do so.

(2) Involuntary singles—those who never married even though they would have liked to, but were unable to find a suitable partner.

(3) Widowed singles—those whose spouse has died.

(4) Divorced singles—those who are divorced and cannot or do not wish to remarry.

*Voluntary Singles*

As suggested above, many people today choose to remain single for a variety of reasons. It is indicative of a broader concept of community and healthy growth that our society is learning to accept voluntary singles. The common view of the past that equated marriage with personal wholeness and viewed single persons as a threat is beginning to pass.

As the number of voluntarily single people increases, society as a whole will become more open to the single state as a way of life. Openness must be true particularly of a Christian society, which is committed to look upon others as fellow members of the People of God. All people—single, married, or religious must seek that level of interpersonal growth that will contribute to the well-being of others.

Further, interpersonal relationship must be developed in the wholeness of one's personhood, and therefore as distinctively male or female. The principles to be used in judging the morality of interpersonal relationships among the voluntarily single are the same as those for other persons, namely, creative growth toward full interpersonal integration. Relationships which foster growth and integration are morally good. The characteristics of healthy relationships between single individuals and others are the same as those described for all human sexuality (Chapter IV): self-liberating, other-enriching, honest and faithful, life-serving, joyful, and socially responsible.

Of particular concern is the question of a relationship between a single person and a married person of the same or the opposite sex. Essentially, such a relationship is governed by the same principles and must have the same characteristics as any other relationship except that it *necessarily* involves a threefold relationship inasmuch as the rights of the other spouse are affected. Therefore, care must be taken that the growth and integration of this third person is not harmed.

Particular note may also be made of so-called "swinging singles."[123] This phenomenon, hardly new to the human scene, involves a casual approach to interpersonal sexual relations, difficult to reconcile with the values suggested as being indicative of healthy human interrelatedness. The danger of becoming self-destructive, exploitative and deceitful toward others, unstable and promiscuous, and consistently non-life-serving seems to be too evident to provide any basis for a true interpersonal growth experience or true human integration. Arguments supporting this way of life as truly freeing and socially responsible among consenting adults are not adequately authenticated. Sexual relations are too much a part of the core of a person's being to admit of such casual treatment.

It must be noted, however, that interpersonal relations between responsible persons need not and should not be devoid of all signs of human warmth and friendship, all signs of human love and affection. In making particular judgments about such relationships, a wise counselor will not resort to overriding prohibitions, but rather will guide the counselee toward a proportionate and gradual deepening of the relationship, a moving toward true growth and full integration. An intimate expression of love between two honest other-centered friends of long standing may be "less immoral" than the same intimate expression between a married couple who are selfish and self-serving, dishonest and irresponsible! The fact of marriage "should" make a difference; too often it does not. In this as in all other matters of sexual relations, the key questions are those concerning true growth and integration, which are necessary to all aspects of human life.

## Involuntary Singles

There have always been individuals in society who were unable to marry. Sometimes due to physical conditions or defects, to appearances or personality, sometimes due to social station or stigma, or even simply a disproportionate imbalance in the number of individuals of the opposite sex—for these and any number of other reasons, society has always had a significant number of "have nots" in the distribution of marriage partners. Too often these individuals become the object of poor humor, ridicule, and social discrimination, or of fear, suspicion, even ill treatment and exploitation. In some instances, without any other qualifications, they have been urged to join religious communities both to their own detriment, the detriment of the communities they joined, and that of society as a whole.

Involuntary singles would be better served if they were urged and helped to live out their lives as true sexual human persons with the same need, right, and opportunity to live as men and women, living in and relating to the world around them, seeking true growth, and full human integration. Such individuals cannot and should not be expected to live as asexual or nonsexual beings. Rather, they can and must find true friendship, true interpersonal relationships that are growth-giving and integrative, and therefore not exploitative or enslaving. Signs of love and friendship proportionate to the depth of the relationship and the limitations of their condition are to be considered proper and appropriate, as long as they demonstrate the characteristics of all human sexual interpersonal relationships that are healthy.

Special note must be made here of the mentally retarded. Everything that has been said of other involuntary singles applies also to them with a special meaning. The retarded are not rendered asexual or nonsexual by their condition. They are not to be denied their sexuality. While needing special care and protection as well as special education and guidance, they cannot be expected to live as non-human persons. They too relate to the world as male or female.

Within the limits of their capability and the good of society as a whole, the retarded, too, need to learn to express the sexual dimension of their personhood so as to achieve that level of growth and integration of which they are capable. Furthermore there is special need for public education in this regard.

The attitude of the public toward the retarded is too often nothing short of cruel in relation to these people.

## Widowed Singles

The widowed can be single voluntarily or involuntarily. Of special concern here are those characteristics that make this particular form of singleness unique. Given the increased longevity in our day, particularly for women, the death of a spouse can leave the remaining partner with the option of either trying to find a suitable second partner or facing the possibility of a long life alone. Two problems seem to be most apparent.

The first is the still prevalent attitude, whereby a widow or widower is kept alienated from the mainstream of society, particularly married society. The need for friends, male and female, the need for healthy interpersonal relations, does not stop with the death of a spouse. The remaining spouse must still interrelate with the rest of the world, and that as a "male or female person." Signs of friendship and love, proportionate with the relationship, must be considered proper and appropriate so long as they are productive of continued growth and integration. Human growth and integration does not stop at any given age, but must continue throughout life. Full integration is achieved only with death and union with the risen Lord. Personal interrelatedness must be part of everyone's life regardless of age or condition. Initial steps are being taken by more progressive homes for the aged to make possible such integrated living. The rest of society ought take note of this and do likewise. Earlier reference has been made to unjust laws that discriminate against the widowed elderly who would want to remarry.[124]

The second problem of the widowed is related to the first and results from the fact that women are outliving men at a higher ratio each year, so that there is a disproportionately higher number of older women to the number of older men. Evidence indicates that older people remain fully sexual human beings, in need of companionship and love, throughout their lives.[125] Suggestions to the contrary are myth. It is also evident that continued sexual activity, continued companionship, continued caring and being cared for make for happy and healthy old age. A society that resists such needs in its elderly, plays a cruel and inhuman, therefore immoral, joke on them.

The right to marry is a basic one, long espoused in Catholic teaching. Steps should be taken to insure this right to the elderly who seek to exercise it. Some social scientists have even suggested a reassessment of the laws against polygamy for the elderly. Given the advanced years of the participants, such a practice cannot be objected to on the basis that it fails to provide for the proper rearing of offspring. It would still seem, however, to offend against the ideal of responsible partnership proposed throughout Christian times as an exemplar of the union of Christ and the Church. Even in the Old Testament, the covenant reality envisioned the Genesis model of "two in one flesh" as the symbol of God's union with Israel. In other words, the danger of human destruction and alienation remains a critical consideration in the evaluation of this and all other emerging patterns of familial living. This danger, however, does not preclude the possibility of further investigation and study by competent authorities, civil and ecclesial, particularly in view of the alienating loneliness experienced by many of the elderly widowed in our society today.

### Divorced Singles

Like the widowed, the divorced can be single, voluntarily or involuntarily. In many respects, the problems they face are similar to those of the widowed. Married society with its exclusive "couple" orientation tends to alienate and exploit the divorced. Too often the problems of adjusting to the single state are only complicated by the lack of loving concern and support from former friends and associates. Further, a life alone after having lived in the married state for many years is sometimes very difficult. This difficulty often goes beyond mere inconvenience and can reach the point of grave psychological and emotional harm. Involuntary singles are often left with only three choices. They must live a life they find unnatural and personally destructive, or seek companionship outside civil and ecclesial norms, or else enter a second marriage. In some cases, recourse to this last option might well be the most moral. The ultimate resolution of this "Catholic Dilemma" is beyond our scope here. We would only call attention to the wealth of material being written on this topic, particularly to an earlier work by a task force of the Catholic Theological Society of America.[126]

Our immediate concern here is the ongoing relationship of the divorced individual to the rest of society. Like the widowed, the divorced cannot be expected to live as nonsexual beings. Their way of being in, and relating to, the world remains essentially that of male or female persons. They have a right to live like sexual beings. Signs of affection and love, commensurate with the depth and degree of each relationship, are proper and moral so long as they are productive of human growth and integration for the individual and all others involved. All too often, the treatment accorded to the divorced by the rest of society is a matter of being more sinned against than sinning. A truly Christian community ought to reach out in loving care and concern to all its members, especially those in most need. Among these must be counted the divorced Christians.

Available statistical data suggest that each of the categories of single individuals discussed above is increasing in American society today. This fact alone calls for a greater effort on the part of the entire Christian community to learn to deal with those in the single state as fully enfranchised members of the Church and of the human race. The tendency of the past to set such people apart, to treat them as members of a suspect minority, must be resisted. Their spiritual and human needs must be addressed. They must be assisted in their interpersonal and intrapersonal growth and be fully integrated into the larger community.

### CELIBATE AND VIRGINAL SEXUALITY

In keeping with the definition of sexuality as "the way of being in, and relating to, the world as male or female person,"[127] it is appropriate to include here a discussion of sexuality in the lives of those who choose to live a life of celibacy or virginity.

In another age, such a discussion would have been judged highly inappropriate because of the prevailing concept of the celibate life and the ordinary preparation for it. Even today, resistance is not lacking to the suggestion that men and women who live in consecrated celibacy or virginity are called, like other human persons, to "experience and express both the incompleteness of their separate natures as well as their relatedness to each other as male and female" through the vehicle of human sexuality.[128] This resistance is expressed, in the first place, by many celibate priests and religious themselves. However, a sensitive and faithful reading of Scripture (1 Cor 7:7) and of Vatican II,[129] calls for attention not only to the existence of celibacy and virginity in the Church, but also to the humanity of those who seek to live this life.[130]

The ideal of celibacy and virginity has been an important part of the life of the Church from earliest times.[131] This mode of living the Christian life has been intimately related to the mystery of Christian love,[132] to eschatological hope for the Second Coming of the Lord,[133] and to the symbolic significance of the ultimate destiny to which every person is called.[134]

Furthermore, almost from the beginning of the Christian era, celibacy and virginity "for the sake of the kingdom" have been associated with ministerial service in the Church. Because of this emphasis, the value of celibacy and virginity has frequently been perceived in terms of convenience, facilitation, or practicality in the performance of apostolic tasks. While such a view need not be immediately and totally rejected, it clearly introduces a pragmatic aspect, which has at times reduced the understanding of this way of life to a minimum.[135]

Today we are witnessing a revalorization of celibacy and of virginity as evangelical values of great spiritual worth. Vatican II sees these values as charisms necessary for the life of the Church.[136] At the same time, as already indicated,[137] we are aware of a renewed appreciation of some dimensions of human sexuality less frequently recognized in Christian teaching. It is time then to question whether the manner in which Christian men and women are being prepared to live celibate and virginal sexuality in the Church today disposes them to be faithful to their commitment and no less faithful to the values of human dignity perceived in the Creator's summons to creative growth toward integration.[138]

The question of formation in sexuality is critical in the lives of celibates and virgins, as many writers have attempted to demonstrate in recent years.[139] Essential to good formation in this matter is adequate, exact, and positive information—physiological, psychological, and emotional. Generally speaking, it seems that this dimension is not neglected today. Beyond the level of instruction, however, a program of education and of formation is needed, adapted to the specific needs of men and women at every age.

Those who seek to live celibate or virginal sexuality must know how to experience a healthy, affective maturation in their own persons; to give and receive friendship with persons of their own and of the opposite sex; to express "universal" love (*caritas*) in specific concern and care for others; to acknowledge the possibility of a unique, intense, personal encounter that at some moment in their lives invites to an intimate, exclusive, lasting relationship.[140]

The man or woman who has tried to understand celibacy or virginity in terms of covenant,[141] must seek to live sexuality in creative fidelity. He or she must be prepared to be vulnerable, to know pain, to experience loneliness in a most acute way. Out of such stuff, celibates and virgins in solidarity with people everywhere, must seek to forge compassion and give birth to wisdom. They must know that the voice of a living, faithful God can be heard in the heart's solitude.[142] They must never cease to believe that the "desert can be beautiful" because somewhere it hides a spring of living water.[143]

Those Christians who have chosen to live celibacy or virginity in the Church are being asked today to face their sexuality honestly and with positive conviction. Through celibacy and virginity, a certain witness is given to the Holy in an age in which moral values are increasingly ambiguous and shallow. Celibate and virginal sexuality must be lived today with respect for the values of creativity and integration as necessary to the growth of every person "to mature manhood, to the measure of the stature of the fullness of Christ" (Eph 4:13).

The experience of human sexuality within the context of creative fidelity to a covenant commitment must be for the celibate and the virgin what it is for any human person: self-liberating, other-enriching, honest, faithful, socially responsible, life-serving, and joyous.[144] There are signs that such a goal can be achieved. The integration of women into fuller participation in the life of the Church is one factor that has contributed to a more balanced view of sexuality in what was formerly an exclusively male world. More realistic spiritual direction and more responsible programs of continuing formation for candidates to the priesthood and the religious life are further positive factors contributing toward the realization of the goal of healthy sexuality for celibates and virgins.

The specific mode of a witness to Christian love on the horizon of celibate and virginal sexuality can only be more credible, as fidelity to commitment is expressed through those experiences which assure creative growth toward integration. A growing *corpus* of bibliographical material that contains realistic and insightful discussion of this topic is an encouraging sign.[145]

## HOMOSEXUALITY

A study of this nature on human sexuality would be both inadequate and incomplete if it neglected the question of homosexuality. Taking up the topic, however, is rife with difficulties. Clearly there is the danger of being misunderstood, particularly by the careless reader who would open the study at this section without having read the preceding chapters. Homosexuality, as an ethical and pastoral concern, can be understood and evaluated properly only within the context of the foregoing historical, anthropological, and theological considerations. It does an injustice to this study, but more so it is unfair to the countless men and women of homosexual orientation to make moral judgments upon them and their behavior in the name of Christian morals without appreciating the complexity of the Christian attitude toward sexuality in general.

A further danger of treating this topic is the prejudice and passionate hostility it invariably generates, attitudes born of ignorance and fear. Particularly for people not altogether secure in their own sexual identity, homosexuality is a highly emotional subject, not easily permitting of concrete objective discussion.[146] Even among those self-assured in their heterosexuality, popular myths and outright ignorance often give rise to irrational fears of homosexual persons. What gross unfairness can be committed, for example, by those who see all homosexuals as child molesters or constituents of some subversive underground. By even raising the question of the objective morality of homosexual behavior and certainly by pointing out some of the problems in the Judeo-Christian tradition on the subject, this study runs the risk of being rejected out of hand on all counts. But again, justice to the topic of sexual morality and, more importantly, justice to homosexuals demand an unbiased critical analysis of the question. For too long homosexuals have been the victims not only of misunderstanding but also of silence and neglect on the part of theologians and those charged with pastoral care within the Church.

These concerns explain the somewhat more extensive treatment given to this topic in the present study. Even so, the limitations under which such a study labors need to be mentioned here. Obviously there is the limitation of space. The problems and complexity of the issues involved, and the more generic scope and purpose of this study, all preclude a comprehensive treatment of the subject. Even a complete survey of the state of research is out of the question, such is the proliferation of literature that has appeared in the last several years.[147] The physiological, psychological, and sociological aspects of homosexuality have come to be reexamined, and, in many instances, previous conclusions have been revised on the basis of more recent findings.

It is difficult to say anything about homosexuality that is not of a provisional nature. Considerable research has yet to be done in the areas of psychology, sociology, and medicine, as well as theology. Little of a definite nature can be said, for instance, with regard to the pastoral care of homosexuals. But, even with this proviso, there are more than a few questions to be raised, myths to be dispelled, and mistakes to be corrected. Above all, there are matters of justice to be recognized. The alienation, loneliness, and discrimination suffered by homosexuals can be attributed in no little part to the attitudes of the Church. The reasons for these attitudes lie deep within the Judeo-Christian tradition.

## Scripture

Nowhere has homosexual activity been viewed with as much abhorrence as in the Judeo-Christian West. Neither Islam nor Hinduism sees it as taboo. Primitive peoples like the Eskimos, Malaysians, and North American Indians had no difficulty accepting it; ancient Greece institutionalized it. In some primitive cultures, a homosexual was even seen as a kind of shaman or holy man, certainly not as a criminal.[148]

The only adequate explanation for the profound, even phobic, animosity of the Judeo-Christian West is the fact that homosexual behavior is viewed in the Bible as a crime worthy of death (Lev 18-22; 20:13), a sin "against nature" (Rom 1:26), which excludes one from entry into the kingdom of God (1 Cor 6:10). Even more ominous was the punishment visited by God upon Sodom for the *assumed* sin that was named after that ill-fated city (Gen 19:1-29). If these acts called to heaven for vengeance, how could a people and their rulers tolerate such behavior except at the risk of divine displeasure for themselves as well?

There is no doubt but that the Old Testament condemns homosexual practice with the utmost severity. The reason for the condemnation, however, and the severity of the punishment cannot be appreciated apart from the historical background that gave rise to them. Simply citing verses from the Bible outside of their historical context and then blithely applying them to homosexuals today does grave injustice both to Scripture and to people who have already suffered a great deal from the travesty of biblical interpretation. "You shall not lie with a male as with a woman; it is an abomination" (*to'ebah*) (Lev 18:22). "If a man lies with a male as with a woman, both of them have committed an abomination (*to'ebah*); they shall be put to death, their blood is upon them" (Lev 20:13).

The prohibition of homosexual activity between men as a crime worthy of death could not be more explicit. The background to these texts and reasons for the condemnation are equally explicit: "You shall not do as they do in the land of Egypt, where you dwelt, and you shall not do as they do in the land of Canaan, to which I am bringing you. You shall not walk in their statutes" (Lev 18:3). "Do not defile yourselves by any of these things, for by all these the nations I am casting out before you defiled themselves" (Lev 18:24). "So keep my charge never to practice any of these abominable customs which were practiced before you, and never defile yourselves by them: I am the Lord your God" (Lev 18:30).

The fundamental theme of the Levitical Holiness Code is, "Do not defile yourselves," do not make yourselves unclean. Its concern is not ethical but cultic. Even adultery is forbidden because of ritual impurity (Lev 18:20). "Leviticus deals almost exclusively with cultic and ritual matters."[149]

Of particular importance for our consideration is the word "abomination" *(to'ebah)*. Derived from the sphere of cult, the word comes from the verb "to abhor" and designates most commonly some practice or thing loathed on religious grounds. For the Israelites, this particularly meant idolatry. An idol is an abomination (Dt 7:25ff; 27:15; 2 Kgs 23:13; Jer 16:18; Ezek 14:6), and anything that has to do with idolatrous practices is an abomination (Lev 18:27, 29-30; Dt 12:31; 13:14; 17:4; 18:9; 2 Kgs 16:3; 21:2; 11; 2 Chr 33:2; Ezek 5:9, 11; Mal 2:11; *et al.*). Included as an abomination was not only the explicit practice of idolatry, however, but anything that even remotely pertained to it, like the eating of unclean animals and foods (Lev 11; Dt 14:3-21).

For Israel of the Old Testament the worship of Yahweh was unconditionally exclusive. Anything pertaining to the idolatrous cult of Israel's neighbors was an "abomination" that "defiled" an Israelite and rendered him unclean for the cult of Yahweh. The Old Testament law codes, however, "took their origin in a milieu where no sharp distinction was drawn between the cultic and the non-cultic sphere of activity, but where every side of life had its links with cultic celebrations."[150]

Many cultic procedures and customs were taboo in Israel simply because they were regarded as belonging specifically to

, foreign cults. In a world where worship permeated every aspect of life, this prohibition referred not only to apostasy but also to anything even remotely connected with it.[151]

Among the Canaanite practices rejected by the Old Testament was that of cultic intercourse whereby the sexual activity of the gods was enacted ritually by temple functionaries.[152] These sexual rites were to be found in the fertility cults of the whole ancient East, from Cyprus to Babylon, and included not only female temple personnel but males as well.

> There shall be no cult prostitute (*kedeshah*) of the daughters of Israel, neither shall there be a cult prostitute (*kedesh*) of the sons of Israel. You shall not bring the hire of a harlot, or the wages of a dog, into the house of the Lord your God in payment of any vow; for both of these are an abomination (*to'ebah*) to the Lord your God (Dt 23:17-18).

Men engaging in ritual intercourse (kedeshim) are mentioned as active in Israel during the period of the monarchy, performing all the "abominations" of the Canaanites (1 Kgs 14:22-24; 15:12-14; 22:47; 2 Kgs 23:7). Recent discoveries of texts at Ras Shamra, the ancient city of Ugarit, have shed considerable light on the religious practices of the Canaanites, including the cult of the Canaanite fertility goddesses Ashera and Astartex, which involved sacral intercourse (Fragment 8252).

Homosexual activity between men is proscribed in Leviticus for the same reason that it is condemned in Deuteronomy and the Books of Kings. It is an "abomination" because of its connection with the fertility rites of the Canaanites. The condemnation of homosexual activity in Leviticus is not an ethical judgment. "Homosexuality here is condemned on account of its association with idolatry."[153]

Even after the danger of ritual intercourse had passed, the rabbis in the post-Exilic period maintained the prohibition against homosexual activity much as they retained all the dietary prescriptions that had arisen in the same period. The Talmud extended the prohibition, but not the death penalty, to women as well, who were not included in the Levitical injunction. The Talmud treated homosexual activity and bestiality as similar crimes on the assumption that "the one like the other had its origin in the licentiousness of the heathen Canaanites."[154]

Even though a Christian does not read the legislation of the Old Testament in the same way as an Orthodox Jew, the Levitical prohibition against homosexual acts has had considerable indirect influence on the Church. Certainly it colored St. Paul's estimation of the sexual practices of first-century Hellenism. More directly influential, however, and historically more significant for the Christian attitude toward homosexual behavior was the Genesis story of Sodom and Gomorrah (Gen 19).

Throughout the Old and New Testaments allusions are made to Sodom as a symbol of utter depravity. So great was Sodom's sin that it merited complete destruction. The Fathers of the Church had no doubt that the nature of the wickedness for which Sodom was punished was the homosexual practice of sodomy. The story has a parallel, however, in the account of the wickedness of the townsmen of Gibeah (Jgs 19). In this instance, a similar incident is described involving the sexual abuse of a female concubine. What is common to both stories, however, whether involving the male visitors of Sodom or the female concubine of Gibeah, is *rape*.

Both the stories of Sodom and Gibeah deal with sexual violations. But the fact that the sex victim is interchangeable without lessening the repulsion of the biblical authors shows clearly that it is not homosexuality or heterosexuality that is the primary consideration here, but the violence of rape. If sexuality is involved in the condemnation, it is subordinated to the issues of hospitality and justice. For Sodom as for Gibeah, "the emphasis falls not on the proposed sexual act *per se*, but on the terrible violation of the customary law of hospitality."[155]

As often as it refers to the sinfulness of Sodom, the Old Testament never explicitly identifies Sodom with the practice of homosexuality. In fact, there is no uniform tradition as to the nature of Sodom's offense. For Isaiah it was lack of justice (Is 1:10; 3:9); for Jeremiah, adultery, lying, and the unwillingness to repent (Jer 23:14); for Ezechiel, "pride, surfeit of food, and prosperous ease" together with the fact that Sodom "did not aid the poor and needy" (Ezek 16:49). Old Testament Wisdom literature speaks of Sodom in terms of folly, insolence, and inhospitality (Wis 10:8; 19:14; Sir 16:8). The New Testament presents Jesus as referring to the proverbial wickedness and punishment of Sodom, but with no indication of the specific nature of its sinfulness (Mt 10:14-15; 11:23-24; Lk 10:12; 17:29). No connection is made with sexuality at all, let alone homosexuality.

Not until the late New Testament books of Jude and 2 Peter is any explicit connection made in the Bible between Sodom and sexuality (Jude 6-7; 2 Pt 2:4, 6-10). In Jude the sin of Sodom is described in terms of "fornication" and "going after strange flesh" (Jude 7), with an allusion to the sin of the angels. Evident here is the influence of the apocryphal writings of the inter-testamental period. The *Book of Jubilees* (1st century B.C.) emphasizes the depravity of Sodom as sexual in nature (Jub 16:5-6; 20:5-6) and links the sin of the Sodomites to the Nephilim or giants born of the unnatural union of angels and men, the "sons of God" and the "daughters of men" (Gen 6:1-4).[156]

Philo of Alexandria (c.13 B.C.-c.50 A.D.) appears to be the first author to connect Sodom explicitly with homosexual practices.[157] Even before him, however, a homosexual interpretation of the Sodom story is strongly implied in the apocryphal *Testaments of the Twelve Patriarchs*, written in the late second century or early first century B.C. (Test. Naph. 3:4-5; Test. Benj. 9:1), and in the *Second Book of Enoch* (2 Enoch 10:4). Josephus (37.38-c.96 A.D.) also makes the same connection (*Antiquities*, I, 11, 3). The conclusion seems warranted, therefore that "by the end of the first century A.D. the sin of Sodom had become widely identified amongst the Jews with homosexual practices."[158] This identification can be shown to have had immense influence not only on the New Testament (Jude) but on Christian tradition and legislation thereafter.

Interestingly enough, this new homosexual interpretation of the sin of Sodom had an almost negligible effect upon the Talmud. The apocryphal writings, some of which were highly apocalyptic in character, lay outside the mainstream of rabbinical tradition and were never recognized by orthodox Judaism. The basis for the reinterpretation of the story in Philo, Josephus, and the early Church seems to lie in the association made between the "wickedness of Sodom" and the "lawlessness of the Gentiles" (Test. Naph. 4:1). In the Old Testament tradition, Sodom was no longer simply a locality on the shores of the Dead Sea, laid waste by some natural catastrophe in the dim past. Sodom had become a symbol of every wickedness offensive to Jewish moral sensibilities, above all, pride, inhospitality, and forgetfulness of God. With a change of time and circumstances, there arose a change of interpretation. Sodom became a symbol of the depravity that Jews and later Christians found most abhorrent in Hellenistic society. The conclusion may be drawn, therefore, that:

> There is not the least reason to believe, as a matter either of historical fact or of revealed truth, that the city of Sodom and its neighbors were destroyed because of their homosexual practices. This theory of their fate seems undoubtedly to have originated in a Palestinian Jewish reinterpretation of Genesis 19, and its exponents, and by contempt for the basest features of Greek sexual immorality.[159]

The Hellenistic depravity that gave rise to the reinterpretation of the Sodom story in the first century A.D. likewise provides the background for the isolated references made to homosexual practices in the New Testament. We have no words of Jesus at all on the issue. The epistles make three definite references. In two passages homosexual behavior is simply listed along with the vices rampant in the licentious pagan society of first-century Rome.

> Do you not know that the unrighteous will not inherit the kingdom of God? Do not be deceived; neither *pornoi* (men involved with prostitution), nor idolaters, nor adulterers, nor *malakoi* (men who engage passively in homosexual acts) nor *arsenokoitai* (men who engage actively in homosexual acts), nor thieves, nor the greedy, nor drunkards, nor revilers, nor robbers will inherit the kingdom of God (1 Cor 6:9-10).
>
> The law is not laid down for the just but for the lawless and disobedient, for the ungodly and sinners, for the unholy

and profane, for murderers of fathers and murderers of mothers, for manslayers, *pornois*, *arsenokoitais*, kidnappers, liars, perjurers, and whatever else is contrary to sound doctrines (1 Tim 1:9-10).

Even the most intolerant anti-homosexual cannot help but be taken aback by the apparent equation in these two lists of homosexual acts with patricide, matricide, kidnapping, and robbery. It must be remembered, however, that the New Testament originated in the era of Caligula and Nero. St. Paul was a contemporary of Petronius, whose *Satyricon*, along with the writings of Juvenal and Martial, presents a lurid description of pagan life in the first century. Prostitution, male as well as female, was rampant.[160] Slaves, men and women, were sold for sex. Pederasty, child molestation, and seduction were commonplace. Dissolute heterosexuals engaged freely in homosexual liaisons for diversion. Violence was coupled with every sort of perversion and possibility of dehumanization. Confronted by such degeneracy, a Hellenistic Jew like St. Paul could not but be repulsed. The foregoing catalogues of vice do not seem to be exaggerations; neither, however, are they examinations of conscience nor careful theological considerations. Both are simply mosaic descriptions of the chaotic moral climate of Hellenistic Roman society. Significantly, neither list singles out homosexual behavior in any way, nor sees it as posing special problems or difficulties.

There can be no doubt that St. Paul considered homosexual acts as perversions of the natural, divinely instituted order of human existence. Writing from Corinth, notorious for its prostitutes, to Rome with a reputation no better, St. Paul makes the only extended reference to homosexuality in the New Testament:

> For the wrath of God is revealed from heaven against all ungodliness and wickedness of men who by their wickedness suppress the truth. . . . Claiming to be wise, they became fools, and exchanged the glory of the immortal God for images resembling mortal man or birds or reptiles. Therefore God gave them up in the lusts of their hearts to impurity, to the dishonoring of their bodies among them-

selves, because they exchanged the truth about God for a lie
and worshipped and served the creature rather than the Creator, who is blessed forever! Amen. For this reason God gave
them up to dishonorable passions. Their women exchanged
natural relations with women and were consumed with passion for one another, men committing shameless acts with
men and receiving in their own persons the due penalty for
their error. And since they did not see fit to acknowledge
God, God gave them up to a base mind and to improper
conduct (Rom 1:18; 22-28).

The most important point to note in this passage is that
the reference to homosexuality is almost parenthetic. It is not
the principal consideration at all. Rather, homosexuality is
used as an illustration of the chaos that follows as a result of
idolatry, the real object of St. Paul's attack. Three times Paul
uses the phrase "God gave them up" to demonstrate the inner
connection between sin and punishment. The Gentiles sin in
that they have "exchanged" (1:23) the true God for idols. The
punishment for this idolatrous confusion is a corresponding
sexual confusion, whereby natural sexual relations are "exchanged" for the unnatural (1:26).[161]
As a Hellenistic Jew conditioned by the Levitical legislation of the Old Testament and appalled at the depravity of the
age, St. Paul understandably rejected homosexual perversion,
whether by men or women. (His mention of women in Rom
1:26 is the only reference to lesbianism in the Bible.) The question needs to be raised at this point, however: can St. Paul's
references to homosexuality simply be applied without qualifi-
cation to all homosexual activity, particularly in the light of
what we know today about inversion?
It has been suggested that, in discussing homosexual behavior in terms of "leaving," "giving up," or "exchanging," St.
Paul is not speaking here at all of the invert, the true homosexual for whom the "natural" use of sex creates not only an aversion but even, in some cases, an impossibility. Paul has been interpreted as speaking here only of those who *deliberately*
choose homosexual over heterosexual relations.[162] Obviously,
St. Paul knew nothing of inversion either as an inherited trait
or a condition fixed in childhood. The Bible regards all homo-

sexual behavior as deliberate and therefore as perversion. "St. Paul's words can only be understood in the sense which he himself would have attached to them."[163]

If the distinction between deliberate perversion and indeliberate homosexual orientation cannot validly be read into St. Paul, the same is true of the rest of the Bible. "Inversion as a constitutional condition is a phenomenon which lies totally outside the biblical perspective and considerations."[164] Until recent findings of medical science and research came to light, inversion lay outside Christian tradition and theological consideration altogether.

### Tradition

There is no need here for a detailed examination of the post-biblical Christian tradition regarding homosexuality. Its essential features extend the basic lines already drawn. The Fathers of the Church were unwavering in their denunciations of homosexual behavior, no doubt with good reason in the case of recent Christian converts from a dissolute pagan life-style. The following citation from St. Augustine's *Confessions* may serve as typical:

> These shameful acts against nature, such as were committed in Sodom, ought everywhere and always to be detested and punished. If all nations were to do such things, they would (equally) be held guilty of the same crime by the law of God, which has not so made men that they should use one another in this way.[165]

St. John Chrysostom was particularly emphatic in denouncing homosexual practices as unnatural, and he made it clear that the Fathers viewed such behavior as deliberate perversion. He held that no one "can say that it was by being hindered of legitimate intercourse that they came to this pass, or that it was from having no means to fulfill their desire that they were driven to this monstrous insaneness."[166]

Something quite striking about patristic thinking on homosexuality is the fact that by far the predominant influence exerted on the Church Fathers came not from St. Paul but the Sodom story, understood historically and interpreted sexually. A survey of Christian tradition reveals that "the effect of the reinterpreted Sodom story upon the mind of the Church was in fact more profound than that of either the Levitical laws or the teaching of the New Testament."[167]

The Sodom story affected not only the Fathers of the Church but civil legislation as well. To pre-Christian laws protecting minors from homosexual violation, the Code of Theodosius and the Code of Justinian added the prohibition of all sodomistic practices under pain of death by fire. An explicit motivation behind these prohibitions and their severe penalty was the protection of the state. Homosexual practices had to be eradicated in order to protect the state from the wrath of divine judgment and any possibility of a catastrophe such as that which befell Sodom. The sixth-century Code of Justinian had considerable impact on both the ecclesiastical and civil laws of the Middle Ages. Indirectly it has influenced civil law in the West well into our own time.[168]

Official Church teaching and legislation is not wanting regarding homosexual practice, beginning as early as the fourth century with the Council of Elvira. It is surprising, however, that the condemnations are relatively few and sporadic. The Church has commonly been accused of sustaining an unrelenting persecution of homosexuals. Careful study of the historical documents indicates nothing of the kind. One finds councils and synods denouncing sodomy from time to time, but invariably in conjunction with other carnal sins. Homosexuals are rarely singled out for special hostility. "We look in vain for that obsessive concern with this one offense which many have imagined that they have detected in the records of ecclesiastical legislation."[169] How small a place has been given to homosexuality in the official teaching of the Church is demonstrated concretely by the manuals of moral theology. While all of them describe sodomy as gravely sinful, their argumentation is limited almost exclusively to an appeal to Scripture and theological reasoning on the natural law. Magisterial pronouncements are noticeably meager. While one cannot accuse the Church of conducting an unrelenting persecution of homosexuals, it should be admitted, however, that it did contribute ideologically to the persecution of homosexuals by the state. The Church shares in the responsibility for the long history in the West of civil persecution of homosexual behavior.

St. Thomas Aquinas is typical of Catholic tradition on

homosexual behavior. Although he cites the biblical teaching, he mainly emphasizes theological reasoning regarding the natural law. St. Thomas treats of homosexual acts in connection with the sins against temperance, specifically lust.[170] He lists sodomy along with masturbation and bestiality as "unnatural vices."[171] His judgment is predicated on the Stoic assumption that any pursuit of sexual pleasure outside of the purpose of all sexual acts, namely, procreation, offends against nature and reason.[172]

St. Thomas and scholastic theology since his time have consistently regarded masturbation, sodomy, and bestiality (in that order of gravity) as sins *contra naturam* and, as such, from the standpoint of chastity considered in itself, more serious than fornication, incest, or adultery. These other vices offend against other virtues as well, like justice and charity; but from the standpoint of chastity alone, nothing offends more than the "unnatural vices." Needless to say, this moral evaluation labors under the influence of a theory of natural law untenable today for its narrow equation of nature with biology. The Stoic conception of nature and natural law, its disparagement of venereal pleasure and its ideal of *apatheia*, had taken hold of medieval consciousness and permeated it. St. Thomas was simply a man of his time in seeing sexuality in terms of biology, solely for the sake of procreation.

An anomaly within the Christian tradition, deserving some mention, is the double standard that prevailed with regard to homosexual acts performed by women. Although a consistent thinker like St. Thomas treats them as equally serious, the medieval penitentials, Church legislation, and Christian tradition in general penalize homosexual acts by men with uncommon severity, while virtually disregarding those by women. An explanation for the inequity cannot be found either on philosophical or theological grounds. It seems to lie instead in the sexist androcentrism of the West and a reverence for semen that borders on superstition. Ignorant of human physiology and dependent on the medical philosophers of antiquity, the Fathers of the Church and medievals after them looked upon the male sperm as *met' oligon anthropon*, as something "almost human."[173]

This conception of semen as a substance "almost human" overshadowed the sexual thought, not only of antiquity, but of the whole Western world until the sixteenth century, and has left its mark upon our own ideas of sexual conduct and morality. It has undoubtedly been responsible in no small measure for the fact that society has always tended to reprobate and punish the homosexual practices of males while more or less ignoring those of females, since the matter, involving "waste" of the precious fluid, could be dismissed as mere feminine lewdness.[174]

In its treatment of homosexual actions Catholic moral theology, until recently, made no substantial changes from that found in St. Thomas. The manuals of moral theology treated sodomy along with masturbation and bestiality as a sin against nature and always gravely sinful. As already indicated, the magisterial teaching to which they appeal is remarkably thin.[175] The theological reasoning is still that of St. Thomas and the Stoics, and the appeal to Scripture still includes the literal, historical interpretation of the Sodom story.[176] In short, post-biblical tradition simply continued the blanket condemnations of the Bible, without recognizing their historical origins. Thus a Levitical prescription became an ethical norm, and its sanction a part of the Western criminal code.

From St. Paul through St. Thomas Aquinas to our own day and the 1975 Vatican Declaration on Sexual Ethics, Catholic tradition has consistently judged all homosexual acts as against nature and hence gravely sinful. Underlying this tradition are not only a pre-scientific physiology and unhistorical interpretation of Scripture but also the Stoic conviction that procreation alone justifies the enjoyment and use of sexual pleasure. Even in Catholic circles this Stoic principle no longer goes without question. Scientific research and recent discoveries in medicine and psychology have brought to light the need to modify traditional preconceptions on a number of counts.

Scientific research has revealed homosexuality to be a phenomenon of bewildering complexity, defying classification according to rigid, pre-determined notions. True sexual inversion is for all practical purposes irreversible. Obviously, the condition itself is morally neutral. But what of homosexual acts in the case of an irreversible homosexual? Are they to be regarded in the same light as the acts of a pervert who deliberately opts for homosexual over heterosexual relations? Are acts that true homosexuals maintain to be entirely natural to their condition to be judged as unnatural simply because they are such for the dominant heterosexual majority?

Those dealing with homosexuals are often faced with the delicate and difficult task of providing moral and spiritual guidance for true homosexuals, assessing their moral behavior, yet doing justice to their personal problems and at times considerable personal suffering. A pastor or counselor cannot help feeling frustrated at the thought that our Christian tradition affords little or no direct assistance. The Christian tradition knows only one kind of homosexual behavior—perversion. To the perplexing problem of inversion, it has only indirect relevance.

This is not to say that homosexual acts are not sinful. They may very well be, to a greater or less degree, even in the case of fixed inversion. But the morality of homosexual acts, like that of all human acts, must be determined by the principles of Christian ethics and moral theology. We must look to reason, aware of the data afforded by contemporary science, guided by the ideals and motives of Christian faith. We cannot simply appeal for answers to tradition or to revelation, as if the question had been decided once and for all by divine decree on the shores of the Dead Sea.

### Current Approaches to the Morality of Homosexuality

The morality of homosexuality has been the subject of much debate and discussion in current theological literature. Surveying the field, one can divide the various approaches into four distinct categories:

(1) *Homosexual acts are "intrinsically evil."*

This position is best represented in the recent publication of the National Conference of Catholic Bishops entitled *Principles to Guide Confessors in Questions of Homosexuality.* The following paragraph indicates the theological framework of this approach:

The objective morality of sexual acts is based upon the teaching of the Church concerning Christian marriage: Genital sexual expression between a man and a woman should take place only in marriage. Apart from the intentions of the man and of the woman, sexual intercourse has a twofold meaning. It is an act of union with the beloved, and it is procreative. Neither meaning may be excluded, although for a variety of reasons, the procreative meaning may not be attained. By their nature homosexual acts exclude all possibility of procreation of life. They are therefore inordinate uses of the sexual faculty. It is assumed, moreover, that the only ordinate use of the sexual faculty must be oriented toward a person of the opposite sex. Sexual acts between members of the same sex are contrary not only to one of the purposes of the sexual faculty, namely, procreation, but also to the other principal purpose, which is to express mutual love between husband and wife. For these reasons homosexual acts are a grave transgression of the goals of human sexuality and of human personality, and are consequently contrary to the will of God.[177]

A similar position is reflected in the 1975 Vatican Declaration on Sexual Ethics:

In the pastoral field, these homosexuals must certainly be treated with understanding and sustained in the hope of overcoming their personal difficulties and their inability to fit into society. Their culpability will be judged with prudence. But no pastoral method can be employed which would give moral justification to these acts on the grounds that they would be consonant with the condition of such people. For according to the objective moral order, homosexual relations are acts which lack an essential and indispensable finality. In Sacred Scripture they are condemned as a serious depravity and even presented as the sad consequence of rejecting God. This judgment of Scripture does not of course permit us to conclude that all those who suffer from this anomaly are personally responsible for it, but it does attest to the fact that homosexual acts are intrinsically disordered and can in no case be approved of.[178]

Such an approach does not regard the homosexual condition itself as morally evil or wrong, but does consider homosexual acts as intrinsically evil and always forbidden. Where there is hope of changing the sexual orientation, this is regarded as the course to be followed. Where such a change is not possible, the homosexual is advised through prayer, the sacraments, spiritual direction, self-discipline, and the formation of a stable relationship with one person to sublimate his sexual impulses in the pursuit of service to God and neighbor. If repeated actions occur, the counselee is to be admonished to break off any relationship and avoid any situations that are conducive to such overt expression.

This approach views human sexuality as an activity restricted to the marriage state and regards full genital experience as acceptable only in the context of a biological openness to procreation. Methodologically, it evaluates the morality of homosexual genital experience on the basis of a biological analysis of the act that it regards as intrinsically evil. Support for this position is sought by an appeal to Scripture but without due consideration of the fuller context and meaning of the passages. It points to the historical evidence as confirmatory without exploring the source or rationale for this historical condemnation. Homosexual activity is assumed to be always destructive of human personhood without due regard for the empirical evidence that raises questions regarding this assumption. Finally, a pastoral solution is suggested (sublimation and abstinence) that has proven practical and successful only in a minority of cases.[179] This position requires much more proof before it can become convincing.

(2) *Homosexual acts are "essentially imperfect."*

A second approach looks upon homosexual behavior as "essentially incomplete" (Presbyterian Report),[180] "not normative" (McCormick),[181] "not human expression at full term" (Kennedy),[182] one that "can never become an ideal" (Curran).[183]

The arguments advanced for this position are summarized by Charles Curran in the following manner:

> Thus the biblical data indicates that the biblical authors in their cultural and historical circumstances deemed homosexual acts wrong and attached a generic gravity to such

acts, but there appears to be no reason for attaching a special heinousness or gravity to these acts.

The Christian tradition has constantly accepted the view that homosexuality goes against the Christian understanding of human sexuality and its meaning. I would agree that historical circumstances could have influenced the condemnation of a particular form of behavior. Likewise, it is possible that the Christian tradition could have been wrong at a particular point. However, there seems to be no sufficient evidence for such a judgment in the case of homosexuality. Despite all the methodological shortcomings and one-sidedness of the natural law approach proposed by Aquinas, it still seems to correspond to a certain human connaturality condemning homosexuality as wrong. Also, the majority of all the data from the human sciences seems to point to the fact that human sexuality has its proper meaning in terms of the love union of male and female.

Pastorally, even though this position recognizes that homosexual acts are wrong, it does not necessarily condemn every form of homosexual expression or union as absolutely immoral. It acknowledges that in the reality of human life, not everyone is capable of realizing the ideal and therefore it may be necessary at times to accept, albeit reluctantly, homosexual expressions and unions as the lesser of two evils or as the only way in which some persons can find a satisfying degree of humanity in their lives.

Writing in this vein, H. Kimball Jones is able to say:

> Thus, we suggest, that the Church must be willing to make the difficult, but necessary, step of recognizing the validity of mature homosexual relationships, encouraging the absolute invert to maintain a fidelity to one partner when his only other choice would be to lead a promiscuous life filled with guilt and fear. This would by no means be an endorsement of homosexuality by the Church.[184]

This approach is far more objective in its use of the data from Scripture, history, and the behavioral sciences. The position is developed on what might be called the preponderance of evidence, without attempting to hide or deny the tentativeness of its conclusions. Acknowledgment is given to the meaning and purpose of human sexuality beyond marriage and procreation even while the heterosexual relationship is suggested as the ideal. The wholistic approach to moral evaluation based on the total well-being of the person makes this approach far more flexible and responsive to pastoral solutions even though not always fully consistent with the ideal. Greater justice is accorded to the developmental nature of the human being and to the reality of sin and its effect upon our lives.

Nonetheless, this approach does have some overall weaknesses: it leaves unproven its basic assumption that heterosexual behavior is always the ideal; it has a tendency to attribute too much to the power of sin; and it fails to answer adequately the question why behavior which contributes to a person's well-being in the maximum way possible must be considered wrong. If the ideal is utterly unrealizable and incompatible with one's personality structure, can it truly be considered an ideal? Or can the failure to pursue what one is constitutionally incapable of pursuing be properly considered wrong? Although this position permits greater respect for individuals and their rights, its negative view of homosexuality as non-ideal can be a substantial violation of human rights and dignity if the presumed thesis is not correct (namely, that heterosexuality is the ideal). Although such an approach based on the preponderance of evidence seems reasonable to follow, one must be careful to recognize its limitations and avoid imposing it as absolute truth.

(3) *Homosexual acts are to be evaluated in terms of their relational significance.*

A third approach to homosexuality insists that meaningful and wholesome sexuality need not always be evaluated in terms of its relationship to procreation. The nature and quality of the relationship provide a more adequate criterion. This position maintains that homosexual expressions are in themselves neutral and become moral to the extent that they are "expressive of self-giving love" (Michigan Episcopal Diocese Report),[185] "capable of grounding friendship and fostering mutuality" (Baum),[186] "generating friendship that enables the partners to grow and become more fully human" (Salvatorian Gay Task

Force).[187] Where such conditions exist, homosexual expressions ought not to be regarded as morally wrong or forbidden. Guidance would obviously center on evaluating homosexual expressions and unions in terms of their ability to call forth human growth, friendship, and unselfish commitment to another.

The following passages from a report on homosexuality issued by the Episcopal Diocese of Michigan provide the rationale for this approach:

> A great virtue of the traditional teaching about sex lies in the fact that it is interpreted as God's creation, and therefore good. It is not characteristic of Christianity to identify bodily life with evil in any way, although specific Christian groups have often acted as if it were. Not only does sexual differentiation provide for the continuation of the human race, it forms the foundation for human community itself. . . . This is why the accent in Christian sexual thought is on lifetime personal commitment, a couple's taking of responsibility for one another, mutual love and faithfulness. . . . Caring for one another is a reflection of the essence of God's care for mankind.
>
> A Christian understanding of sexuality, therefore, requires a responsible, sacrificial use of sexuality as a necessary component of spiritual maturity.
>
> We also discovered, however, that it is impossible to perceive these values in Christianity's traditional sexual teachings and automatically condemn all homosexual persons or relationships. Heterosexual partners by no means possess a monopoly upon sacrificial love and it was far from clear to the Commission that a homosexual relationship is in and of itself incapable of expressing sacrificial love. Social circumstances do indeed make it more difficult for homosexuals than for heterosexuals to aim at sacrificial love in their relationships with each other, but we found no inherent reason for assuming that they could not do so and we know that some homosexuals seriously do. Therefore we contend that it is wrong and presumptuous to deny Christian value to any human relationship which involves attachment to another person in the spirit of sacrificial or self-giving love. Homosexuals seriously seeking to build such relationships with one another are surely as deserving as heterosexuals of

encouragement and help from the Church and its ministry.

To begin with, the Commission has discovered that it is impossible to study homosexuality in depth without recognizing an element of mystery in the phenomenon that refuses to be wholly dispelled. No scientist has managed convincingly to isolate the "causes" of the homosexual personality. Nor did the theological literature examined by the Commission display any unanimity on how homosexuality was to be assessed. The traditional negativism of the Church on the subject to which we have alluded turned out to be less justified and less convincing than the Commission anticipated. We are persuaded that we are faced less with an aberration than with a mystery: the nature of love itself.[188]

In line with such reasoning, Gregory Baum draws the appropriate pastoral conclusions:

If it is true that some people are constitutively homosexual and that homosexual relations allow for mutuality, then, from the viewpoint of Christian theology, it is the task of homosexuals to acknowledge themselves as such before God, accept their sexual inclination as their calling, and explore the meaning of this inclination for the Christian life.[189]

This approach works out of an understanding of human sexuality that is totally relational. Human sexuality seems to be viewed simply as a vehicle of human intercommunication and is to be assessed accordingly. It fails to address the question of the procreative or life-serving element of human sexuality. The contention that a Christian understanding of human sexuality requires a responsible and sacrificial use of sexuality and that it must reflect mutual love, faithfulness, and caring for one another certainly expresses a basic minimum for wholesome human sexuality. The question remains: is that enough? It would seem that the elements of mutual love, fidelity, and caring need more detailed and specific explanation if this approach is to provide a suitable pastoral norm for counseling homosexuals.

(4) *Homosexual acts are essentially good and natural.*

This fourth approach to homosexuality regards the homosexual orientation and its expression as unequivocally good, "not contrary to human nature" and "the finest bloom of human friendship." Persons who consciously discover and view themselves as basically homosexual are to be encouraged to accept this orientation and live accordingly. Others also are to be encouraged to be free to choose this form of expression as a legitimate variant or preference in sexual experience. Usually this self-expression is urged in the context of mutuality and with a view toward building friendship (very similar to the preceding approach), but it is also recognized by many as acceptable for purely recreational purposes without any deeper personal commitment. The main thrust suggested in counseling from this position is to assist the homosexual in accepting his or her sexual orientation without regret or self-pity and to enable guilt-free, self-affirming sex expression to occur.[190]

A former director of the Mattachine Society of New York reflects this attitude in the following statement given in an interview:

> In my experience, male homosexual relationships usually start out with sex, sex, sex. After a week or two, it gets a little bit tiring. After the first year, you've probably had it. Then if you've got anything going for you outside of bed, you can stay together. Which my lover and I do. We're very compatible as personalities. We like one another an awful lot. We like the same things, we do things together incessantly.
>
> Most gay couples have to make some kind of decision about sex after a while. Not only because of boredom, but because sexuality has so many meanings to a homosexual. It's a reinforcement of the fact that you're still attractive, which is important in the gay world.
>
> It's also a means of communication. It's usually your first relationship with another person. Most of my friends are people I first picked up and had sex with and we liked one another and continued seeing one another and became friends.
>
> Sex has a lot of meanings. So, we recognized the fact that he was going out and I was going to go out. He goes to work on the subway and he gets offers, and I go to work at Mattachine and I get offers, and you get tired of saying

"No" all the time. So we "trick out" as we say—without guilt. . . . One of the great things about being homosexual is that you can have sex as often as you want with no hassle whatsoever.[191]

Such an approach reflects the extreme position of the Gay Liberation Movement. It has little respect for Scripture[192] and is patently selective in its use of historical and scientific evidence. The only foundation for moral evaluation it appears to acknowledge is personal experience. This renders the judgment narrow and biased. From an ethical point of view such an approach can hardly be taken seriously and one wonders if such facile statements proceed more from desperate efforts at self-justification and political strategy than from genuine conviction. In any case, there is little of any biblical, historical, scientific, or theological support for such an oversimplification of the question.

These varied approaches to the moral evaluation of homosexual behavior reflect the limited knowledge and understanding currently available in regard to this phenomenon. It would seem wise for the counselor not to assume too categorical or judgmental an attitude when dealing with homosexual behavior. For this reason, the first and fourth approaches can be said to lack sufficient support to be able to serve as a reliable framework for effective pastoral counseling. The second and third approaches are more compatible with the understanding of human sexuality advanced in this report. Applying the principle of creative integration and the values characteristic of wholesome sexual expression would seem to enhance either approach by providing a more specific and objective norm for evaluating such behavior. In any case, the confessor or counselor must be careful not to render "infallible" judgments or impose serious moral restrictions on counselees whenever clear certitude is lacking.

Henri J. M. Nouwen's advice on this matter seems to the point. He says that if a person

. . . prefers homosexual circles and homosexual friends and does not show any desire or willingness to change, it does not make sense to push him or try to change him. It is much more important to relate to him on the basis of reality, to show understanding and to prevent any form of rejection of him as a human being who needs love and charity. . . . Our general attitude towards homosexuality should be free from anxiety and fear, not to speak of disgust and rejection. By a relaxed and understanding relationship to our homosexual fellow man, we might help him more than by an overly moralistic concern which requires changes as a condition for friendship.[193]

## Pastoral Reflections

In 1973 the committee on pastoral research and practice of the National Conference of Catholic Bishops approved for distribution and published a paper entitled, *Principles to Guide Confessors in Questions of Homosexuality*. Although not put to a formal vote of approval by the Catholic bishops of the United States, this paper may serve as an accurate indication of official Catholic teaching and pastoral practice today regarding homosexuality.

Vast strides are made in this quasi-official document. Homosexuality is finally recognized as a "complex question" (Foreword). Recognition is also given to the fact that a "man or woman does not will to become homosexual," but at a certain point in life "discovers" the fact, usually with "a certain amount of trauma" (p. 5). Confessors are encouraged to "avoid both harshness and permissiveness" (p. 8) and are advised not to insist that a homosexual seek psychiatric treatment when it has become clear that there is no hope for any change in sexual orientation (p. 11). The deep need for human relationships that homosexuals have like anyone else is affirmed. Homosexuals are to be encouraged to form stable friendships among both men and women (p. 9), among both heterosexuals and other homosexuals (p. 11).

Although the paper is open to the possibility of reduced culpability of homosexual acts subjectively, in respect to their objective morality it remains adamant: "Homosexual acts are a grave transgression of the goals of human sexuality and of human personality, and are consequently contrary to the will of

God" (p. 4). The reasons advanced for this judgment are the ones discussed above at some length. Sexuality is equated with genitality, and "genital sexual expression between a man and a woman should take place only in marriage" (p. 3). The twofold meaning of sexual intercourse is unitive and procreative, and neither meaning may be excluded. Because homosexual acts exclude all possibility of procreation, they are "inordinate uses of the sexual faculty" (p. 4), whether performed by heterosexuals or homosexuals. Besides the Stoic natural law argument with its biological bias, biblical teaching against homosexual acts is cited as conclusive, this time felicitously omitting any appeal to the Genesis story of Sodom. Reference is also omitted, however, to the cultic origins of the Old Testament condemnations and the historical circumstances that influenced St. Paul's remarks.

Since all homosexual acts are assumed to be intrinsically evil by nature apart from any other consideration, confessors are advised to help homosexuals to work out an "ascetical plan of life" (p. 9). "Each homosexual has the obligation to control his tendency by every means within his power, particularly by psychological and spiritual counsel" (p. 8). Compulsiveness may mitigate responsibility in some cases, but even prisoners, who "frequently submit to homosexual acts under terror," are "not entirely inculpable" (p. 10). "The worst thing a confessor can say is that the homosexual is not responsible for his actions" (p. 9). "It is difficult for the homosexual to remain chaste in his environment, and he may slip into sin for a variety of reasons, including loneliness and compulsive tendencies and the pull of homosexual companions. But, generally, he is responsible for his actions" (p. 9).

Warm commendation is warranted for the many advances this paper has made over the harsh, often unenlightened attitudes and practices that have long characterized the pastoral approach to homosexuals. It is evident, however, that there are several fundamental differences between that paper and our own position. For one, we do not view sin as something one can "slip" into; it is a fundamental option that determines a person's total moral posture. Moreover, we see sex as including more than genitality, and the purposes of sexuality—creativity and integration—as broader than biological procreation and physical union. Finally, in our estimation, the objective moral evaluation of a person's action must take into consideration the context of that person's total moral stance, the circumstances of the action, and the effects that issue from it. These differences in fundamental moral theory give rise to several differences in practical pastoral application.

There is little that can be said on the subject of homosexuality that enjoys conclusive evidence or undivided opinion. A variety of theories has prevailed on the origin of the homosexual condition; current research seems to favor the probability of multiple contributing factors. Authorities disagree as to whether homosexuality should be seen as a disease, a disorientation, or simply a departure from a prevalent social pattern (Chapter III). Current research and the direction taken by the American Psychiatric Association admit the possibility of healthy homosexuality, in which there is no inherent connection between homosexual orientation and clinical symptoms of mental or emotional illness.

Research today continues on the etiology of homosexuality, the impact of homosexual behavior on society, and the possibility of altering or modifying the homosexual condition. So too with regard to the pastoral care of homosexual persons. Research is being conducted by those in pastoral ministry in both Catholic and Protestant churches, most extensively in Holland.[194] There are still many questions regarding the proper pastoral care of homosexuals, questions not susceptible of easy answers. In the wake of research in the theological and social sciences and of the experience of those already involved in the pastoral care of homosexuals, the following pastoral guidelines can be offered with some degree of moral certitude:

(1) Before attempting to provide spiritual guidance or moral counseling to a homosexual, persons involved in pastoral ministry need to become aware of the complexity not only of the questions but of the homosexual condition itself. Homosexuality or inversion is commonly defined as the erotic, sexual attraction of a person toward members of the same sex. A more accurate description should also include the absence of attraction toward members of the opposite sex, sometimes to the ex-

tent of positive disgust at the thought of sexual relations with the opposite sex. Recent research has brought to light the impossibility of categorizing all people simply as either heterosexual and homosexual (See Chapter III). Empirical evidence suggests that sexual orientation in a few individuals is totally exclusive. In those individuals in whom heterosexual orientation is dominant, there seems to exist a latent potentiality for homosexual interest, which may or may not rise to consciousness. It has been suggested that Western cultural pressures mask an awareness of this interest and create a deceptive picture of rigid polarity between heterosexual and homosexual orientations.

It is also estimated that some four percent of American men are exclusively homosexual all their sexual lives, as are a smaller percentage of women, comprising approximately five percent of the total population. Five percent may be a relatively unappreciable minority statistically, but in terms of human beings we are speaking conservatively of some ten million people in America, some one hundred people in an average parish of one thousand families. In terms of human lives and human anguish, this is certainly no small number and calls for concern on the part of all persons engaged in pastoral ministry and leadership.

(2) Before attempting to provide spiritual guidance or counseling to a homosexual, persons involved in pastoral care need to examine their own attitudes. Unconscious prejudices resulting from biased education or societal attitudes do serious injustice to the homosexual and render effective counseling impossible. No real benefit can be expected unless the pastor or counselor clears away all trace of the myths that make real encounter impossible:

- The myth that every homosexual is attracted to children and adolescents and wishes to have physical contact with them. There are heterosexuals with the same inclinations; in fact, it would seem that, proportional to their numbers in the population, heterosexuals are more prone to child molestation than homosexuals.
- The myth that male homosexuals are easily identifiable as ef-

feminate, or female homosexuals as masculine; that homosexuals recognize each other and form a veritable secret society; that homosexuals invariably tend toward particular
professions.

- The myth that all homosexuals are unstable or promiscuous,
  unable to form enduring relationships.
- The myth, perhaps the worst of all, that homosexuals simply
  require will power to correct their condition or an experience of heterosexual intercourse or heterosexual marriage. A
  pastoral minister should never encourage a homosexual to
  contract a heterosexual marriage; in fact, such action should
  be positively discouraged.

(3) Professional psychiatric treatment or psychological
counseling is by no means a proven remedy for the homosexual
condition. More often than not, it proves to be an expensive
and frustrating experience that only heightens the homosexual's anxiety. Counselors should suggest psychological testing
to determine whether a person is a true homosexual, that is,
exclusively or predominantly homosexual, as opposed to a
"transitional" homosexual, that is, one passing through a temporary phase of psychological development. In the case of true
homosexuals or inverts, professional therapy may be helpful to
assist them in accepting their condition positively; but therapy
never should be suggested in a way that raises false expectations of a reverse or modification of the homosexual condition.

(4) One of the most important aspects of homosexuality is
the awareness of being different from the majority of people.
This consciousness of being "different," of belonging to a minority, leads homosexuals to suffer from the same problems as
all minority groups, with the added factor that their "dif-
ferentness" is secret and thereby leads to an even more profound alienation. In a society that treats them as objects of
cruel jokes and contempt, homosexuals commonly suffer from
lack of self-esteem and a loneliness that heterosexuals find difficult if not impossible to comprehend. Hiding their identities
in ordinary mixed society, homosexuals cannot help but feel
like strangers. They need friendship and association with one
another in order to share, like everyone else, their deepest feel-

ings, fears, and emotions. They need friendship to construct their lives, and the kind of association that they cannot find except with one another. Homosexuals have the same rights to friendship, association, and community as heterosexuals.

(5) Homosexuals have the same rights to love, intimacy, and relationships as heterosexuals. Like heterosexuals, they are also bound to strive for the same ideals in their relationships, for creativity and integration (see Chapter IV). The norms governing the morality of homosexual activity are those that govern all sexual activity, and the norms governing sexual activity are those that govern all human ethical activity.

The question arises at this point: Are homosexuals, by reason of their condition, denied by God and nature the right enjoyed by heterosexuals to the intimate, sexual expression of love? The homosexual is one for whom an exclusive or predominant homosexual orientation is for all practical purposes natural and irreversible. This irreversible condition is no more a matter of free choice for a homosexual than is the orientation of the heterosexual. Is it to be presumed that homosexuals by virtue of their condition, have been guaranteed by God the "charism" of celibacy? (The data of the behavioral sciences seem to indicate the contrary.) Is it to be presumed that homosexuals *ipso facto* have the vocation and obligation to work out an ascetical plan of life beyond the vocation and obligation of heterosexuals? Heterosexuals are free to choose or not to choose a life of celibacy. Are homosexuals denied that free choice? Heterosexuals may see continence as a call in life. Must homosexuals see continence as their destiny?

It is our considered opinion that Christian sexual morality does not require a dual standard. Homosexuals enjoy the same rights and incur the same obligations as the heterosexual majority. Homosexuals, like the heterosexual majority, are required to examine and evaluate their behavior in the light of the same values and according to the same moral norms to determine whether or not their actions are indicative of the same characteristics of wholesome human sexuality. A pastor or counselor should attempt to help a homosexual make a moral judgment upon his or her relationships and actions in terms of whether or not they are self-liberating, other-enriching, honest, faithful, life-serving, and joyous. Like everyone else, homosexuals are bound to avoid depersonalization, selfishness, dishonesty, promiscuity, harm to society, and demoralization. In helping homosexuals come to such a moral assessment, a pastor or counselor should direct consideration to the broader context of their total life, all their actions and relationships, in particular their relationship to God and the state of their spiritual life of prayer and participation in the sacramental life of the Church.

(6) Given the fact that their friendships and relationships are not sustained by the normal approval and supports that society provides for heterosexual relations, homosexuals tend to suffer the very real temptation of promiscuity. Inadvertently, Catholic pastoral practice has promoted the incidence of promiscuity among homosexuals precisely by advising them against forming intimate or exclusive friendships. Homosexuals living together have been regarded as living in a proximate occasion of sin; they were counseled to desist or else be denied absolution in the sacrament of penance. Dissuaded from deep, lasting relationships, homosexuals who found themselves unable to practice complete continence were driven to multiply superficial relationships.

Faced with the problem of promiscuity, a pastor or counselor may recommend close, stable friendships between homosexuals, not simply as a lesser of two evils but as a positive good. Such friendships need not be seen as occasions of sin. Friendship is always a positive good. It is the homosexual orientation and not the friendship that provokes the difficulties.

The situation arises with ever more frequency of a pastor or minister being asked to bless or solemnize liturgically what is termed a "gay union" or a "homosexual marriage." Since historically marriage has been understood in terms of a heterosexual union, it seems to us inappropriate and misleading to describe a stable relationship between two homosexuals as a "marriage." Anything suggesting a sacramental celebration of marriage, therefore, would also be inappropriate and misleading. At the same time, prayer, even communal prayer, for two people striving to live Christian lives, incarnating the values of fidelity, truth, and love, is not beyond the pastoral possibilities of a Church whose ritual tradition includes a rich variety of blessings.[195] The advisability of such an action must be determined by pastoral prudence and consideration of all possible consequences, including social repercussions.

(7) Christian homosexuals have the same needs and rights to the sacraments as heterosexuals. In determining whether or not to administer absolution or give Holy Communion to a homosexual, a pastor can be guided by the general principle of fundamental moral theology that only a morally certain obligation may be imposed. *Ubi dubium, ibi libertas.* An invincible doubt, whether of law or of fact, permits one to follow a true and solidly probable opinion in favor of liberty.[196]

In light of remaining doubts and unanswered questions regarding homosexuality, the historical circumstances at the basis of the biblical and traditional prohibition, the divided opinions among theological authorities, and the argumentation advanced in behalf of seeing homosexual acts as other than intrinsically evil—in the light of all these considerations, solidly probable opinion can be invoked in favor of permitting a homosexual freedom of conscience and free access to the sacraments of reconciliation and the eucharist.

Homosexuality is not a problem to which a pastoral minister need only to propose and implement proper solutions. On the contrary, homosexuality is a question that moral theology has only recently come to appreciate in all its complexity, ambiguity, and uncertainties. Given the limits of our knowledge, counselors and confessors must keep in mind that they have no right to impose unproven views or questionable opinions on others, thereby interfering with their fundamental freedom of conscience. All else being equal, a homosexual engaging in homosexual acts in good conscience has the same rights of conscience and the same rights to the sacraments as a married couple practicing birth control in good conscience.

(8) If a homosexual seems to have been given the grace of continence, the confessor or counselor should certainly encourage him or her to cooperate generously with that grace and to embrace it freely. No one, however, is ever bound to the morally impossible. An experienced pastor or spiritual director knows that absolute continence is ultimately a grace of God, not given to all. Where it apparently has not been given, no al-

ternative remains for the pastoral minister but to accept the homosexual condition as a given and to assist the homosexual to live a life in accord with the same moral standards as heterosexuals, striving for the same goals of creativity and integration.

(9) The priesthood, according to the present discipline of the Roman Catholic Church, and the religious life both require of their members not only a healthy emotional and sexual maturity but also the voluntary embrace of a way of life not expected of those outside the priesthood or religious vows.[197] All the requirements and expectations made of heterosexual priests and religious hold for those with homosexual inclinations as well.

In the case of a person exclusively or predominantly homosexual and contemplating entry into the priesthood or religious life, the pastor or counselor must obviously distinguish between erotic attraction and overt activity, between an incidental homosexual act and consistent homosexual behavior. Candidates for the priesthood or religious life should be confident that they can live the ideals and expectations of a celibate life, particularly since priests and religious commonly find themselves in a monosexual environment. Even when indications exist that they can live a celibate life, homosexuals should never be encouraged to enter the seminary or the religious novitiate simply as an escape from confronting their sexuality and making it a creative force in their lives.

(10) The traditional Christian attitude toward homosexuality down the centuries makes the Church responsible at least indirectly for much of the prejudice and discrimination that homosexuals suffer in society today. As representatives of Jesus Christ, Church leaders have a serious responsibility to work toward the elimination of injustices that continue to be perpetrated on homosexuals by society. This includes discriminatory practices in both housing and employment. Particularly in the sphere of legislation and civil rights, Church leadership would do well to follow the lines set down by the *Westminster Report* commissioned by the former Catholic Archbishop of London, Bernard Cardinal Griffin (1956): "Penal sanctions are not justified for the purpose of attempting to restrain sins

against sexual morality committed in private by responsible adults." The following year, 1957, the celebrated *Wolfenden Report*, prepared for the British Parliament after encouragement by the Church of England, made a similar recommendation, "that homosexual behavior between consenting adults in private be no longer a criminal offense."[198]

It should not be too much to expect that the Church and its leaders serve as more than a barometer of public moral opinion, that they take a lead in advance of the civil courts in championing the civil rights of homosexuals by working to change unjust social conditions, even when this is not a particularly popular cause. Eliminating discrimination on the basis of race and religion should extend logically to eliminating discrimination and injustice on the basis of sexual orientation.

(11) As a group that has suffered more than its share of oppression and contempt, the homosexual community has particular claim upon the concern of the Church and its leaders. Homosexuals have a right to enlightened and effective pastoral care from pastoral ministers who are properly trained to meet their particular needs. The Church in America would do well to learn from the pioneering pastoral efforts and experience in this field being made by the joint efforts of the Catholic and Protestant Churches in Holland.

Homosexuals have a right to expect understanding and acceptance from their pastors and counselors along with a constant challenge to maturity and integration in their lives and relationships. To this end, homosexuals need encouragement and support from their spiritual mentors. They need the supportive atmosphere of attitudes that Jesus exhibited to the despised and oppressed of his day.

(12) It bears repeating that there is much that is uncertain and provisional about the subject of homosexuality. Much research needs yet to be done, much pastoral experience yet to be accumulated before more than tentative pastoral guidelines can be formulated. It bears repeating, however, without provision, that where there is sincere affection, responsibility, and the germ of authentic human relationship—in other words, where there is love—God is surely present.

## SPECIAL QUESTIONS

*Masturbation*

There is no clear explicit moral prohibition of masturbation in either the Old or New Testament. Several passages are occasionally cited as condemning this practice (Lev 15:16; Dt 23:9-11; Gen 38; 1 Thes 4:3-4; Rom 1:24 and 1 Cor 6:10), but contemporary biblical exegesis finds no convincing proof that the authors were addressing themselves in these texts to the morality of masturbation.[199] The testimony from tradition on the other hand is quite consistent in regarding masturbation as a serious moral wrong. Authors, however, have not always been in agreement regarding the reason for the evil of masturbation.

Originally, the deliberate wasting of the seed of life was deemed by most as the reason for the grave and intrinsic evil of masturbation. Because the male seed was regarded as the only active element in the procreative process, many authors even into the present century concluded on this basis that female masturbation did not share in the same moral evil as that of the male.[200] Other authors placed greater emphasis on the deliberate pursuit of complete venereal pleasure outside the marriage act as the source of the moral evil.[201] When it was realized that some prostitutes find no pleasure in their involvement in sexual activity but engage in sex for other reasons, this argumentation too was found to be inadequate. They were still judged guilty for their willingness to provide pleasure for others for monetary gain.[202] Still others considered masturbation as evil because it constituted a threat to propagation of the human race; it was supposed that if masturbation were permitted, men would not be anxious to enter marriage and procreate children. Most recently, there seems to be emerging a consensus that places the moral malice of masturbation in a "substantial inversion of an order of great importance."[203]

Throughout most of Catholic tradition every act of masturbation was regarded as gravely and intrinsically evil; if performed with full knowledge and consent, it was considered a mortal sin. But the widespread and repeated practice of masturbation, especially among males, created serious difficulties for many when drawing the logical conclusions. Human experience and common sense seem to be in sharp conflict with the formulations of theology. On the pastoral level, this clash was often mitigated and harsh judgments tempered by maintaining that full knowledge and consent were often lacking in such activity and consequently mortal sin was not committed.

During the last decade much discussion has centered around the question as to whether a single act of masturbation constitutes such a substantial inversion of the sexual order that it must always be regarded as intrinsically grave matter. The discussion stemmed from the theological developments regarding the nature of mortal sin and from an improved understanding of the complex nature of the phenomenon of masturbation. In what must be regarded as a significant theological breakthrough in this matter, Charles Curran successfully argued that every act of masturbation of itself need not be considered as constituting a deordination "which is always and necessarily grave."[204] This is not meant to imply that masturbation is not sinful or that masturbation can never involve serious sin. It maintains simply that not every deliberately willed act of masturbation necessarily constitutes the grave matter required for mortal sin. The vast majority of contemporary theologians would seem to agree with Curran's conclusion.

### Magisterium

A review of some of the magisterial pronouncements on masturbation reflects much of the historical development:

1054—Pope Leo IX issued the first official teaching on masturbation, when he declared that "masturbators should not be admitted to sacred orders."[205]

1679—Pope Innocent XI condemned as at least scandalous and dangerous in practice the opinion of Caramuel that "masturbation is not forbidden by the law of nature; therefore, if God had not forbidden it, it would be good and sometimes gravely obligatory."[206]

1904—The Sacred Penitentiary declared that complete masturbatory acts of a woman during the absence of her husband are gravely illicit and that any confessor who approves this practice should be denounced to the Holy See.[207]

1929—The Holy Office responded to an inquiry as follows:

Q. "Whether direct masturbation is permitted for the purpose of obtaining semen for the scientific detection of the contagious disease 'blenorragia' and its cure."

A. In the negative.[208]

1952—Pius XII in his encyclical on the *Christian Education of Youth* made the following statement:

> We reject, therefore, as erroneous the affirmation of those who regard lapses as inevitable in the adolescent years, and therefore as not worthy of being taken into consideration, as if they were not grave faults, because, they add, as a general rule, passion destroys the liberty requisite if an act is to be morally imputable.[209]

1961—The Sacred Congregation for Religious issued the following instruction to spiritual directors of candidates for the religious life:

> Any candidate who has the habit of solitary sins and who has not given well-founded hope that he can break this habit within a period of time to be determined prudently, is not to be admitted to the novitiate. . . . A much stricter policy must be followed in admission to perpetual profession and advancement to Sacred Orders. No one should be admitted to perpetual vows or promoted to Sacred Orders unless he has acquired a firm habit of continency and has given in every case consistent proof of habitual chastity over a period of at least one year. If within this year . . . doubt should arise because of new falls, the candidate is to be barred from . . . Sacred Orders.[210]

1971—*The Ethical and Religious Directives for Catholic*

*Health Care Facilities* promulgated by the National Conference of Catholic Bishops states:

> The use of the sex faculty outside the legitimate use by married partners is never permitted even for medical or other laudable purposes, e.g., masturbation as a means of obtaining seminal specimens.[211]

1974—The Sacred Congregation for Catholic Education in *A Guide to Formation in Priestly Celibacy* gives the following advice:

> One of the causes of masturbation is sexual imbalance. The other causes are generally of an occasional and secondary nature, albeit contributing to its appearance and continuation. In education, efforts should be directed rather towards the causes than to attacking the problem directly. Only in this way can one promote the effective development of boyish instincts—which means an interior growing up towards domination of instinct. This is the growth that the causes mentioned above tend to obstruct.
>
> Fear, threats, physical or spiritual intimidation are best avoided. These could encourage the formation of obsessions and compromise the possibility of a balanced sexual attitude, making him turn further in on himself instead of opening himself to others. Success as always will depend on the degree of awareness of the real causes of the problem. This is what formation needs to be particularly concerned with.
>
> Self-abuse upsets the kind of life which is the educator's aim. He cannot remain indifferent to the close-up attitude which results from this. Nevertheless, he should not overdramatize the fact of masturbation nor lessen his esteem and goodwill for the individual afflicted. As he comes into deeper contact with the supernatural and self-sacrificing love of the educator, the youth is bound to be aware of his place in the communion of charity and will begin to feel himself drawn out of his isolation.
>
> In trying to meet each difficulty, it is better not to offer a readymade take-it-or-leave-it solution. Rather, using the occasion for real interior growth, help and encourage the

sufferer in such a way that he finds his own remedy. Not only will he then solve this one problem, but will learn the art of resolving all other problems which eventually he will have to face.[212]

1975—The Vatican *Declaration on Certain Questions Concerning Sexual Ethics* prepared by the Sacred Congregation for the Doctrine of the Faith states as follows:

The traditional Catholic doctrine that masturbation constitutes a grave moral disorder is often called into doubt or expressly denied today. It is said that psychology and sociology show that it is a normal phenomenon of sexual development, especially among the young. It is stated that there is real and serious fault only in the measure that the subject deliberately indulges in solitary pleasure closed in on self ("ipsation"), because in this case the act would indeed be radically opposed to the loving communion between persons of different sex which some hold is what is principally sought in the use of the sexual faculty.

This opinion is contradictory to the teaching and pastoral practice of the Catholic Church. Whatever the force of certain arguments of a biological and philosophical nature, which have sometimes been used by theologians, in fact both the Magisterium of the Church—in the course of a constant tradition—and the moral sense of the faithful have declared without hesitation that masturbation is an intrinsically and seriously disordered act. The main reason is that, whatever the motive for acting in this way, the deliberate use of the sexual faculty outside normal conjugal relations essentially contradicts the finality of the faculty. For it lacks the sexual relationship called for by the moral order, namely, the relationship which realizes "the full sense of mutual self-giving and human procreation in the context of true love." All deliberate exercise of sexuality must be reserved to this regular relationship. Even if it cannot be proved that Scripture condemns this sin by name, the tradition of the Church has rightly understood it to be condemned in the New Testament when the latter speaks of "impurity," "unchasteness" and other vices contrary to chastity and continence.[213]

*Current Theology*

In reviewing the current theological literature, one can find three widely varying approaches to the morality of masturbation:

(1) *Masturbation is an objectively grave evil.*

This position maintains that every act of masturbation objectively constitutes a grave moral deordination and hence serious sin. It often appeals subjectively to mitigating circumstances to lessen imputability for repeated falls. Generally, however, it insists on the regular confession of each individual act in an attempt to eradicate this practice entirely from the life of the individual. The following excerpt from a recent publication exemplifies this approach:

Self-abuse is a serious rejection of God's plans for the individual. Aside from the harm to the individual, each of us —from God's point of view—is a kind of window. If we are to give a clear view of him, we cannot pull the shades down on our personality and its development. And yet, this is exactly what self-abuse does. It constitutes a closing off of self to others and to real self. It is playing a game with life. This has to be a serious rejection of God and his designs, even if such persons claim they are not rejecting God or his plans.

Where do we stand? Of itself, the act of self-abuse is an intoxication or poisoning from within. Obviously, this is seriously offensive to self and God. However, since responsibility is measured by people's knowledge and strength of character, it could well be that because of their lack of awareness or weakness they suffer little or no guilt from their actions. It would be similar to a child or dazed person pulling the trigger of a loaded gun. The action is deadly but little or no guilt can be assigned to the one who pulled the trigger.

Such persons have, however, a responsibility to seek out help. Not to seek help, because of shame or attachment to their actions, could be serious, providing they have sufficient awareness and strength to seek help. As we have said, perhaps the final weighing of morality must be left to God. Those who are guiding such persons must not compromise on the goal. The way can be made smooth with kindness and understanding, but self-abuse should not be made light of. The goal is self-liberation not self-imprisonment.[214]

(2) *Masturbation, generally speaking, is objectively neutral.*

This position would maintain that occasional masturbation (with some periods of greater frequency and intensity caused by anxiety) is statistically, psychologically, and morally normal. As one writer puts it: "Masturbation is no less inevitable and no less a part of the psycho-physical development of adolescence than is nocturnal emission."[215] Some psychologists and educators suggest that the only thing wrong with masturbation is the misinformation, the myths, and religious taboos that surround it.

Some authors have even waxed poetic in their defense of masturbation, concluding that far from being the vice combatted by teachers and moralists, it is "the natural passage by which is reached the warm and generous love of youth and later the calm and positive matrimonial love of maturity."[216] Another outspoken author defending this view of masturbation as amoral, states:

> It is necessary to have the courage to speak frankly to the child about masturbation and to recognize what are its rights. For the benefit of both parents and child, it must be said once and for all that the masturbation of the child and of the adolescent is a normal act which has no unfavorable consequences, either physical or moral, as long as one does not make the mistake of placing these acts on a moral plane, with which they have nothing to do.[217]

Those who hold this view of masturbation thus advise youngsters that it is a perfectly natural and normal sexual outlet, and that they need not fear any harmful consequences or experience feelings of guilt for having expressed themselves in this manner.

(3) *Masturbation is a "symptom" capable of many meanings.*

This approach regards masturbation as a symptom that must be carefully read to discern its true human and moral meaning. The 1974 statement from the Sacred Congregation for Catholic Education reflects this approach, which is very much in accord with the finding of the behavioral sciences, recent theological developments, and the judgment of human experience. It insists that any attempt to change or eliminate masturbatory activity will be successful only to the extent that one discovers and responds to the underlying cause or source of such activity.

The following categories would be illustrative of the varying meanings that masturbation can have and indicate the varying pastoral responses that are needed in dealing with this phenomenon:

(a) *Adolescent Masturbation:* Puberty signals the onset of important changes in the life of the adolescent. The curiosity awakened by the first experience of the sexual tension that arises in the adolescent quite naturally leads to a process of self-discovery that results in a certain tendency to close in on oneself. The fact that at this age sexuality is not oriented as yet toward a partner of the opposite sex complicates the problem and quite often leads to a search for release and satisfaction for these tensions within oneself. The youngster at this stage needs support and direction that will bring reassurance and foster growth and development in terms of reaching out to others. Directing attention to each act of masturbation can hamper this development by focusing attention on self and deepening the youngster's sense of inadequacy. Directing the young person to activities that strengthen self-confidence and encourage growth and interrelationship with others is the most important help that can be given. As the adolescent reaches out to others and progresses in personal development, the masturbation in most instances will gradually disappear.

(b) *Compensatory Masturbation:* Where youngsters find their healthy growth toward autonomy and personal responsibility repressed by tyrannical parents or smothered by over-solicitous ones, it is not unusual for them to turn to masturbation as a sign of reaction. The root of the problem in these instances is the unhealthy family life, which needs to be changed if the problem is to cease. Where changing the family atmosphere is impossible, teachers and friends can be of great help by showing interest and encouraging involvement in activities that provide opportunity for self-expression and autonomy.

(c) *Masturbation of Necessity:* The very strength of the biological urge that is part of human sexuality especially for some persons or at least at certain times for others finds in masturbation a relief from the tremendous sexual tensions that may be deprived of their normal outlet. Early habits may add to the difficulty of dealing with this tension by simple resistance. Celibates, married men away from home on business or in military service or prison, or spouses who for health or other reasons must abstain from intercourse for long periods of time often find themselves in this predicament. The use of masturbation to obtain reasonable relief from excessive sexual tension or to preserve fidelity would seem to be a matter of prudent choice of values. Moral malice in such instances ought not be imputed.

(d) *Pathological Masturbation:* Psychological maladjustment can at times be the root cause of masturbatory behavior. This is especially indicated when the impulse to masturbation seems to be a compulsion, bringing little or no satisfaction and yet frequently repeated even though there is no rational explanation for the behavior. Likewise, persons who regularly prefer masturbation even in the presence of opportunities for intercourse are seen to be operating out of a sexuality that has not been fully integrated. Counseling to help discover the deeper causes of such behavior would be appropriate.

(e) *Medically Indicated Masturbation:* Masturbation is generally accepted as the standard clinical procedure for obtaining semen for fertility testing or for diagnosing certain venereal infections. Such procedures do not constitute a substantial inversion of the sexual order but rather serve to preserve or promote the life-serving quality of human sexuality. In keeping with our understanding of human sexuality and the principles indicated for evaluating such behavior, procedures of this kind should not be viewed in any way as sinful or immoral.

(f) *Hedonistic Masturbation:* Masturbation simply for the sake of the pleasure involved, without any effort at control or integration, can be indicative of self-centeredness, isolation, and evasion of relational responsibility. Cases of this type deserve the serious attention of the counselor-confessor. Exploitation of one's sexuality freely, deliberately, and consistently in this manner creates a serious obstacle to personal growth and integration and constitutes the substantial inversion of the sexual order—an inversion that is at the heart of the malice of masturbation. Pastoral prudence will indicate that little can be gained by simply highlighting and condemning the sinfulness of each individual act. A far more radical conversion is needed in regard to the very nature and meaning of human sexuality and human personhood.

### Pastoral Reflections

1. Masturbation is a subtle and complex phenomenon. To condemn every act of masturbation harshly as mortal sin or to dismiss it lightly as of no moral consequence fails to do justice to the symptomatic nature of masturbation capable of many meanings. The sensitive pastoral approach outlined in the Sacred Congregation's *Guide to Formation in Priestly Celibacy* (1974), which insists on discovering and responding to the cause of such behavior, deserves serious consideration and implementation.

2. A single act even of willful masturbation seldom achieves that substantial deordination in a matter of great importance, which is generally considered to constitute the serious moral malice of masturbation. Such substantial deordination requires a consistent, deliberate, self-centered pursuit of pleasure, which refuses to acknowledge or respond to one's relational responsibility toward others. Persons who occasionally masturbate must not, therefore, be automatically judged as being in the state of mortal sin.

3. Persons seriously struggling with the task of integrating their sexuality, especially adolescents, should be encouraged to receive the eucharist at every opportunity even though occasional incidents of masturbation may occur. The presumption should be that such persons have not sinned gravely and consequently have not lost their right to receive the sacraments. The regular celebration of the sacrament of reconciliation and

the wise counsel of a prudent confessor can provide additional support in the struggle toward integration.

4. Little benefit appears to be gained from focusing directly on the masturbatory behavior. Highlighting the malice of each act of masturbation only serves to compound the problem and drive the person further into self. For this reason, directing the counselee to activities that are other-centered appears to be the most effective remedy for treating adolescent masturbation. Immediate confession after each act of masturbation ought not to be encouraged, though periodic discussion of one's progress in this area can prove helpful to the counselee or penitent.

5. Professional psychological consultation should be recommended only in those instances in which it is clear that the masturbatory behavior stems from serious psychological maladjustment and the counselee could benefit from such professional therapy.

### SEXUAL VARIANTS

### *Bestiality*

Bestiality is the use of animals to obtain sexual excitation and gratification. The actual sexual pattern may involve masturbation by means of friction against the animal, fellatio, masturbation of the animal by the human subject, or actual sexual intercourse.

In the Old Testament we find the practice punishable by death (Ex 22:19; Lev 20:15) though the exact reason why it was considered such a grievous crime is not always clear. According to the Kinsey report (1948) about one male in twelve or fourteen of the general population has had sexual experience with animals. Among boys reared on farms about sixteen percent reported experiencing orgasm through animal contacts.[218]

The lack of adequate heterosexual opportunities in many isolated farm areas appears to be the major reason for the substitution of animals for sexual purposes. At times it may be caused by a fear of inadequacy in approaching members of the opposite sex. Where the individual prefers sexual relations with animals when heterosexual outlets are available, the condition is regarded as pathological.

In responding to the problem of bestiality, the counselor-confessor would do well by looking for the cause that produces this form of behavior and attempting to eliminate the source of the problem. There is no question but that this practice renders impossible the realization of the personal meaning of human sexuality. Persons so involved need to be gently led to a deeper understanding and appreciation of the full meaning and significance of human sexuality.

## Fetishism

Fetishism involves the use of clothing or parts of the body as a means of obtaining sexual pleasure and gratification. In some cases, the origin of this behavior is rooted in early childhood experience. In psychoanalytic theory, the fetish objects become substitutes for infantile sexual objects.

Most instances of fetishism reveal a person with an immature approach to, and understanding of, sexuality although in some cases the behavior seems to be associated with more extensive maladjustment. Persons of this kind would seem to benefit more from effective professional counseling than from condemnation, rejection, and harmful moralizing.

## Transvestism

Transvestism involves a marked preference for wearing clothing of members of the opposite sex. It expresses a psychosexual conflict that appears to be a combination of homosexuality and fetishism. Since the cause of such behavior is generally found in the failure to resolve unconscious psychosexual conflicts, the approach to this type of behavior should focus on effective therapeutic counseling. As with other forms of sexual deviation, there is good reason for questioning serious moral culpability because of the psychological factors causing the deviation.

## SEX CLINICS

The sex clinic is a rather recent addition to the efforts being made to cure sexual dysfunction. Rather than relying solely on psychotherapy and counseling, the clinics in addition employ more active and direct methods designed to help patients experience erotic excitement and achieve orgasm in intercourse. For the most part the clinics work with married couples.[219] No ethical question seems involved where the therapeutic sexual activity is between married partners who are attempting to help one another. Potential moral questions arise when the therapy indicated or advised is solitary self-stimulation or sexual exercises and coition to be engaged in by non-married pairs, whether this involves a spouse-surrogate or a volunteer sex partner. For legal and, perhaps more importantly, therapeutic reasons, surrogates are no longer widely used.[220] More common is the situation where the unmarried patient is encouraged to obtain the help of a volunteer sex partner for purposes of the therapy.

Applying the ethical norm adopted in this study, namely, that sexual expression to be moral must be "creative and integrative" for the parties involved, it might seem on first reflection that the sexual activity prescribed in serious therapy would present no moral difficulty. Self-stimulation oriented to healthy sexual intercourse fits the norm without difficulty. Sex partners truly intent on being the means of making the other whole and capable of relating sexually to his or her beloved would also seem to be engaged in a moral use of genital sex. Theoretically, this would be true whether they be married couples, unmarried lovers, surrogates or volunteer partners of unmarried patients. In fact, however, there is serious doubt within the experienced scientific community that sexual "stand-ins" really help overcome, in any effective way, the sexual difficulties that afflict an existing relationship.[221] Their use does, in fact, risk weakening an ailing relationship further. Since it is not at all clear that the use of surrogates is necessary even to achieve the limited objective of erotic arousal and may be counterproductive in achieving the long term therapeutic objective of curing a sexual dysfunction in the context of a specific human relationship, the use of stand-ins does not seem morally justified at this time.

Sex therapy suggests another issue that has been receiving attention recently. It is the question of the morality of the therapist himself or herself engaging in erotic stimulation of the patient. Apparently the practice is not uncommon and is defended by some psychiatrists and lay-therapists.[222] Officially the professional societies continue to condemn it for reasons of law, public confidence, and therapy effectiveness. (The American Psychiatric Association specifically prohibits it. However, the American Psychological Association code of ethics does not mention it, and a resolution prohibiting sexual activity with clients failed to pass at the 1975 convention of the association.)

Applying the norms adopted in this study, we would have to say that in a hypothetical case wherein erotic expression between therapist and patient in fact results in making the patient whole without harm to the other relationship of therapist and patient, such direct involvement of the therapist might be moral. However, the overwhelming majority of professionals in the field deny the possibility of such an outcome. The burden, therefore, would be upon the therapist to justify morally the risks attendant on such practice, considering the individual and social dimensions in each case.

Finally, given the high incidence of sexual dysfunction in American marriages and the increasing willingness of couples to seek help, "sex clinics" have begun to proliferate. The pastoral counselor can offer needed assistance in steering those seeking his advice to medically responsible centers and away from well-intentioned but inadequately trained personnel. At the present time there is little or no state regulation of those holding themselves out as marriage and sex counselors.

### TRANSSEXUALISM

Transsexualism is a "disturbance of gender identity in which the person manifests, with constant and persistent conviction, the desire to live as a member of the opposite sex, and progressively takes steps to live in the opposite sex role, full time."[223]

Various theories have been advanced to explain the cause of this disturbance, but none thus far have proven to be convincing or conclusive. Psychotherapeutic efforts to remedy this condition invariably fail. At the present time, surgery coupled with hormonal treatments and supportive counseling is the only therapy of any possible value. The incidence of transsexual surgery or sex reassignment of male to female outnumbers the reverse procedure by nine to one.

The surgical approach to this problem is relatively recent, with the first operation in modern times being performed in Europe in 1931. It was not until the 1950's that the procedure received much public attention. The Johns Hopkins Gender Identity Clinic established in 1966 was the first clinic set up in the United States for such procedures and was followed shortly thereafter by the Minnesota Gender Clinic. The following criteria are used for selecting patients who will be eligible for surgical sex reassignment:

1. The patient must have lived in the desired sex vocationally and socially for a long enough period of time to prove his or her ability to function in society in the changed sex.
2. The patient must be at least twenty-one years of age and a U.S. citizen.
3. The patient must have a clean police record, though impersonation convictions are allowable.
4. If the patient has a history of temporal lobe epilepsy, he would require a neurosurgical work-up, with a view to relief of both seizure and psychosexual symptoms as a sequel to brain surgery.
5. The patient must be legally free of any previous marriage bond.
6. The patient must live within accessible traveling distance to the hospital in order to insure concientious followup.
7. The patient must designate a next-of-kin as an additional informant willing to give written operative consent. The reason for this rule is (a) to safeguard against erroneous

personal and social history-giving, (b) to safeguard against malpractice charges on the part of the next-of-kin, (c) to have the guarantee of at least minimal family acceptance of the operated patient, should there arise an emergency in the future, and (d) to improve the social chances of rehabilitation.[224]

The overall evaluation of the results of the procedures performed in recent years has been generally favorable. Randell who conducted a study of the pre-operative and post-operative status of many of these patients concluded:

The post-operative results indicate that the majority of males and females undergoing operation for sex reassignment are subjectively and objectively improved both in their adjustment to their environment and in their own feelings of well-being and satisfaction in their gender role.[225]

In view of the incomplete knowledge surrounding many aspects of this disturbance and in the absence of a more adequate and effective treatment, transsexual surgery must be regarded as a highly experimental procedure subject to the usual conditions involving human experimentation. It seems unrealistic to reject the procedure as totally unacceptable because it involves the mutilation of healthy organs. Mutilation procedures that serve the good of the whole person can be justified when there is a proper proportionality between the good achieved and the loss suffered. In evaluating the procedures that have been performed to the present, there seems to be abundant evidence that that proportionality has been safeguarded. Experts from the various fields of science ought not to be deterred from searching for a more adequate and satisfactory solution to the problem.

### PORNOGRAPHY AND OBSCENITY

Perhaps no category in a discussion of human sexuality admits of as much cultural conditioning as that of pornography and obscenity. Scripture does not deal with the topic explicitly, in fact, several parts of the Bible have been considered obscene enough to be bowdlerized by translators. The command not to covet thy neighbor's wife is often appealed to as a source for divine direction concerning the question of pornography and obscenity; such, however, does not seem to be the mind of the Israelites of the Old Law. Jesus is pointed in his judgment of those who look at a woman with lust in their hearts; the force of his words, however, seems to point to a radical view of the implications of the law of love, rather than to a general rejection of any specific material.

The larger view of history, the arts and literature of the bulk of the Western World and even more so that of the Far East suggest a less rigoristic view concerning sexually explicit material. Attitudes today are perhaps best understood in the light of the puritanism of our past, the mores of the Victorian age, the traditional suspicion of sexual pleasure in the Western Churches, and, conversely, the almost hedonistic pursuit of pleasure in contemporary Western culture.

One can see today a radical change from previous generations in the degree of specificity concerning sexual matters in public media. This is demonstrated by even the most casual survey of materials available in the average city bookstore or magazine counter, not to mention the movie advertisements and daily television fare. Nor is this specificity limited to materials dealing explicitly with sexual topics. It is also evident in the average content of popular materials, including advertising, news and feature magazines and publications. As a result of this proliferation, explicit sexual information is available not only to those who previously had to seek it out in sources of hard-core pornography, but to almost everyone in every conceivable form of media presentation.

This situation has resulted in a variety of changes, not the least of which is a new freedom of language. Words that once were not used in polite society (and at times were not even known!) have today become part of the common vocabulary. Likewise, details of the anatomy and of the psychology of sex, even to the point of the mechanics of sexual stimulation, are commonly available. The overall situation has reached the point that various publications are being geared to the sexual interests of various socio-economic groups and to various levels

of educational attainment. Concomitant with this easy availability has come a radical change in the attitudes of the majority of the population, most noticeably among the younger element. Various sociological studies suggest that for the bulk of
the population, the materials on sexual topics bring about little
or no ill effects.

Further complicating this problem is the difficulty encoun-
tered in defining what precisely constitutes "pornography" and
"obscenity." This is no small task, as attested to by the Supreme Court of the United States. The Supreme Court Justices
offered the following criterion: "Whether to the average person, applying contemporary community standards, the dominant theme of the material taken as a whole appeals to prurient
interest." In practice this principle becomes extremely relative
to place and time. Given the wide divergence of opinion, the
possibility of any agreement in specific cases seems to be highly
unlikely.

In the light of the principles outlined above (Chapter IV),
the following guidelines may be helpful:

(1) Explicit sexual material is harmful, regardless of how
it is categorized, when the result is the exploitation of persons.
Anything that tends to depersonalize sexuality, to regard persons as objects to be used, is obviously immoral. Further, those
objects or presentations that foster immaturity and autoerot-
icism obviously do not lead to personal growth and interpersonal integration. They tend to dehumanize and thus are counterproductive to human development.

(2) Further special attention must be given to those who
would profit from human weakness in others by exploiting it
for personal gain or profit. Such exploitation fails to give due
respect to human dignity.

(3) Finally, rather than becoming preoccupied with determining which objects or portrayals are within the definition of
pornography or obscenity, we would place the emphasis on
what is happening to people in the process of viewing these objects or exhibitions or using a given vocabulary. Less attention
can be given to explicit sexual materials and their objective
"goodness" or "badness," and more attention centered on the
overall effects and directedness of the materials. The test or

criterion must be to what extent the language or sexual material is truly productive or counterproductive of creative growth toward mature Christianity, toward full integration of human personal and interpersonal relations. Viewed from this perspective, we would see a goodly amount of explicitly sexual material to be neuter or amoral to most adults. Concomitant with these suggestions, we would conclude that a sex education program stressing both the facts and values involved in human sexuality is a matter of paramount importance. It would help to mitigate and control the exploitation of the uninformed by those interested in making a profit selling commercial pornography.

### PROGRAMS OF SEX EDUCATION AND FORMATION

The concept of adequate and proper instruction in sexual matters is not a new development in Christianity. What is new today is the systematic programming of sex education, based on the findings of studies in the human sciences and presented through group instruction outside the family. The development of such programs in Church-related schools and other institutions can be attributed to at least three factors: (1) the breakdown of Christian family life, (2) the sexism of contemporary American society, (3) the availability of programs of sexual education that emphasize information without reference to ethical standards, moral norms, or the formation of conscience.

Sex education, acknowledged as necessary in a survey of the Sacred Congregations for the Clergy, the Religious, and for Catholic Education (April 1973) must extend beyond that called for in the home and permeate all areas of educational development. We acknowledge that there are powerful forces at work in the United States and Canada today that would curtail such programs, pleading that they are out of harmony with Christian principles and practice and insisting that such education belongs in the home only. We would point out that such education in the home does not generally take place (as attested to by numerous studies), and that it is sorely needed to stem the tide of hedonism and to instill wholesome attitudes and values regarding human sexuality.

Programs of education consonant with the understanding of sexuality presented in this report call for guidelines that respect the Christian concept of human dignity and the goal of human destiny to which all persons are called in Jesus Christ. Because sexuality must not be divorced from a wholistic view of life, sex education must grow out of life experiences. It must be adapted to the age and readiness of the individual and be appropriate to the life situation of the child or the adult. It must be realistic, challenging, and inspiring.

Where programs of education are given to supplement and/or correct the formation provided in the home, an effort must be made to awaken respect for life and reverence for love. Such programs should be of a nature to prepare every human being for an experience of sexuality that fosters "creative growth toward integration" within the framework of a chosen life-style.

Instruction in sexuality must be adapted to the age and condition of the person to be educated. The material of sex education programs should foster the formation of a right conscience, a sense of freedom in responsibility, and enthusiastic appreciation for the gifts of God to men and women.

Sex education for adults who have not previously had adequate instruction is not to be neglected. This is particularly necessary where puritanical or Jansenistic influences have produced a negative, pessimistic concept of sex and the role of sexuality in the human experience.

Men and women preparing for a life of celibacy or virginity in Christian witness are to be prepared for an experience of human sexuality that is creative and integrative for them within the context of their commitment to a specific state of life.

A special effort is needed to further the important project of providing appropriate sex education for the handicapped, whether their disabilities be physical, mental, or emotional. Very little research has been pursued along this line. It is especially needed, in order to provide the fullest human development possible to these persons.

Programs of sex education for the handicapped should also provide for the preparation of those who are to work in caring for disabled human beings. Proper education can offset the unreasonable apprehension, unrealistic expectations, and the danger of exploitation that tend to develop when some persons are acutely dependent on others.

# Postscript

Throughout this study on human sexuality, it has been our purpose to provide "some helpful and illuminating guidelines" for moral direction in this sensitive and central area of life, filled as it is presently with confusion for so many people, including those in pastoral ministry. It is this moral and pastoral perspective that has determined the principal focus of our work.

We have attempted in our methodology to remain faithful to the best elements of Christian Catholic moral tradition—a tradition that recognizes both revelation and reason as indispensable sources of moral guidance and enlightenment. So it is that we have taken into account evidence from Scripture, tradition, theology, and the empirical sciences, convinced that only in this way could we be credible to the contemporary American Catholic mind. We have given particular attention to magisterial statements regarding sexuality; but, where new knowledge and insights have rendered traditional understanding and formulations inadequate, we have not hesitated to suggest new directions that would be, we hope, more useful to present circumstances yet still faithful to the sources of Christian moral guidance. We see our efforts as contributing not to dissent but rather development of Church teaching. As Avery Dulles, S.J., stated in his 1976 Presidential Address to the Catholic Theological Society of America, "Recognizing the stern demands of intellectual integrity, theology must pursue truth for its own sake no matter who may be inconvenienced by the discovery. Unless we are true to this vocation, we shall not help the Church to live up to its calling to become, more than ever before, a zone of truth."

Our study in no way pretends to be a comprehensive treatment of human sexuality. Many topics could have received far more extensive consideration were it not for the limitations of time, resources, and the scope of this study. In retrospect, we recognize our undertaking to be so vast in its proportions and implications as to have been almost foolhardy. Yet we assumed the task commissioned by the Catholic Theological Society because our own pastoral experience indicated a critical need for it. We are gratified that the 1976 Call to Action Conference sponsored by the National Council of Catholic Bishops gave expression to a similar perception of this need.

May we conclude this study with a threefold appeal:

To our colleagues in the theological and other sciences— we invite your serious criticism and encourage continuation of scholarly dialogue on the topic of human sexuality. We hope that our study will provide a stimulus for the kind of theological discussion that will contribute to a better understanding and more effective articulation of the Christian values we share in common.

To our co-workers in pastoral ministry, counselors, and educators—we encourage your careful reading of our study and cautious consideration of our recommendations. We hope that the recognized limitations of this work, the tentativeness of our conclusions, and the unanswered questions will not prove disheartening. How blessed we would be if pastoral counseling could be put aside until all theological questions had been fully researched, completely thought out, and finally, definitively, absolutely resolved. Unfortunately, such is not the nature of pastoral ministry nor of the human condition. We have attempted to place at your service the best available information of the moment and thus enable you to respond to people and their needs with pastoral prudence and sensitivity in a way that is healing and integrating. At the same time, we recommend continuing openness to further developments and better insights that are sure to follow.

To our fellow Catholics and other Christians—we wish to remind you of the ultimate moral responsibility all of us bear as Christians to strive to conform our behavior in the pattern of Jesus Christ to the deepest convictions of a well-formed conscience. Human dignity and our vocations as Jesus' disciples require us to respond freely and out of conviction rather than from simple conformity to rules or the mere external imposition of authority. We hope that our reflections will help you form your conscience with a better understanding of the teachings of Christ and the Church and in a way that enables you to respond to today's challenges freely and maturely, out of genuine conviction.

Finally, we hope that our efforts will serve to foster the creative growth toward integration that will enable all of us to appreciate more deeply and realize better the ultimate purpose of the beautiful reality that is human sexuality: "God created man in his own image, in the image of God he created him, male and female he created them."

# NOTES

*Introduction*

1. Given the purpose of this study and the limitations of space, primary consideration has been given to the Roman Catholic tradition. Eastern Orthodox and Protestant traditions often take differing views.

2. Reinhold Niebuhr, *The Nature and Destiny of Man* (New York: Scribner, 1964), p. 5.

3. Indicative of the classical view of human nature was the play on the Greek words for "body" (*soma*) and "tomb" (*sema*).

4. Because the Septuagint translated the Hebrew *nephesh hayya* (Gen 2:7) by the Greek psyche (soul), the English version rendered it as "man received a soul," implying Greek dualism. The Hebrew *nephesh hayya* is now properly translated in modern versions as "man became a living being." While the Bible speaks of certain bodily functions as rendering one ritually unclean for the purposes of temple worship, it in no way implies a metaphysical or moral statement on the body as such.

5. Biblical Hebrew has no word for "body" in the current sense of the term (as conditioned by medieval scholasticism). The nearest the language comes to any such meaning is in a word for "corpse." See Edmond Jacob, *Theology of the Old Testament* translated by A. W. Heathcote and P. J. Allcock (New York: Harper and Row, 1958), pp. 180-2.

6. Niebuhr, p. 18.

*Chapter I*

1. It is an assumption of this study that neither the Old nor the New Testament can be simply identified with revelation. The Bible constitutes an inspired witness to the revelation not of propositions or decrees but of God himself, in a history which finds its fullness in Jesus Christ. (Vatican Council II, *Constitution on Divine Revelation*, no. 2).

2. Cf. Claus Westermann, *Genesis, Biblischer Kommentar* (Neukirchen: Neukirchner Verlag, 1973), pp. 192-4.

3. Cf. Claus Westermann, *Schöpfung* (Stuttgart: Kreuz Verlag, 1971), pp. 117-18.

4. Dietrich Bonhoeffer, *Creation and Fall, Temptation* (New York: Macmillan, 1959), p. 62.

5. Donald Goergen, *The Sexual Celibate* (New York: Seabury Press, 1975), pp. 14-6.

6. Gerhard Von Rad, *Theology of the Old Testament*, 2 vols. (Edinburgh: Oliver and Boyd, 1962-1965), 1:27, 146; 2:249.

7. This attitude was not peculiar to Israel. The 4th century A.D. biography of Pythagoras (6th, 5th century B.C.) recounts the advice of Pythagoras to women: "If you come from your marital consort, it is a divine privilege even on that very day to visit the holy shrines; but by no means, of course, if you are coming from forbidden intercourse." H. Schelkle, *Theology of the New Testament: Morality,* translated by W. A. Jurgens (Collegeville, Minn.: Liturgical Press, 1970), 3:265.

8. Recent evidence from Ugarit shows that even the prohibition of transvestism (Dt 22:5) and of intercourse with animals (Lev 18:23) must be seen as motivated by opposition to the sacred cult of Canaan rather than as expressing a biblical sexual ethic. Prof. Cyrus Gordon in an article discussing "Ugarit and Its Significance," [*Arts*, The Journal of the Sydney University Arts Association, 9 (1974):26-27] explains the commands in this way:

> In the Baal cycle, Baal mates with a heifer and sires a bull calf (UT, 67 V 17-23; III 33-37). Variations of the pagan cult reverberate as the Golden Calf in Sinai and as the Golden calves worshipped at Dan and Bethel . . . Leviticus 18:23 prohibits copulation with animals precisely because it was an abomination wherewith the older inhabitants of the Promised Land had defiled themselves and the Land (verses 24-25) . . .

> The biblical prohibition against transvestism can now be explained as opposition to what was sacred in Canaan. In the Epic of Daniel, the murder of Aqhat is avenged by his sister Rughat, who wears a man's garb and wields a man's sword (1 Aght 206-7). It is interesting to note that Dt 22:5 not only outlaws transvestism, but also the bearing of men's weapons by women. Again Ugarit provides the background against which Israel reacted.

This is not to say, of course, that the repulsion felt by the biblical authors toward these practices is not pertinent to the development of a biblically founded sexual ethic, but simply that the prohibitions in themselves do not directly constitute such an ethic.

9. See *Dictionary of the Bible,* 1965 ed., s.v. "Woman," by John L. McKenzie.

10. Roland deVaux, *Ancient Israel* (New York: McGraw-Hill, 1961), 1:40.

11. It is not clear whether the laws prohibiting sexual intercourse or marriage with a brother's wife (Lev 18:16, 20:21) presume levirate marriage as an exception or intend to prohibit it.

12. Thomas and Dorothy Thompson, "Some Legal Problems in the Book of Ruth," *Vetus Testamentum* 18 (1968): 79-99.

13. George E. Mendenhall, *The Tenth Generation* (Baltimore: John Hopkins Press, 1973), pp. 110-12 presents some of the limited amount of contemporary evidence for the ancient practice of ritual intercourse.

14. John L. McKenzie, *A Theology of the Old Testament* (New York: Doubleday, 1974), p. 207.

15. See Martin McNamara, *Targum and Testament* (Grand Rapids, Michigan: Eerdmans, 1972), p. 8; See also Bab. M. 30b, 88a: "Why were the shops of Beth Hino destroyed . . . because the shopkeepers stuck to the letter of the law and did not advance to equity."

16. Leonard Swidler, "Jesus was a Feminist," *Catholic World* 212 (1971): 177-83.

17. H. Strack and P. Billerbeck, *Kommentar zum Neuen Testament aus Talmud und Midrasch* (München: C. H. Beck, 1926-1928), 1:312-14.

18. Ibid., p. 320.

19. Herman Schelkle, pp. 243ff; H. Balz, "Sexualitat und Christliche Existenz," *Kerygma und Dogma* 14 (1968): 279ff.

20. Dom J. Dupont, *Mariage et divorce dans l'Evangile, Matthieu 19, 3-12 et paralleles* (Bruges: Abbaye de Saint Andre, 1959), pp. 161-222; Quintin Quesnell, "Made Themselves Eunuch for the Kingdom of Heaven," *Catholic Biblical Quarterly* 30 (1968): 335-58.

21. Cf. Quintin Quesnell, pp. 344-6, comparing Mt 22:1-6 with Lk 14:15-24; Mt 22:2 with Lk 14:16.

22. Pseudo-Demonsthenes, 59, 122, cited in Balz, p. 277.

23. For example, Cicero: "In libidine esse peccatum est etiam sine effectu," Cic. Fin., III, 9, 32, cited in G. Kittel, *Theological Dictionary of the New Testament,* 1965 ed., s.v. "epithumia."

24. A special consideration of the biblical position on homosexuality will be given in chapter five.

25. Shelkle, p. 255.

26. Ibid., p. 259.

27. Cf. Karl Barth, *Church Dogmatics* (Edinburgh: T. and T.

Clark, 1960), vol. 3, p. 2; S. Bailey, *Common Sense about Sexual Ethics* (New York: Macmillan, 1962), p. 80.

28. J. M. Pohier, "Recherches sur les fondements della morale sexuelle chrétienne," *Revue des Sciences Philosophiques et Théologiques*, 54 (1970): 3-23, 201-26.

## Chapter II

1. Cf. pp. 17, 20-21, 26, 30.
2. Cf. pp. 20-21, 26, 30.
3. Cf. pp. 17, 22, 30.
4. According to the Encratites, the gospel counsels to renunciation were addressed to all and were meant to be taken as laws. Every Christian is necessarily called to be an ascetic and to practice continence (cf. "Marriage," L. Godefroy, *Dictionnaire de theologie catholique* XI, cols. 2078-2080).
5. The Gnostic conceived matter as the result of a principle of evil in the world and thus a source of impurity for the soul. The best known representative of Gnostic Encratism is Marcion, whose errors were refuted by Tertullian (cf. *Adversus Marcionem*, PL II). No Christian community in the second century so strictly insisted on renunciation of the world as the Marcionites. Harnack remarks that this asceticism was "reluctantly acknowledged by the Church Fathers," who did not always find the same zeal in members of the orthodox community. Cf. *History of Dogma I*, Neil Buchanan, trans. (New York: Dover Publications, Inc., 1961), p. 278.
6. The Montanists were one of those heterodox or schismatic groups which proclaimed sexual abstinence the matter of a promise, rather than a law. It constituted the preliminary condition for the "Prophet" who was to receive the oracles and vision of God. The most zealous defender of Montanism was Tertullian who extolled this sect's concern for perfection and their eschatological state of expectancy for the imminent end of the world but who, even as a Montanist, refused to adopt their outright condemnation of marriage (cf., *De monogamia*, PL I).
7. The Novation schism was characterized by a rigorous asceticism in reaction to the Church's pardon of the *lapsi,* following a time of persecution in the third century. The Novatians condemned second marriages.
8. The Council of Toledo (A.D. 447) condemned the Priscillian rejection of marriage, seemingly the consequence of Gnostic or Manichaean doctrines. Cf. J. D. Mansi, *Sacrorum conciliorum nova et amplissima collectio* III, col. 1004; Hefele-Leclercq II, p. 487.
9. Since the Gnostics regarded the soul as the "bride of God,"

sexual activity was understood by some to contribute to union with the Divine Spirit.

10. This term refers to the custom of a communal life in which ascetics of both sexes lived together under one roof. Objections against the *virgines subintroductae*, as they are sometimes called are found for the first time in Church literature towards the middle of the third century.

11. Cf. Clement of Alexandria, *Stromata* III, 649: PG VII. Clement gives an account of the life style of members of the circles of ascetics found in every Christian community from earliest times.

12. Cf. Athenagoras, *Embassy for the Christians*, ANCIENT CHRISTIAN WRITERS, 23, Joseph H. Crehan, S.J., trans. (Westminster, Md.: The Newman Press, 1956), 33:74.

13. Tertullian protested this move to set up a "higher" morality for the clergy and a "lower" for the laity. The Christian community came to reject this "higher" standard, as soon as it claimed to be the one authoritative norm. Societies which persisted in applying the highest demands to all Christians ended in secession from the great Church.

14. Clement declares that the married man may even be superior to the celibate: "One is not really shown to be a man in the choice of a single life; but he surpasses men, who, disciplined by marriage, procreation of children, and care for the house, without pleasure or pain, in his solicitude for the house has been inseparable from God's love, and withstood all temptation arising through children and wife and domestics and possessions. But he that has no family is in a great degree free of temptation. Caring then for himself alone, he is surpassed by him who is inferior, as far as his own personal salvation is concerned, but who is superior in the conduct of life" (*Stromata* 7, 12; PG VIII). This text is cited in Johannes Quasten, *Patrology* (Westminster, Md.: The Newman Press, 1964), 2:35.

15. Cf. Methodius of Olympus, *Banquet of the Ten Virgins* 7, 3. PG 18, cols. 127-30.

16. Cf. Tertullian, *De resurrectione carnis* LXIII, PL II, cols. 933-34.

17. Cf. S. Athanasius, *Epistola ad Amunem monarchum*, PG XXVI, cols. 1173, 1174. Gregory of Nyssa, *De Virginitate* VII, PG XLVI, cols. 353, 354.

18. Cf. St. John Chrysostom, *De Virginitate* ii, PG XLVIII, cols. 539-40.

19. Cf., e.g., Tertullian, *Adversus Marcionem* I, xxix, PL II, col. 280; *De baptismo*, XVII, PL I, col. 1219; *Ad uxorem*, II, 9 PL I, cols. 1302-4; Ignatius of Antioch, *Ad Polycarpem* 2, PG V, cols. 723-

24; Justin Martyr, *Apologeticum* I, 29, PG VI, col. 373; Irenaeus, *Adversus haereses* I, XXIV, 5, PG VII, col. 678; Clement of Alexandria, *Stromata* I, III, ix, PG VIII, col. 1169; Gregory of Nyssa, *De virginitate* VII, PG XLVI, cols. 353-54.

20. Cf., e.g., the doctrine of St. John Chrysostom in his commentaries on Scripture, his sermons, and homilies, and even in the treatise, *De Virginitate*, PG LIII, col. 180; LVIII, cols. 122, 123, 136; LXII, cols. 464ff; LXVIII, cols. 539, 540, 547; Basil the Great, *Liber de vera virginis integritate* 38, PG XXX, cols. 745-46.

21. Cf. *Chrétiennes des Premiers Temps*, Jean-Claude Guy, S.J., et Francois Refoule, O.P., eds., (Paris: Les Editions du Cerf, 1965), pp. 33-6 for a discussion of the role of Greek rhetoric and philosophy in the apparent preference of the Fathers for some Christian values to the apparent devaluation of others.

22. *Ad Polycarpem* V, 2, PG V, cols. 717-28.

23. *Ad uxorem* 11, 9, PL I, col. 1302; *De monogamia* XI, PL I, col. 943.

24. *Dictionnaire de théologie catholique* (DTC) IX, cols. 2077ff. addresses this question, with reference to L. Godefroy, *Le mariage aux temps des Perès*.

25. *Commentoriorum in epistolam ad Ephesios* I, III, V, PL XXVI, cols. 530-7.

26. Samuel Laeuchli (*Power and Sexuality, the Emergence of Canon Law at the Synod of Elvira* [Philadelphia: Temple University Press, 1972]) explores the possible motivation for the attitudes of the early Church toward the discipline of celibacy and sexual behavior for Christians.

27. For one author's discussion of this question cf. John J. Hugo, *St. Augustine on Nature, Sex and Marriage* (Chicago: Scepter, 1969). The author's position should be qualified by Warren T. Reich's critique in a review of this work; cf. *The American Ecclesiastical Review* 163 (1970): 351-54.

28. *De bono conjugali* 11, PL XL, col. 381.

29. *De conjugiis adulterinis* 11, 12, PL XL, col. 479.

30. *Opus imperfectum contra Juliani* VI, 23, PL XLV, col. 1557.

31. *Contra secundinum manichaeum* xxii, PL XLII, col. 598.

32. *De bono conjugali* 9, PL XL, col. 380.

33. Cf. DTC I, col. 2431 on Augustine's use of "sacrament" in reference to marriage.

34. Augustine insists that the ascetic life is an ideal for the individual, but that faith, hope, and charity alone are of decisive importance for Christian perfection. He also affirms that grace blots out

the guilt of original sin, but that evil sexual lust remains in man. Although Augustine teaches that chastity in marriage, like virginity, is a gift of God, his Manichaeistic tendencies in other discussions of marriage cannot be denied (cf. *De civitate Dei* XIV).

35. The Manichees saw sexual desire itself as sinful because of the compulsion and shame which accompany sexual lust. Augustine opposed the Pelagian contention that man was connaturally equipped to overcome concupiscence by virginity and continence, declaring that sin is rooted in our nature and propagated with it.

36. Here, the efforts of Faustus and Caesarius of Arles to combat Semi-Pelagianism must be recalled. In granting approbation to the twenty-five canons of the Synod of Orange, Boniface II confirmed Western Christianity in an Augustinian view of marriage and procreation as the means by which original sin is transmitted.

37. Cf. DTC I (cols. 2469ff) and IX (cols. 2132ff) for Augustine's influence on later thinkers.

38. The development of monastic spirituality from Christian catechesis and liturgy was followed by a subsequent influence of monasticism on Christian spirituality. The Golden Age of the Fathers was dominated by an asceticism which grew out of the eremetical, monastic experience. The fundamental and primary characteristic of this asceticism was abstinence from sexual relationships.

39. There have been many discussions of this. One representative view can be found in John L. Thomas, "The Catholic Tradition for Responsibility in Sexual Ethics" in *Sexual Ethics and Christian Responsibility*, J. C. Wynn, ed. (New York: Association Press, 1970).

40. Cf. nn. 14 and 20, supra.

41. Cf. DTC IX, cols. 2101-9.

42. Cf. Gregory Nazianzen, *Oratio* XXXVII, PG XXXVI, cols. 281-308.

43. Cf. Gregory Nazianzen, *Oratio* XLIII, xii, PG XXXVI, cols. 510ff.

44. Cf. John Chrysostom, *Sermonem* XII, 6, PG XLIX, cols. 135-36.

45. Cf. Cyril of Jerusalem, *Catecheses* XVII, 7, PG XXXIII, col. 978.

46. Report of Most Reverend Michael F. McAuliffe, Chairman, Ad Hoc Sub-Committee on Women in Society and the Church to the National Conference of Catholic Bishops, 18 November 1975, p. 3.

47. The Christian community gradually developed the ability to discriminate and evaluate the works of pagan philosophers and poets.

A growing articulation of the doctrine of the Incarnation brought about the need to assess alien sexual systems, even as it became necessary to refute heretical Christological tendencies. In time, the appearance of Christian families contributed to a Christian doctrine on chastity, on equality of the sexes before God, on the value of human life, and on the sanctity of the marriage bond.

48. McAuliffe, p. 3.

49. John T. McNeill, Helen M. Gamer, "The Penitentials of Finnian," *Medieval Handbook of Penance* (New York: Octagon Books, Inc., 1965), p. 95.

50. On this question, cf. F. X. von Hornstein, A. Faller, *Sex-Love Marriage* (New York: Herder and Herder, 1964), p. 282.

51. The Penitential of Theodore states:

> Moreover, women shall not in the time of impurity enter into a church, or communicate—neither nuns nor laywomen; if they presume (to do this) they shall fast for three weeks . . . in the same way shall they do penance who enter a church before purification after childbirth, that is, forty days . . . But he who has intercourse at these seasons shall do penance for twenty days . . . For intercourse at the improper season he shall fast for forty days.

Canon 46 of the Penitential of Finnian decrees as follows:

> We advise and exhort that there be continence in marriage, since marriage without continence is not lawful, but sin, and (marriage) is permitted by the authority of God not for lust but for the sake of children, as it is written, "and the two shall be in one flesh," that is, in unity of the flesh for the generation of children, not for the lustful concupiscence of the flesh. Married people, then, must mutually abstain during three forty-day periods in each single year, by consent for a time, that they may be able to have time for prayer for the salvation of their souls; and on Sunday night or Saturday night they shall mutually abstain, and after the wife has conceived he shall not have intercourse with her until she has born her child, and they shall come together again for this purpose, as saith the Apostle. But if they shall fulfill this instruction, then they are worthy of the body of Christ. Cf. McNeill, Gamer, pp. 197, 96.

These restrictions seem more the result of the Manichean Stoic influence in the early Christian community than a development from the Old Testament sexual ethic. Sexual abstinence and extreme asceticism were not seen as virtues by the mainstream of Jewish tradition. In contradistinction to this early Christian view banning intercourse on Sundays and Holydays, which implies that intercourse will profane their holiness, intercourse can even be encouraged on the Sabbath in the Jewish tradition.

52. Cf. In IV Sent., d. 26. See also E. Schillebeeckx, *Marriage Human Reality and Saving Mystery* (New York: Sheed and Ward, 1965), 2:339ff.

53. Cf. *Summa Theologica* I-II, 82, 2 ad 4.

54. This emphasis is quite apparent in Thomas' treatment of lust, *Summa Theologica* II-II, 154.

55. Even St. Thomas concurred in this view, suggesting that except for procreation, any human task was better done with the aid of another man; cf. I, 92 a.1.

56. Both Albert the Great and Abelard held rather positive views concerning matters sexual. John Noonan, *Contraception* (Cambridge: Harvard University Press, 1965), p. 288, comments on a rather striking text from Albert the Great to the effect that there is no sin of matrimonial copulation (nullum autem peccatum concubitus matrimonialis, *Summa Theologica*, 2. 18. 122. 1. 4). This text suggests a "sacramental" end of intercourse, apart from the intent of procreation. Thomas did not comment on this text, and it remained obscure throughout the early Scholastic period.

57. An example would be Hugh of St. Victor, who spoke of marriage as a *unio animarum*.

Thomas was generally unwilling to depart from Augustine, even when his mentor Albert did so, as noted above. Thomas distinguished three aspects of marriage. There was the natural office which called for procreation, the civil office which encompassed the anthropological reality of marriage and included friendship and mutual concern (the unitive aspect later developed), and the sacramental office which was grace giving and significant of the union of Christ and the Church. Cf. the development of Thomas' theory in Schillebeeckx, pp. 339ff.

58. For a discussion of the Augustinian influence on Thomas in particular, as well as those in the Thomistic tradition, see D. Doherty, *The Sexual Doctrine of Cardinal Cajetan* (Rogensburg: Pustet, 1966), pp. 43ff. Also, J. Fuchs, *Die Sexualethik des hl. Thomas v. Aquin* (Köln, 1949). For a discussion of the decline of Augustinian pessimism, see Noonan, pp. 315ff.

59. This is the standard division found in every major treatise on sexuality during this period. *Bibliotheca Canonica, Juridica, Moralis, Theologica* 1767 ed., s.v. "Luxuria," by Lucio Ferraris.

60. How extreme the emphasis on venereal pleasure as a criterion for evaluating the morality of sexual expressions became, is reflected in the following conclusions of Davis:

> It is grievously sinful in the unmarried deliberately to procure or to accept even the smallest degree of true venereal pleasure; secondly, that it is equally sinful to think, say, or do anything with the intention of arousing even the smallest degree of this pleasure. . . . the smallest amount of this pleasure is an inducement to indulgence in the fullest amount of it. Cf. *Moral and Pastoral Theology* (London: Sheed and Ward, 1936), 2:182.

61. Noonan, p. 307.

62. Ibid., p. 324.

63. Ibid., p. 320.

64. Ibid., p. 342.

65. Ibid., p. 441.

66. John Ford and Gerald Kelly, *Contemporary Moral Theology* (Westminster, Md.: Newman Press, 1963), 2:16ff.

67. Ibid., p. 246.

68. *Acta Apostolicae Sedis* 22 (1930), translation from Paulist Press edition, pp. 259-60.

69. Ibid.

70. Ibid., p. 548.

71. AAS, 43 (1951): 843.

72. Ford and Kelly, pp. 256ff.

73. Robert Hoyt, ed., "On Responsible Parenthood"—Final Report of the Papal Commission, *The Birth Control Debate* (Kansas City, Mo.: National Catholic Reporter, 1968), pp. 87-8.

74. "Pastoral Approaches" from the Papal Commission, in Hoyt, pp. 106-7.

75. Walter Abbott and Joseph Gallagher, "The Church in the Modern World," *The Documents of Vatican II* (New York: America Press, 1966), no. 51.

76. Cf. footnote #173 in *The Church in the Modern World* by W. Abbott, J. Gallgher.

77. Paul VI, *Humanae Vitae* (Rome, July 25, 1968), no. 11.

78. *Population Bulletin: Catholic Perspectives on Population Issues* (Washington, D.C.: Population Reference Bureau, n.d.), no. 6, 30:25.

79. Hoyt, pp. 143-74.

80. Ibid., pp. 175-97.

81. Andrew Greeley, *The Catholic Priest in the United States: Sociological Investigations* (Washington, D.C.: U.S. Catholic Conference, 1972), pp. 106ff; *Origins*, 11 January 1973, p. 158.

82. *The Church in the Modern World*, no. 51.

83. Ibid.

84. Ibid., no. 49.

85. Ibid., nos. 47, 50.

86. Ibid., no. 48.

87. *Declaration on Certain Questions Concerning Sexual Ethics* (Rome: Sacred Congregation for the Doctrine of the Faith, 22 January 1976).

88. Ibid., no. 1.

89. Ibid., no. 5.

90. Ibid., no. 3.

91. Ibid., nos. 7, 8, 9.

*Chapter III*

Adler, A., "The Homosexual Problem," *Alienist and Neurology* 38 (1917): 268-87.

Adler, A., *Social Interest* (London, 1938), chapter 11.

Adler, A., *The Practice and Theory of Individual Psychology* (New York 1939), pp. 184-96.

American Statistical Association, *Statistical Problems of the Kinsey Report on Sexual Behavior in the Human Male* (Washington, D.C.: American Statistical Association, 1954).

Anderson, W. J., *How to Understand Sex* (Minneapolis, 1966).

Athanasiou, R., Shaver, P., Tavris, C., *Sexual Psychology Today* (July 1970), pp. 39-50. A study of 20,000 subjects, well educated and of high socioeconomic status.

Avebury, L., *Pre-historic Times* (New York, 1902).

Bartell, G. D., "Group Sex Among Mid-Americans," *Journal of Sex Research,* 6 (1970): 113-30.

Beach, F. A., "Evolutionary Aspects of Psychoendocrinology," *Behavior and Evolution* (New Haven, 1958).

Bell, A. P., Weinberg, M., *Sex Research, Studies from Kinsey Institute* (London, 1976).

Bell, R. R., *Marriage and Family Interaction* (Homewood, Ill., 1971).

Bell, R. R., Chaskes, J. B., "Premarital Sexual Experience Among

Co-eds, 1958 and 1968," *Journal of Marriage and the Family* 32 (1970). Reports a controlled comparison of the two classes in the same large urban university.

Benjamin, H., *The Transexual Phenomenon* (New York, 1966).

Benson, L., *The Family Bond* (New York, 1971).

Bergler, E., *Kinsey's Myth of Female Sexuality* (New York, 1954).

Bieber, I., "Advising the Homosexual," *Medical Aspects of Human Sexuality* 2 (March 1968).

Bieber, I., et al., *Homosexuality: A Psychoanalytic Study of Male Homosexuals* (New York, 1962).

Bieber, I., "The Lesbian Patient," *Medical Aspects of Human Sexuality* 3 (January 1969).

Brown, N., *Love's Body* (New York, 1966).

Burgess, E. W., Wallin, P., *Engagement and Marriage* (Philadelphia, 1953).

Buytendijk, *La Femme* (Paris, 1954).

Calderone, M. S., *Sex, Love, and Intimacy* (New York: Siecus, 1971).

Christensen, H. T., Gregg, C. F., "Changing Sex Norms in America and Scandinavia," *Journal of Marriage and the Family* 32 (1970): 616-27.

Clathworthy, N. M., an associate professor of sociology at Ohio State completed a study to be published seemingly indicating that trial marriages are no help in choosing compatible mates.

Coleman, J. C., *Abnormal Psychology and Modern Life*, 4th ed. (Chicago, 1972).

Cory, D. W., "Homosexuality," *The Encyclopedia of Sexual Behavior*, ed., A. Ellis and A. Abarbanel, vol. 1 (New York, 1961).

Curran, C. E., "Is There a Catholic and/or Christian Ethic?" *Proceedings, The Catholic Theological Society of America*, 29 (1974). In the course of his paper Curran provides a convenient review of Catholic positions on natural law and critically surveys current literature on the subject. He addresses the question of human experience in Catholic ethics.

Davis, K. B., *Factors in the Sex Life of 1200 Women* (New York, 1969).

Davis, K. E., "Sex on Campus: Is There a Revolution?" *Medical Aspects of Human Sexuality.* (January, 1971). Findings generally support Kinsey's 1953 report.

Denfield, D., *Human Behavior* (Spring, 1974).

Denfield, D., Gordon, M., "The Sociology of Mate-swapping," *Journal of Sex Research* 6 (1970).

Dreikurs, R., *The Challenge of Marriage* (New York, 1946), p. 95.

Earle, W., "Love and Metaphysics," *Experience, Existence and the Good* (Southern Illinois University Press, 1961).

Ellis, A., "Constitutional Factors in Homosexuality: A Re-examination of the Evidence," *Advances in Sex Research* (New York, 1963).

Ellis, A., "A Rational Sexual Morality," *The New Sexual Revolution*, ed., L. A. Kirkendall (New York, 1971).

Ellis, A., *The Civilized Couple's Guide to Extra-Marital Adventure* (New York, 1972).

Ellis, A., *The Theory and Practice of Rational-Emotive Psychotherapy* (New York, 1964).

Ellis, A., *Homosexuality: Causes and Cures* (New York, 1965).

Ehrman, W., "Premarital Sexual Intercourse," *The Encyclopedia of Sexual Behavior*, ed. A. Ellis and A. Abarbanel, vol. II (New York, 1961).

Erikson, E., *Identity, Youth and Crisis* (New York, 1968). The discussion of "Inner Space and Womanhood" originally appeared in *Daedalus*, Spring, 1964. See also *Childhood and Society* (New York, 1950).

Fenichel, O., *The Psychoanalytic Theory of Neurosis* (New York, 1945).

Ferenzi, "The Nosology of Male Homosexuality," *Sex in Psychoanalysis* (New York, 1950).

Folson, J. K., review of Kinsey Report in *American Sociological Review* 13 (1948).

Foote, N., "Sex as Play," *Social Problems* (April 1954).

Ford, C. S., Beach, F. A., *Patterns of Sexual Behavior* (New York, 1951).

Ford, C. S., Beach, F. A., "Self-Stimulation," *Sexual Behavior and Personality Characteristics*, ed. M. F. DeMartino (New York, 1963).

Frede, M. C., *Sexual Attitudes and Behavior of College Students at a Public University in the Southwest*, dissertation, University of Houston, 1970, cited by J. L. McCary in *Human Sexuality* (New York, 1973), p. 310.

Freuchen, P., "Love Among the Eskimos," *American Weekly* (Sept. 16, 1956).

Freud, S., "Contributions to a Discussion on Masturbation," *Works*, standard ed., 12 (London: Hogarth, 1958), 239-54 (original German ed. 1912).

Freud, S., *Three Essays on a Theory of Sexuality* (1905).

Gadpaille, W. J., "Talk About Sex," *Sexual Behavior and Sex Research* (April 1966).

Gagnan, J. H., "The Lesbians," *Sexual Deviance* (New York, 1967).

Green, R., "Change of Sex," *Medical Aspects of Human Sexuality* 3 (October 1969): 96-113.

Green, R., *Sexual Identity Conflict in Children and Adults* (New York, 1974).

Gustafson, J. M., "Response to Professor Curran—I," *Proceedings The Catholic Theological Society of America*, 29 (1974). Gustafson's words are: . . . we are not going to get ethics unqualified until we get rational minds unqualified by affectivity, or persons unqualified by particular histories; or knowledge of a moral order unqualified by historical and embodied experiences."

Hampson, J. L., Hampson, J., "The Ontogenesis of Sexual Behavior in Man," *Sex and Internal Secretions* (Baltimore, 1961).

Harper, R. A., "Extramarital Sex Relations," *Encyclopedia of Sexual Behavior*, 1 (New York, 1961).

Hoffman, M., "Homosexuality," *Psychology Today* (July 1969).

Hooker, E., "An Empirical Study of Some Relations between Sexual Partners and Gender Identity in Male Homosexuals," *Sex Research, New Developments*, ed. J. Money (1965).

Hooker, E., "The Adjustment of the Male Overt Homosexual," *Journal of Projective Techniques* 21 (1957).

Hooker, E., "Male Homosexuality in the Rorschach," *Journal of Projective Techniques* 22 (1958).

Jeanniere, A., *The Anthropology of Sex* (New York, 1967).

Jung, C. G., *Psychological Types*, Collected Works, vol. 6 (Princeton, 1974), p. 471.

Kaplan, H. S., Sager, C. J., "Sexual Patterns at Different Ages," *Medical Aspects of Human Sexuality* 5 (June, 1971).

Kaye, H. E., "Lesbian Relationships," *Sexual Behavior* 1 (April, 1971).

Kinsey, A. C., et al., *Sexual Behavior in the Human Male* (Philadelphia, 1948).

Kinsey, A. C., et al., *Sexual Behavior in the Human Female* (Philadelphia, 1953).

Kirkendall, L. A., *Premarital Intercourse and Interpersonal Relationships* (New York, 1961).

Kirkendall, L. A., *The New Sexual Revolution* (New York, 1971), Epilogue.

Kirkendall, L. A., "Developing Human Sexuality," *The New Sexual Revolution* (New York, 1971).

Koats, G. R., Davis, K. E., "The Dynamics of Sexual Behavior of College Students," *Journal of Marriage and the Family* 38 (1970).

Lee, P. and Stewart, R., ed., *Sex Differences* (New York, 1976).

Largey, G., Taft, L., analysis of data collected in a national sampling by the National Opinion Research Center as reported in the *National Catholic Reporter* (January 24, 1975).

Levitt, E., Klassen, A., Paper presented to Orthopsychiatric Association convention, 1973, published in part in *Journal of Homosexuality*, vol. 1, 1974 as "Public Attitudes toward Homosexuality."

Maccoby, E., Jacklin, C., *The Psychology of Sex Differences* (Stanford University Press, 1974).

Marcuse, H., *Eros and Civilization* (London, 1956).

Marmor, J., *Sexual Inversion* (New York, 1965).

Maslow, A., "Self-Esteem and Sexuality in Women," *Journal of Social Psychology* 16 (1942).

Maslow, A., "Volunteer Error in the Kinsey Study," *Journal of Abnormal and Social Psychology* 47 (April 1952).

Maslow, A., "Love in Self-Actualizing People," *Sexual Behavior and Personality Characteristics,* ed. M. F. DeMartino (New York, 1966).

Maslow, A., *Motivation and Personality* (New York, 1954).

Masters, W. H., Johnson, V. E., *Human Sexual Response* (Boston, 1966).

Masters, W. H., Johnson, V. E., *Human Sexual Inadequacy* (Boston, 1970).

Masters, W. H., Johnson, V. E., *The Pleasure Bond* (New York: Bantam edition, 1976).

Masters, W. H., et al., "Plasma Testosterone and Semen Analysis in Male Homosexuals," *New England Journal of Medicine*, 285 (1971). The report states that exclusively homosexuals or predominantly homosexuals displayed "diminished plasma testosterone and impaired spermatogenesis." Bisexuals did not differ from heterosexuals in these factors. In a conference at Chicago on May 19, 1974 Masters indicated he was about to release the results of extensive studies that he believed would support the view that homosexual mode of sexual expression can be a satisfactory one.

McCary, J. L., *Human Sexuality* (New York, 1973).

McCormick, R.A., "Response to Professor Curran—II," *Proceedings, The Catholic Theological Society of America*, 29 (1974). McCormick suggests that the Christian community has historically been exposed to privileged influences which may have rendered it "less vulnerable to long-term cultural distortions of our basic value-judgments." He further suggests that the Catholic experience has additionally been privileged with a "facilitating vehicle" for preserving and sharing these moral insights within the Christian community, namely the *magisterium*. Thus, for McCormick, the experience of the Church helpfully contributes to its moral reflection.

Mead, M., "An Anthropologist Looks at the Report," *Problems of Sexual Behavior* (New York, 1948).

Mead, M., Male and Female, *Sexes in a Changing World* (New York, 1949).

Mead, M., *Sex and Temperament* (New York, 1950).

Mead, M., *Women and Analysis* (New York, 1974).

Merleau-Ponty, M., "The Body in Its Sexual Being," *Phenomenology of Perception* (London, 1962), chapter 5.

Merleau-Ponty, M., *Structure of Behavior* (Boston, 1942).

Meyers, L., "Hyponatology, Sex Role Concepts, and Human Sexual Behavior," *The Family Coordinator* (July 1973). Dr. Meyers is associated with the Midwest Population Center in Chicago. She is a forceful proponent of bisexual behavior.

Meyer, L., Leggit, H., "A New View of Adultery," *Sexual Behavior* 2 (February 1972).

Money, J., "Imprinting and The Establishment of Gender Role," *Archives of Neurological Psychiatry* 77 (1957).

Money, J., "Sex Hormones and Other Variables in Human Eroticism," *Sex and Internal Secretions*, vol. 2 (Baltimore, 1961).

Money, J., "Determinants of Human Sexual Identity and Behavior," *Progress in Group and Family Therapy*, ed. by C. J. Sager and H. S. Kaplan (New York, 1972).

Money, J., *Transsexualism and Sex Reassignment* (Baltimore, 1969).

Murdock, G. P., *Our Primitive Contemporaries* (New York, 1934).

Murdock, G. P., *Social Structure* (New York, 1949).

National Opinion Research Center Report, reported in *Critic* (January, 1975).

Neiger, F. H., "Mate Swapping: Can It Save a Marriage?" *Sexology* (January, 1971).

Otto, H. A., "The New Sexuality: An Introduction," *The New Sexuality* (1971).

Paci, E., "Per una fenomenologia dell'eros," *Nuovi Argomenti* (1961), transl. in *Facets of Eros*, eds. Smith/Eng. (The Hague, 1972), pp. 1-22.

Packard, V., *The Sexual Wilderness* (New York, 1968).

Pomeroy, W. B., "Why We Tolerate Lesbians," *Sexology* (1965).

Pomeroy, W. B., *Boys and Sex* (New York, 1968).

Pomeroy, W. B., "Parents and Homosexuality," *II Sexology* (April 1966).

Pomeroy, W. B., "Homosexuality, Transvestism and Transsexualism," *Human Sexuality in Medical Education and Practice*, ed. C. E. Vincent, (Springfield, Illinois, 1968).

Reevey, W. R., "Child Sexuality," *The Encyclopedia of Sexual Behavior*, vol. 1, ed., A. Ellis and A. Abarbanel (New York, 1961).

Reiss, I. L., "Premarital Coitus and Marital Happiness," *Medical Aspects of Human Sexuality* 4 (October 1970).

Renshaw, D., "Understanding Masturbation," *Journal of School Health* (1976): 46.

Rosen, H. S., "A Survey of Sexual Attitudes and Behavior of Mate-Swapping in Houston" (University of Houston Press, 1971).

Rosenberg, B. G., Sutton-Smith, B. *Sex and Identity* (New York, 1972).

Rosenzweig, S., "Human Sexual Autonomy as an Evolutionary Attainment, Anticipating Proceptive Sex Choice and Idiodynamic Bisexuality," *Contemporary Sexual Behavior: Critical Issues in the 1970's* ed., J. Zubin and J. Money (Baltimore, 1973).

Rubin, I., "New Sex Findings," *Sexology* (November 1969).

Rubin, I., "Sex Over 65," *Advances in Sex Research*, ed. H. G. Beigel (New York, 1963).

Sagarin, E., "Sex Research and Sociology," *Studies in the Sociology of Sex*, ed. J. M. Henslin (New York, 1971).

Sagarin, E., "Ideology as a Factor in Consideration of Deviance," *Journal of Sex Research*, 4 (1968).

Salisbury, W. W., Salisbury, F. F., "Youth and the Search for Intimacy," *The New Sexual Revolution*, ed. L. A. Kirkendall (New York, 1971).

Simpson, G., "Nonsense About Women," *Sexual Behavior in American Society*, ed. J. Hammelbach and S. Fava (New York, 1955).

Smith, F. J., English, E., eds., *Facets of Eros* (The Hague, 1972), Introduction.

Smith, F. G., Smith, J. R., "Co-marital Sex and the Sexual Freedom Movement," *Journal of Sex Research* 6 (1970).

Smith, F. G., Smith, J. R., Paper delivered at 61st Annual Meeting of the American Psychopathological Association and published in *Contemporary Sexual Behavior: Critical Issues in the 1970's* (Baltimore, 1973).

Sonnenschein, D., "The Ethnography of Male Homosexual Relationships," *Journal of Sex Research* 4 (1968).

Spitz, R. A., "Authority and Masturbation," *Psychoanalytic Quarterly* 21 (1952): 490-527.

Stiller, R., "Wife Swapping," *Sexology* (May 1961).

Sullivan, P. R., "What is the Role of Fantasy in Sex?" *Medical Aspects of Human Sexuality* 3 (April 1969).

Terman, L. M., Miles, C. C., *Sex and Personality* (New York, 1936).

Thorpe, L. D., *The Psychology of Abnormal Behavior* (New York, 1961).

Tripp, C. A., *The Homosexual Matrix* (New York, 1975). See chapter 10 for discussion of homosexual politics. Author also offers a good cross-cultural report on homosexual practice.

Walsh, R. H., "The Generation Gap in Sexual Belief," *Sexual Behavior* 2 (January 1972).

Watts, A., *Nature, Man and Woman* (London, 1958).

Weinberg, M., Bell, A. P., *Homosexuality: An Annotated Bibliography* (New York: Harper and Row, 1972). The bibliography contains 1200 scholarly publications.

Yankelovich, D., Report of the Carnegie Corporation published as *The New Morality, A Profile of American Youth in the 70's* (New York, 1974).

*Chapter IV*

1. Walter Abbott and Joseph Gallagher, "Pastoral Constitution on the Church in the Modern World," *The Documents of Vatican II* (New York: Association Press, 1966), no. 62.

2. Ibid.,

3. Ibid., no. 12.

4. Ibid., no. 44.

5. Henry Davis, S.J., *Moral and Pastoral Theology* (London: Sheed and Ward, 1936), 2:173.

6. Ibid., p. 182.

7. *Declaration on Certain Questions Concerning Sexual Ethics*, no. 1.

8. Cf. Gen 2:17, as interpreted by Karl Barth, *Church Dogmatics* (Edinburgh: T. and T. Clark, 1961), III/1, pp. 184-87; III/4, pp. 116-18.

9. *Church in the Modern World*, no. 51.

10. *Canon* 1013, no. 1.

11. Cf. Herbert Vorgrimler, *Commentary on the Documents of Vatican II* (New York: Herder, 1969) 5: 239ff.

12. *Church in the Modern World*, no. 51.

13. *Declaration on Certain Questions Concerning Sexual Ethics*, no. 1.

14. Ibid., no. 12.

15. Ibid., no. 62.

16. Bernard Haring, *The Law of Christ*, translated by E. G. Kaiser (Westminster, Md.: Newman Press, 1963), 1:35-53.

17. Richard McCormick, "Ambiguity in Moral Choice," (Washington, D.C.: Kennedy Center for Bioethics, Georgetown University, 1973), p. 65.

18. Joseph Fuchs, S.J., "The Absoluteness of Moral Terms," *Gregorianum* 52 (1971): 415-58. For a good evaluation of the recent literature and developments in this direction consult McCormick's comments on the "Understanding of Moral Norms," in *Theological Studies* 36 (March, 1975): 85-100.

19. John A. Robinson, *Honest to God* (London: SCM Press, 1963), p. 115; Joseph Fletcher, *Situation Ethics: The New Morality* (Philadelphia: Westminster Press, 1966), pp. 18ff; A. Heron, ed., *Towards a Quaker View of Sex* (London: Friends Home Service Committee, 1963), are representative of such an approach. Cf. Gene Outka and Paul Ramsey, *Norm and Context in Christian Ethics* (New York: Scribner, 1968), pp. 3ff for a fuller discussion of this matter.

20. Sources which have contributed to a renewed appreciation of this point include: *Declaration on Certain Questions Concerning Sexual Ethics*, no. 1; Peter Bertocci, *Sex, Love and the Person* (Mission, Kansas: Sheed and Ward, 1969): John Milhaven, "Conjugal Sexual Love," *Theological Studies* 35 (December 1974): 692-710; Michael Valente, *Sex, The Radical View of A Catholic Theologian* (New

York: Bruce, 1970), especially pp. 132ff; E. Kennedy, *What a Modern Catholic Believes About Sex* (Chicago, Ill.: The Thomas More Press, 1971), pp. 25ff.; "Theological and Psychological Aspects of Habitual Sin," by Jerome Hayden, O.S.B., *Proceedings of CTSA* (1956): 130-63.

21. The Vatican Constitution on *The Church in the Modern World* (no. 49) speaks eloquently on this characteristic of human love in the context of marriage and the more recent Vatican *Declaration on Certain Questions Concerning Sexual Ethics* implies the same for non-marital sexuality (no. 1).

22. Cf. *Sex and Morality: A Report Presented to the British Council of Churches* (Philadelphia: Fortress Press, October 1966), pp. 29-30; Matthias Neuman, O.S.B., "Friendship Between Men and Women in Religious Life," *Sisters Today* 46 (October 1974): 89-92.

23. Richard Roach, S.J., "Sex in Christian Morality," *Way* 11 (1971): 148-61, 235-42.

24. The report of the British Council of Churches reflects this kind of concern when it suggests with regard to the rules of abstinence before marriage and fidelity within it "even if such rules do not completely coincide with the rights and wrongs of each case taken in isolation, yet they do prescribe what is normally good for our society. In this case we may have a duty to uphold the rule even at some sacrifice of personal liberty." *Sex and Morality*, p. 27.

25. The Christian Catholic tradition has generally maintained that the procreative and unitive aspects of human sexuality are in some sense inseparable. In what precise manner the relationship between the two elements is to be understood and harmonized is far from agreed upon. See Chapter V of this study under "Call to Responsible Parenthood," for more complete discussion of this problem.

26. *Church in the Modern World*, no. 50.

27. The final report of the Papal Commission studying the problem of birth control and responsible parenthood treats this aspect of human sexuality especially well. Cf. Robert Hoyt, ed., *The Birth Control Debate* (Kansas City, Mo.: National Catholic Reporter, 1968), pp. 83ff.

28. The important role of the erotic element in human sexuality has received increased attention in the writings of recent authors on the subject. Milhaven and Greeley especially have made important contributions in this area. Cf. John Milhaven, pp. 692-710; Andrew Greeley, *Sexual Intimacy* (Chicago, Illinois: Thomas More Press, 1973); Andrew Greeley, *Love and Play* (Chicago, Ill.: Thomas More Press, 1975).

29. *Church in the Modern World*, no. 51.

30. Richard McCormick, "Notes on Moral Theology," *Theological Studies* 36 (March 1975): 85-100.

31. Cf. 1970 edition of *Medico-Moral Guide* Preamble approved by Canadian Catholic Conference.

*Chapter V*

1. Henry Davis, S.J., *Moral and Pastoral Theology*, (London: Sheed and Ward, 1936), 2:172.

2. Ibid., p. 173.

3. *Declaration on Certain Questions Concerning Sexual Ethics*, no. 11.

4. Donald Goergen, *The Sexual Celibate* (New York: The Seabury Press, 1974), p. 226.

5. Cf. Edward Schillebeeckx, *Marriage Human Reality and Saving Mystery* (New York: Sheed and Ward, 1965), pp. 177ff, for an excellent commentary on this passage and its significance for marriage.

6. H. Noldin, S.J., "De Sexto Praecepto et De Usu Matrimonii," *Theologiae Moralis* (Austria, 1922), no. 67, p. 73.

7. Ibid., no. 94 (1 b), p. 106.

8. Ibid., no. 68d, p. 76.

9. Ibid., no. 92, #2, p. 103.

10. Ibid.

11. AAS 22 (1930): 559-60.

12. *The Church in the Modern World*, no. 48.

13. Ibid., no. 49.

14. Ibid.

15. Ibid.

16. Ibid.

17. Ibid., no. 51.

18. Thomas and Dorothy Thompson, "Some Legal Problems in the Book of Ruth," *Vetus Testamentum* 18 (1968): 79-99.

19. John Dedek, *Contemporary Medical Ethics* (New York: Sheed and Ward, 1975), pp. 73ff.

20. *Church in the Modern World*, no. 50.

21. Ibid., no. 51.

22. Ibid., no. 50.

23. Ibid.

24. Ibid., no. 51.

25. Pope Paul VI, *Humanae Vitae* (Rome: 25 July 1968), no. 12.

26. Ibid., no. 13.

27. Cf. Bernard Haring, "The Inseparability of The Unitive-Procreative Functions of the Marital Act," *Contraception: Authority and Dissent*, ed. by C. E. Curran (New York: Herder and Herder, 1969), pp. 190ff.

28. *Church in the Modern World*, no. 51.

29. Haring, pp. 190-191.

30. Robert Hoyt, ed., "On Responsible Parenthood," and "Papal Approaches"—Documents from the Papal Commission, *The Birth Control Debate*, pp. 87, 106-7.

31. Charles E. Curran, *Contemporary Problems in Moral Theology* (Notre Dame, Ind.: Fides Publishers, 1970), p. 174.

32. *Humanae Vitae*, no. 17.

33. Herbert Vorgrimler, ed., *Commentary on the Documents of Vatican II*, (New York: Herder and Herder, 1969) 5: 242-3.

34. Bernard Haring, *What Does Christ Want* (South Bend, Indiana: Ave Maria Press, 1968), pp. 110-11.

35. Some recent sources regarding this question include: J. Billings, *Natural Family Planning: The Ovulation Method*, 2nd American ed. (Collegeville, Minn.: Liturgical Press, 1972); John and Sheila Kippley, *The Art of Natural Family Planning* (Cincinnati: The Couple to Couple League International Inc., 1975); Wm. Uricchio, ed., *Proceedings of a Research Conference on Natural Family Planning* (Washington, D.C.: The Human Life Foundation, 1973).

36. *Casti Connubii*, no. 72; AAS 22 (1930): 565.

37. AAS 23 (1931): 119.

38. Ibid.

39. AAS 32 (1940): 73.

40. AAS 43 (1951): 845-46; Pope Pius XII, "Apostolate of The Midwife," trans. by *Catholic Mind* 50 (January 1952): 55-56.

41. AAS 45 (1953): 675.

42. *Humanae Vitae*, no. 14.

43. *Ethical and Religious Directives for Catholic Health Facilities* (Washington, D.C.: USCC, 1971), no. 2, p. 6.

44. Letter of Most Rev. Joseph L. Bernardin (Washington, D.C.: National Conference of Catholic Bishops, April 14, 1975).

45. Gerald Kelly, "Pope Pius XII and the Principle of Totality," *Theological Studies* 16 (1955): 282-84.

46. Hoyt, p. 93.

47. *Policy Manual for Committee to Advise on Requests for*

*Obstetrical/Gynaecological. Sterilization Procedures* (London, Ontario: St. Joseph's Hospital, 1973).

48. Bernard Haring, *Medical Ethics*, edited by L. J. Gabrielle (Notre Dame, Ind.: Fides Publ., 1972), p. 90.

49. Thomas Wassmer, *Christian Ethics for Today* (Milwaukee: Bruce, 1969), p. 192.

50. *Church in the Modern World*, no. 43.

51. Cf. Leonard Paolillo and Anthony Walsh, *Emerging Attitudes Toward Alternate Family Forms*, paper presented to meeting of the Pacific Sociological Association, Portland, Ore., April 13, 1972. Also James Schulte, *The Phenomena of Child Free Marriage in American Society Today: A Theological Appraisal,* incomplete dissertation, Marquette University.

52. AAS 43 (1951): 845-46.

53. Canons 1013, 1086, 1092.

54. Cf. Canon 1068, no. 3.

55. Pope Pius XII's discussion here seems to be in harmony with this discussion of the "inward molding" and "perfection" of spouses as a purpose of marriage, by Pope Pius XI in his encyclical on marriage.

56. Child-free marriage is here considered a variant form of marriage, but different from the other "variant forms" discussed elsewhere in this study because there is no question here as to "fidelity" or of a clandestine relationship. Rather, it is a question which more properly fits under a discussion of responsible parenthood.

57. Rustum and Delly Roy, *Honest Sex* (New York: New American Library, 1968), chap. 8.

58. Cf. Lawrence Casler, "Permissive Matrimony: Proposals for the Future," *The Humanist* 34 (March/April 1974): 4-8.

59. It bears repetition that the empirical data is quite incomplete as to the long and short range effects of this kind of activity, and therefore quite inconclusive (Chapter III). Further, there are a variety of other consequences that can take place that do not admit of empirical study, e.g., the effects upon the spiritual life on the individuals involved. All of this must enter in the moral consideration of these forms of behavior.

60. This social dimension in moral decision making is necessary to uphold the value of being socially responsible. In the past, this information was largely contained in the tradition and/or laws of a given community, e.g., the laws of the Church. Today, in accord with the suggestion of Vatican II to take note of the data of empirical

science, we look to various reports of measured human behavior and attitudinal studies, taking due note of the limitations of such studies. It is essential to avoid seeing the decision making process as a purely "private matter." The norms and ideals of the rest of society must be considered.

61. Cf. p. 92.

62. Cf. p. 93.

63. *Ibid.*

64. Cf. p. 86.

65. Cf. p. 60.

66. Cf. p. 13.

67. Cf. pp. 14ff.

68. Cf. p. 20.

69. Cf. pp. 22ff.

70. Immanuel Kant, *Critique of Practical Reason,* transl. by Lewis White Beck (New York: Bobbs-Merrill, 1956), pp. 90, 136.

71. H. Nolden, "Fornicatio est copula soluti cum soluta ex mutuo consensu," *De Sexto Praecepto,* I, 3, 1.

72. According to St. Thomas, the sins against chastity but not against nature are fornication, adultery, incest, seduction, rape, and sacrilege, that is, intercourse involving irreligion. Sins against both chastity and nature are masturbation, birth control, homosexual practice, and bestiality. *Summa Theologica,* American ed. (New York: Benziger, 1947), II-II, q. 154.

73. Noldin, I, 3, 1.

74. Aquinas, II-II, q. 154, a.2; A. Liguori, *Theologia Moralis* (Rome: Vaticana, 1905), III, 432; Noldin, I, 3, 1.

75. For a detailed account of the reasoning behind the tradition, cf. B. Schlegelberger, *Vor-und Ausserehelicher Geschlechts-verkehr* (Remscheid: St. Paulus Mission, 1970).

76. Liguori, III, 412.

77. Arthurus Vermeersch, *De Castitate* (Rome: Gregoriana, 1919), n. 304. The fact that Catholic moralists continued, even after him, to cite the Old Testament as forbidding premarital intercourse, indicates how little attention moralists often paid to critical scriptural exegesis in the past. Cf. B. Schlegelberger, 23, n. 11.

78. Inde colligimus, fornicarios in iram Dei incurrere. Sed quo iure et an graviter *singulae* fornicationes prohibeantur, Scriptura *expresse* non dicit; neque stricte est fornicator, qui semel vel bis fornicatus est. Verum, non apparet cur in sola quadam actuum pluritate, quae ceterum definiri nequit, ratio peccati mortalis primum inesset; satis autem receptum est, Lege nova, si leges de fide et sacramentis excipias, nullum divinum praeceptum promulgari praeter ea quae na-

turali lege continentur (Cf. v.g., *Caietanum*, in 2,2, q. 143, art. 2). Indirecte ergo constat ex sacris litteris omnem fornicationem gravi eaque naturali malitia infici. Vermeersch, n. 306.

79. Paulus ter affirmat *fornicarios excludi a regno Dei*: Gal 5:21; Eph 5:5; 1 Cor 6:9s. Quod hoc ultimo loco dici videtur praecise de ea fornicatione, quae non est adulterina, cum contra adulterium contradistinguatur; utrum autem apostolus hic de facto cogitet de solo meretricio, ut immediate antea (1 Cor 6:12-20), an etiam de aliis relationibus fornicariis, v.g. inter sponsos, non explicite ostenditur. J. Fuchs, *De Castitate et Ordine Sexuali*, 3rd ed. (Rome: Gregoriana, 1963), p. 100.

80. Schlegelberger, p. 27.

81. F. Böckle and J. Köhne, *Geschlechtliche Beziehungen vor der Ehe* (Mainz, 1967), pp. 18-19.

82. In 1679, Pope Innocent XI condemned as erroneous the opinion that fornication is forbidden only because of divine positive law: Tam clarum videtur, fornicationem secundum se nullam involvere malitiam, et solum esse malam, quia interdicta, ut contrarium omnino rationi dissonum videatur. H. Denzinger, A. Schönmetzer, *Enchiridion Symbolorum*, 32nd ed. (New York: Herder, 1963), n. 2148.

83. Peter Lombard, *Sententiarum Libri IV*, 26, 2: "reprehensibilis est malus coitus, nisi excusetur per bona conjugii" (Florence: St. Bonaventure, 1916).

84. Liguori, III, n. 432.

85. Aquinas, II-II, 154, 2.

86. Ibid.; Liguori, III, n. 432.

87. Catholici itaque de intrinseca et gravi fornicationis malitia non dubitant; in assignanda autem ratione satis laborant, ita ut PALMIERI (Opus *theol. mor.* tom. 2, n. 1008) fateatur se non abhorrere ab observatione TAMBURINI (*Expl. Decalogi*, 1. 7. c.1, 2) efficacem rationem qua malitia ista e naturali fonte eruatur exsistere quidem, attamen "eam a priori nondum clare nobis esse compertam." Vermeersch, III, n. 304.

88. Schlegelberger, pp. 62ff.

89. Supra, pp. 85ff; also B. Strätling, "Liebe vor der Ehe?—Zur Frage voreneicher Sexualbeziehungen," *Moral braucht Normen,* F. Schlosser, ed., (Limburg: Lahn, 1970), p. 139.

90. Böckle, Köhne, pp. 19-20.

91. Schlegelberger, p. 217.

92. Aquinas, I-II, 103, 4, ad 3.

93. Sed hic notanda est quaestio illa magna inter doctores: *an cessat lex, cessante fine adaequato legis?* Finis adaequatus est ille, qui

est totalis finis legis: nam si lex plures fines habeat, finis adaequatus ex omnibus illis constituitur.—Hoc posito, certum est quod, cessante fine adaequato seu totali legis in communi, cessat lex: ut si vovisti non ingredi talem domum ob periculum fornicationis, cessante periculo, cessat votum. Ratio, quia lex cum sit inutilis, vim amittit obligande. Ita D. Thomas, et Salmant. cum communi. St. Alphonsus, *Theologia Moralis*, I, n. 199.

94. Schlegelberger, p. 232.

95. Henry Davis, *Moral and Pastoral Theology* (London: Sheed and Ward, 1936), 2:177-78, 180, 182.

96. *Declaration on Certain Questions Concerning Sexual Ethics*, no. 7.

97. For an excellent discussion of various contemporary approaches to the question of premarital sexuality, cf. R. McCormick's comments on the subject in *Theological Studies* 34 (March, 1973): 77-92.

98. Francis Manning, "The Human Meaning of Sexual Pleasure and the Morality of Premarital Intercourse—Part Three," *The American Ecclesiastical Review* 166 (May, 1972): 317.

99. *Sex and Morality: A Report Presented to the British Council of Churches* (Philadelphia: Fortress, October 1966), p. 31.

100. *Blue Book—1970* (182nd General Assembly of the United Presbyterian Church in the United States of America), p. 342.

101. Ibid., p. 349.

102. Lester Kirkendall, "A New Bill of Sexual Rights and Responsibilities," *The Humanist* 36 (Jan/Feb 1976): 5.

103. Eugene Borowicz, *Choosing a Sex Ethic* (New York: Schocken Books, 1969), p. 54.

104. Eleanor Hamilton, *Sex Before Marriage* (New York: Bantam Books, 1969), p. 35.

105. Strätling, p. 39.

106. See chapter III on premarital sex.

107. Strätling, pp. 147-48.

108. Gallup Poll, *Detroit Free Press*, 5 October 1975.

109. Shirley Saldahna et al., "American Catholics Ten Years Later," *Critic*, 33 (1975): 18.

110. Andrew Greeley, *The Catholic Priest in the United States: Sociological Investigations*, The National Opinion Research Center, University of Chicago (Washington, D.C.; The USCC, 1972), p. 101.

111. Goergen, p. 184.

112. Paul Ramsey, "A Christian Approach to the Question of Sexual Relations Outside of Marriage," *The Journal of Religion*, 45 (1965): 109.

113. Ibid., p. 116.

114. Cf. T. C. De Kruijf, *The Bible on Sexuality* (De Pere, Wisconsin; St. Norbert Abbey Press, 1966), pp. 51ff.

115. John T. McNeill and Helen M. Gamer, *Medieval Handbook of Penance* (New York: Octagon Books, Inc., 1965), p. 103.

116. Davis, pp. 180-81.

117. Gerald Kelly, *Modern Youth and Chastity* (Missouri: Liguorian-Queen's Work, 194), pp. 75ff.

118. Schulte, Chapter 2, footnote 37, p. 37.

119. *Ibid.*, footnote 36, p. 37.

120. This practical control of conception is only relatively safe, and there is a growing body of statistics to suggest that many of the young are putting too much stock in that safety factor. The high percentage of abortions among young unmarried girls would argue strongly that the safety factor is not adequately understood by many! Likewise the general increase in the incidence of venereal diseases would suggest some reservations as to the "relative safety" of today's control of conception methods. These statistical indicators have not as yet had much impact on popular attitudes.

121. Kelly, pp. 74ff.

122. Presbyterian Report, p. 348.

123. Cf. p. 147.

124. Cf. p. 146.

125. James McCary, *Sexual Myths and Fallacies* (New York: Schocken Books, 1971), pp. 39ff.

126. *Proceedings of CTSA*, 27 (1972): 233-40.

127. Supra, chapter 4.

128. Ibid.

129. *Gaudium et Spes*, Part II, Chap. I; *Perfectae caritatis*, no. 12.

130. *Gaudium et Spes*, Part I, Chap. I, no. 12.

131. Cf. p. 35.

132. Cf. *Perfectae caritatis*, no. 12.

133. 1 Cor. 7:29-31. This is a favorite theme in the early Christian centuries and in the writings of the Fathers of the Church.

134. Cf. 1 Cor. 7:32-36.

135. This pragmatic point of view has prevailed largely with the religious institutes termed "apostolic." On the other hand, the dimension of community, when sought as a human and a Christian value, helped to neutralize a too utilitarian attitude toward evangelical chastity, expressed in celibacy and virginity.

136. *Lumen Gentium*, no. 21.

137. Supra, chapter IV, the values characteristic of wholesome sexuality.

138. Cf. pp. 83-84.

139. The bibliography (cf. infra), clearly limited and selected, is nonetheless representative of the effort in this direction.

140. Two excellent discussions of these aspects of celibate or virginal sexuality can be found in Philip Keane, S.S., "The Meaning and Functioning of Sexuality in the Lives of Celibates and Virgins," *Review for Religious* 34 (1972): 277-312; Matthias Neuman, O.S.B., "Friendship Between Men and Women in Religious Life," *Sisters Today* 46 (October 1974): 89-92.

141. The term "covenant" can be taken here to represent those dimensions of celibacy and virginity which are embraced in an understanding of the charismatic, symbolic, eschatological values of these life styles.

142. Cf. Hosea 2:14.

143. Antoine de Saint-Exupéry, *Le Petit Prince* (Paris: Gallimard, 1946), p. 78.

144. A more wholistic view of celibate and virginal sexuality is represented in the writings of Teilhard de Chardin, who discusses the "evolution" of chastity: cf. *Toward the Future* translated by Rene Hague (New York: Harcourt Brace Jovanovich Publishers, 1975); cf. also Goergen.

145. Cf. infra, "Celibate and Virginal Sexuality: Bibliography," esp., Goergen, Keane, Matura, Oraison, Raguin.

146. Homophobia is the technical term describing the fear of homosexuality whether the fear that heterosexual persons have of homosexual feelings which they experience in themselves or the fear of contempt that homosexuals themselves manifest. See Martin Weinberg, *Society and the Healthy Homosexual* (New York: St. Martin's Press, 1972).

147. Martin S. Weinberg and Alan P. Bell, eds. *Homosexuality: An Annotated Bibliography* (New York: Harper and Row, 1972) contains 1,265 entries, books and articles published in the English language alone during the years 1940 to 1968. Of especial significance for Catholics is John J. McNeill, *The Church and the Homosexual* (Kansas City, Mo.: Sheed Andrews and McMeel, Inc., 1976).

148. Cf. the cultural studies of Margaret Mead.

149. Martin Noth, *Leviticus, A Commentary* (London: SCM Press, 1965), p. 16.

150. Martin Noth, *The Laws in the Pentateuch* (Philadelphia: Fortress Press, 1967), p. 49.

151. Ibid., p. 52. It may be supposed that what existed as a

neighboring foreign cult in the immediate surroundings of ancient Israel, and might therefore become a temptation to "fall away" to "other gods," was forbidden to Israel, along with all its special features. M. Noth, *Leviticus*, p. 16. This explains, for example, why the eating of pork was forbidden to the ancient Israelites. Every act of slaughtering was considered as sacrificial, and the wild swine was sacred to one of the Canaanite deities. If the swine could not be offered in sacrifice to Yahweh, it could not be slaughtered and therefore could not be eaten. M. Noth, *The Laws in the Pentateuch.* p. 56, no. 138.

152. See Chapter I.

153. N. H. Snaith, *Leviticus and Numbers*, the Century Bible (London: Nelson, 1967), p. 126; see also H.-J. Schoeps, "Homosexualitat und Bibel," in *Zeitschrift für Evangelische Ethik.* 6 (1962), p. 371; and William G. Cole, *Love and Sex in the Bible* (New York: Association Press, 1959), pp. 350-51.

154. Louis Epstein, *Sex Laws and Customs in Judaism* (New York: KIAV, 1968), p. 135.

155. Anthony Phillips, *Ancient Israel's Criminal Law, A New Approach to the Decalogue* (Oxford: Basil Blackwell, 1970), p. 122; see also Gerhard VonRad, *Genesis, A Commentary* (Philadelphia: Westminster Press, 1961), pp. 212-13.

156. For a detailed study of the development of the homosexual interpretation of Sodom in the Pseudepigrapha, see D. S. Bailey, *Homosexuality and the Western Tradition* (London: Longmans, 1955), pp. 11-25.

157. *Questiones et Solutiones in Genesin*, 4, 37; *De Abrahomo*, 26, 134-36.

158. Bailey, p. 23.

159. Ibid., p. 27. See also J. McNeill, *The Church and the Homosexual*, pp. 42-50.

160. McNeill argues that the *malakoi* and *arsenokoitai* condemned by St. Paul should not be exclusively identified with homosexual activity but in the first instance with "soft" dissolute behavior in general, and in the second instance with male prostitution. *The Church and the Homosexual*, pp. 52-53.

161. Otto Kuss, *Der Römerbrief* (Regensburg: Pustet, 1963), p. 52.

162. T. Bovet, *Sinnerfülltes Andersein* (Tübingen, 1959), p. 87, cited in H.-J. Schoeps, "Homosexualität und Bibel," p. 373, n. 17.

163. Bailey, p. 38.

164. Schoeps, p. 373.

165. *Confessions of St. Augustine*, 3, 8.

166. See *In epist. ad Rom. IV.* PG 60, pp. 415-22.

167. Bailey, p. 157.

168. Ibid., pp. 70-81.

169. Ibid., p. 98.

170. Aquinas, II-II, q. 154.

171. Ibid., II-II, q. 154, a. 11-12.

172. Ibid., II-II, q. 154, a. 1.

173. St. Clement of Alexandria, Paed. 10.

174. Bailey, p. 164.

175. The teaching of Pope Alexander VII is cited, to the effect that sodomy must be confessed specifically. Prop. 24. D. 1124. Ecclesiastical censures leveled against clerics for homosexuality in the *Code of Canon Law* (C. 2357, 2358, 2359) are also cited.

176. Cf. Michael Buckley, *Morality and the Homosexual, A Catholic Approach to a Moral Problem* (Westminster: Newman Press, 1959), pp. 116-21.

177. *Principles to Guide Confessors in Questions of Homosexuality* (Washington, D.C.: National Conf. of Catholic Bishops, 1973), p. 3.

178. *Declaration on Certain Questions Concerning Sexual Ethics*, no. 8.

179. John McNeill, S.J., "The Christian Male Homosexual," *Homiletic and Pastoral Review* 70 (1970): 758.

180. "Sexuality and Human Community: Study Document," in *Blue Book - 1970*, p. 322.

181. Richard McCormick, S.J., "Full Sacramental Support Urged for Irreversible Homosexuals," *WNY Catholic Newspaper*, 6 February 1975, p. 17.

182. Eugene Kennedy, *The New Sexuality Myths Fables and Hang-ups* (New York: Doubleday and Co., 1972), p. 180.

183. Charles Curran, *Catholic Moral Theology in Dialogue* (Notre Dame, Ind.: Fides Press, 1972), p. 217.

184. Kimball Jones, *Toward a Christian Understanding of the Homosexual* (New York: Association Press, 1966), p. 108.

185. Episcopal Diocese of Michigan, *The Report and Recommendations of the Commission on Homosexuality* (Detroit, Mich., July, 1973), pp. 1-2.

186. Gregory Baum, "Catholic Homosexuals," *Commonweal* 99 (1974): 479-81.

187. Salvatorian Gay Ministry Task Force, "Human Nature and Homosexuality," (Milwaukee: Salvatorian Task Force, n.d.), p. 2 of Module #6.

188. Episcopal Diocese of Michigan, pp. 1-2.

189. Baum, p. 481.

190. Lewis Willimas, "Walls of Ice—Theology and Social Policy," *Is Gay Good?*, Dwight Oberholtzer, ed. (Philadelphia: The Westminster Press, 1971), p. 178.

191. Dick Leitsch, "Interview with a Homosexual Spokesman," *Sexual Behavior* 1 (1971): 20-21.

192. Thomas Maurer, "Toward a Theology of Homosexuality— Tried and Found Trite and Tragic," in *Is Gay Good?*, p. 98.

193. Henri Nouwen, *Intimacy* (Notre Dame, Ind.: Fides Publications, 1969), p. 52.

194. The National Catholic Mental Health Clinic of Utrecht has been especially active in this regard. Results of their pioneering efforts have been published in *Homosexualiteit*, 4th edition, *Pastorale Cahiers*, (Hilversum: Antwerp) translated into the French as *Homosexualite*, (Paris: Mame, 1967); also *Pastorale Zorg voor Homofielen*, (Utrecht-Anvers: Het Spectrum, 1968) translated into the French as *Dieu Les Aime Tels Qu'ils Sont, Pastorale pour les Homophiles* (Points Chauds: Fayard, 1972).

195. *Roman Ritual*, 1946.

196. Marcellinus Zalba, *Theologiae Moralis Summa* (Madrid: Biblioteca de Autores Cristianas, 1957) 1:475-76.

197. Cf. *A Guide to Formation in Priestly Celibacy* issued by the Sacred Congregation for Catholic Education, (Washington: USCC, 1974), pp. 46ff.

198. *The Wolfenden Report*, Report of the Committee on Homosexual Offenses and Prostitution (New York: Stein and Day, 1963), p. 187.

199. T. C. de Kruijf, *The Bible on Sexuality*, p. 40; J. Dedek, *Contemporary Sexual Morality* (New York: Sheed and Ward, 1971), pp. 49-51; J. Fuchs, *De Castitate et Ordine Sexuali*, 3rd ed. (Roma: Gregoriana, 1963), p. 63.

200. Noldin, p. 76.

201. Ibid., p. 30, n. 29.

202. Ibid., pp. 21-3, n. 18.

203. Fuchs, p. 68.

204. Charles Curran, "Masturbation and Objectively Grave Matter," in *A New Look at Christian Morality* (Notre Dame, Ind.: Fides Press, 1968), p. 214.

205. Henricus Denzinger, A. Schönmetzer, *Enchiridion Symbolorum*, 33rd ed. (Rome: Herder, 1965), n. 688.

206. D.S. 2149.

207. Reprinted in Zalba, II, p. 160, n. 39.

208. D.S. 3684.

209. AAS 44 (1952): 275.

210. *Religiosorum institutio*, no. 30.

211. *Ethhical and Religious Directives*, no. 21, p. 7.

212. *A Guide to Formation in Priestly Celibacy*, no. 63, pp. 53-54.

213. *Declaration on Certain Questions Concerning Sexual Ethics*, no. 9.

214. Russell Abata, CSSR, *Sex Sanity in the Modern World—a Guidebook for Everyone* (Missouri: Liguorian Pamphlet Books, 1975), p. 48.

215. Cf. William Bausch, *A Boy's Sex Life: Handbook of Basic Information and Guidance* (South Bend, Ind.: Fides, 1969).

216. Silveo Venturi, cited in Havelock Ellis, *Psychology of Sex* (London: Pan Books Limited, 1959), p. 97.

217. Dr. Cherbuliez, cited in Paulo Liggeri, *Morale Sessuale e Difficolta Attuali* (Milano: Instituto La Casa, 1958), p. 293.

218. Alfred C. Kinsey et al., *Sexual Behavior in the Human Male* (Philadelphia: W. B. Saunders, 1948), pp. 670-71.

219. Helen S. Kaplan, *The New Sex Therapy* (New York: Brunner-Mazel, 1974), p. 195. Patients without spouses are numerous as well, Ibid., p. 237.

220. Lew and Joanne Koch, *The Marriage Savers* (New York: Coward, 1976), p. 137.

221. This is clearly the opinion of the director of the highly regarded Sexual Dysfunction Center at the Stritch Medical School in Chicago, Dr. Domeena Renshaw. Dr. Renshaw, in an interview with the writer, expressed belief that her opinion is shared by most of her medical colleagues, namely that surrogates are counterproductive when the final objective of therapy is kept in mind. Dr. Kaplan, *supra*, p. 237, does not use surrogates but is not so convinced as is Dr. Renshaw that there might not be a role for them in treating sexual dysfunctions whose genesis is independent of the marital relation. The use of surrogates is more popular on the West Coast and among non-medical practitioners. The Koch report tends to be critical of the existing practice in the use of surrogates.

222. Koch, p. 134; Kaplan, p. 204.

223. John Money, assisted by R. Gaskin, "Sex Reassignment," *International Journal of Psychiatry* 9:249-82.

224. Ibid.

225. J. Randell, "Preoperative and Postoperative Status of Male and Female Transexuals," *Transexualism and Sex Reassignment*, R. Green and J. Money, eds. (Baltimore: Johns Hopkins Press, 1969), chapter 26.

# SELECTED BIBLIOGRAPHY

## CHAPTER I

Baab, O.J. "Marriage," "Sex," *Interpreter's Dictionary of the Bible.* New York: Abingdon Press, 1962.

Bailey, D. S. *Common Sense about Sexual Ethics.* New York: Macmillan, 1962.

Balz, H. R. "Sexualität und christliche Existenz," *Kerygma und Dogma,* 14 (1968): 263-306.

Barth, K. *Church Dogmatics.* Edinburgh: T. and T. Clark, 1960.

Blinzler, J. "Eisin eunouchoi," *Zeitschrift für die Neutestamentliche Wissenschaft,* 48 (1957): 254-70.

Bloemhof, F. "Sexualethik," in *Die Religion in Geschichte und Gagenwart,* 5 (1957-65): 804.

Cole, W. G. *Sex and Love in the Bible.* New York: Association Press, 1959.

de Jong, B. "Christian Anthropology: the Biblical View of Man," *Sex, Family, and Society in Theological Focus.* ed. by J. C. Wynn. New York: Association Press, 1966.

de Kruijf, T. C. *The Bible on Sexuality.* De Pere, Wisconsin: St. Norbert Abbey Press, 1966.

Dubarle, A. M. *Love and Fruitfulness in the Bible.* De Pere, Wisconsin: St. Norbert Abbey Press, 1968.

Dupont, J. *Mariage et divorce cans l'Evangile, Matthieu 19, 3-12 et paralleles.* Bruges: Abbaye de Saint-André, 1959.

Grelot, P. *Man and Wife in Scripture.* New York: Herder and Herder, 1964.

Hauck, F. *Theological Dictionary of the New Testament.* ed. by G. Kittel, c.1964-1974, s.v. "Moicheuo."

Hauck, F., and Schultz. *Theological Dictionary of the New Testament.* s.v. "Porne."

Horner, T. *Sex in the Bible.* Rutland, Vermont: Charles E. Tuttle, 1974.

Humbert, A. "Les Peches de Sexualite dans le Nouveau Testament," *Studia Moralia* 8 (1970): 149-83.

McKenzie, J. L. *Dictionary of the Bible.* New York: Macmillan, 1965.

McKenzie, J. L. *A Theology of the Old Testament.* New York: Doubleday, 1974.

Niebuhr, R. *The Nature and Destiny of Man.* New York: Scribners, 1964.

Piper, O. "Sex in Biblical Perspective," *Sexual Ethics and Christian Responsibility*, ed. by J. C. Wynn. New York: Association Press, 1970.

Pohier, J.-M. "Recherches sur les Fondements de la Morale Sexuelle Chrétienne," *Revue des Sciences Philosophiques et Theologiques* 54 (1970): 3-23, 201-26.

Quesnell, Q. "Made Themselves Eunochs for the Kingdom of Heaven," *Catholic Bible Quarterly* 30 (1968): 335-58.

Ringeling, H. *Ethik des Leibes.* Hamburg: Furche-Verlag, 1965.

————, *Theologie und Sexualität.* Gutersloh: Gerd Mohn, 1968.

Schelkle, K. H. *Theology of the New Testament*, vol. 1, *Creation*, vol. 3, *Morality.* Collegeville, Minn.: Liturgical Press, 1971.

Stamm, J. J. and M. E. Andrew. *The Ten Commandments in Recent Research.* Naperville, Illinois: Alec R. Allenson, Inc., 1967.

Strack, H. and P. Billerbeck. *Kommentar zum Neuen Testament aus Talmud und Midrasch.* München: C. H. Beck, 1926-1928.

Swidler, L. "Jesus was a Feminist," *Catholic World* 212 (1971): 177-83.

Thompson, T. and D., "Some Legal Problems in the Book of Ruth," *Vetus Testamentum* 18 (1968): 79-99.

Vollebregt, G. N. *The Bible on Marriage.* De Pere, Wisconsin: St. Norbert Abbey Press, 1965.

Von Rad, G. *Theology of the Old Testament.* Edinburgh: Oliver and Boyd, 1962.

Weber, L. M. "Geschlechtlichkeit," *Lexikon für Theolgie und Kirche*, vol. 4. Freiburg: Herfer, 1957-67.

Westermann, C. *Biblischer Kommentar, Genesis.* Neukirchen: Neukirchner Verlag, 1973.

————, *Schopfung.* Stuttgart: Kreuz Verlag, 1971.

CHAPTER II

Abbott, W. and J. Gallagher. *The Documents of Vatican II.* New York: Guild Press, 1966.

Abailard, *Abailard's Ethics*, tr. by J. Ramsay McCallum. Oxford: Basil Blackwell, 1935.

————, *Historica Calamitatum*, tr. by Henry Adams Bellows. St. Paul: Boyd, 1922.

Aquinas, T. *Summa Theologica.* Roma: Marietti, 1950.

Aubert, Jean-Marie. *Sexualite, Amour et Mariage. (Doctrine pour le peuple de Die).* Paris: Beauchesne, 1970.

Bianchi, E. and R. R. Reuther. *From Machismo to Mutuality.* New York: Paulist Press, 1976.

Blonkinsopp, J. *Sexuality and the Christian Tradition.* Ohio: Pflaum Press, 1969.

Brown, P. *Religion and Society in the Age of Saint Augustine.* New York: Harper and Row, 1972.

Cayré, F. A. A. *Patrologie et Histoire de la Theologie* (vols. I, II). Paris, Tourmai, Rome: Desolée et Cie., 1945.

Charue, A. M. et al. *Priesthood and Celibacy.* Milano: Editrice Ancora, 1972.

Cole, W. G. *Sex and Love in the Bible.* New York: Association Press, 1959.

*Corpus Iuris Canonici.* Ex officina Bernhardi Tauchnitz, Lipseae, 2 vols., 1879.

Davis, H. *Moral and Pastoral Theology,* 4 vols. New York: Sheed and Ward, 1936.

*Declaration on Certain Questions Concerning Sexual Ethics.* Rome: Sacred Congregation for the Doctrine of the Faith (January 22, 1976).

Delhaye, P. "The Development of the Medieval Church's Teaching on Marriage," *Concilium,* 55 (1970).

Denzinger, *The Sources of Catholic Dogma.* St. Louis: B. Herder, 1957.

de Riencourt, A. *Sex and Power in History.* New York: Dell Pub. Co., 1974.

Doherty, D. *The Sexual Doctrine of Cardinal Cajetan.* Regensburg: Pustet, 1966.

Ford, J. C. and G. Kelly. *Contemporary Moral Theology,* vol. 2. Westminster, Maryland: The Newman Press, 1963.

Harnack, A. *History of Dogma,* vols. 1-7, tr. by Neil Buchanan. New York: Dover Publications, 1961.

Hoyt, R., ed. *The Birth Control Debate.* Kansas City, Mo.: National Catholic Reporter, 1968.

Hugh of St. Victor. *Hugh of St. Victor on the Sacraments of the Christian Faith,* tr. by Roy Deferrari. Cambridge: The Medieval Academy of America, 1951.

Hugo, John J. *St. Augustine on Nature, Sex and Marriage.* Chicago: Scepter Press, 1969.

Jedin, H. *Geschicte Des Konzils von Trient,* Band III. Freiburg: Herder, 1970.

Kucharek, C. *To Settle Your Conscience.* Huntington, Indiana: Our Sunday Visitor, 1974.

Laeuchli, S. *Power and Sexuality, the Emergence of Canon Law at the Synod of Elvira.* Philadelphia: Temple University Press, 1972.

Lea, H. C. *History of Sacerdotal Celibacy in the Christian Church.* University Books, Inc., 1966.

LeBras, G. "La doctrine du marriage chez les theologions et les canonist dupuis L'an mille," *Dictionnaire de Théologie Catholique.* Paris: Librairie Letouzey et Ane, vol. 9 (1927), cols. 2123-17.

Ligorio, A. *Theologia Moralis,* vol. 7 Mechliniae, 1845.

Lombard, P. *Sententiarum Libri IV,* Ex Typographia Colegii S. Bonaventurae, 1916.

McNeill, H. T. and H. M. Gamer. *Medieval Handbooks of Penance.* New York: Octagon Books, Inc., 1965.

Migne, J. P. *Patrologia Latina.* Parish: Garnier fratres, 1880.

Murphy, F. *Moral Teaching in the Primitive Church* in Guide to the Fathers of the Church Series. New York: Paulist Press, 1968.

Noldin, H. *De Praeceptis.* Barcelona: Herder, 1951.

Noonan, J. *Contraception.* Cambridge, Massachusetts: Harvard Univ. Press, 1965.

Paul VI. *Humanae Vitae.* (Rome: 25 July 1968).

*Population Bulletin: Catholic Perspectives on Population Issues* Washington, D.C.: Population Reference Bureau, vol. 30 (n.d.), no. 6.

Quasten, J. *Musik und Gesang in Den Kulten Der Heidnischen Antike und Christlichen Frühzeit.* Munster: Aschendorffsche Verlagsbushhandlung, 1973.

———, *Patrology II.* Westminster, Maryland: The Newman Press, 1964.

Reuther, R. R., ed. *Religion and Sexism.* New York: Simon and Schuster, 1974.

Schillebeeckx, E. *Marriage: Human Reality and Saving Mystery.* New York: Sheed and Ward, 1965.

Societas Georessina, ed. *Concilium Tridentinum.* Friburgi Brisgoviae, vol. 13 (1964).

Taylor, G. *Sex in History.* New York: Harper and Row, 1970.

Taylor, M., ed. *Sex: Thoughts for Contemporary Christians.* New York: Doubleday and Company, Inc., 1972.

Vermeersch, A. *De Castitate.* Romae: Universita Gregoriana, 1919.

Von Hildebrand, D. *In Defense of Purity.* New York: Sheed and Ward, 1935.

Von Horstein, A. Faller. *Sex-Love Marriage.* New York: Herder and Herder, 1964.

Weber, L. M. "Geschlechtlichkeit," *Lexikon für Theologie und Kirche*, 4.

Willis, J., ed. *The Teachings of the Church Fathers*. New York: Herder and Herder, 1966.

Zalba, M. *Theologiae Moralis Summa*, vol. 2. Matriti: Biblioteca de Autores Christianos, 1957.

Ziegler, J. *Die Ehelehre des Ponitentiarsummen von 1200-1350*. Regensburg: Pustet, 1956.

CHAPTER III

See notes on Chapter III.

CHAPTER IV

Abbott, W. and J. Gallagher. *The Documents of Vatican II*. New York: Association Press, 1966.

Bertocci, P. *Sex, Love and the Person*. Mission, Kansas: Sheed and Ward, 1969.

Davis, H. *Moral and Pastoral Theology*. London: Sheed and Ward, vol. 2, 1936.

*Declaration on Certain Questions Concerning Sexual Ethics*. Rome: Sacred Congregation for the Doctrine of the Faith (January 22, 1976).

Duhamel, J. S. "Psychiatric Aspects of Habitual Sin,"—I. "Theological Aspects," *Proceedings of CTSA* (1956), pp. 130-167.

Fletcher, J. *Situation Ethics: The New Morality*. Philadelphia: Westminster Press, 1966.

Fuchs, J. "The Absoluteness of Moral Terms," *Gregorianum* 52 (1971): 415-58.

Greeley, A. *Love and Play*. Chicago, Ill.: Thomas More Association, 1975.

_____ *Sexual Intimacy*. Chicago, Ill.: Thomas More Press, 1973.

Haring, B. *The Law of Christ*, Trans. by E. G. Kaiser, vol. 1. Westminster, Md.: Newman Press, 1963.

Hayden, J. "Theological and Psychiatric Aspects of Habitual Sin." *Proceedings of CTSA* (1956): 130-67.

Heron, A., ed. *Towards a Quaker View of Sex*. London: Friends Home Service Committee, 1963,

Hoyt, R., ed. *The Birth Control Debate*. Kansas City, MO.: National Catholic Reporter, 1968.

Kennedy, E. *What a Modern Catholic Believes About Sex and Marriage*. Chicago, Ill.: The Thomas More Press, 1975.

McCormick, R. "Notes on Moral Theology," *Theological Studies*, 36 (March 1975): 85-100.

————, "Ambiguity in Moral Choice," Washington, D.C.: Kennedy Center for Bioethics, Georgetown University, 1973.

Milhaven, J. "Conjugal Sexual Love," *Theological Studies*, 35 (December, 1974): 692-710.

Neuman, M. "Friendship Between Men and Women in Religious Life," *Sisters Today* 46 (October, 1974): 89-92.

Outka, G. and P. Ramsey. *Norm and Context in Christian Ethics.* London: Friends Home Service Committee, 1963.

Roach, R. "Sex in Christian Morality," *Way* 11 (1971): 148-61, 235-42.

Robinson, J. A. *Honest to God.* London: SCM Press, 1963.

*Sex and Morality: A Report Presented to the British Council of Churches.* Philadelphia: Fortress Press. (October, 1966).

Strojnowski, J. *Eros i Czlowiek.* Znak: Krakow, 1976.

Valente, M. *Sex, the Radical View of a Catholic Theologian.* New York: Bruce, 1970.

Vorgrimler, H. *Commentary on the Documents of Vatican II*, vol. 5. New York: Herder, 1969.

CHAPTER V

*Sexuality and Personhood*

Davis, H. *Moral and Pastoral Theology*, vol. 2. London: Sheed and Ward, 1936.

*Declaration on Certain Questions Concerning Sexual Ethics*, Rome: Sacred Congregation for the Doctrine of the Faith (January 22, 1976).

Smolenski, S. "Norma Personalistyczna," *Analecta Cracoviensia* 3 (1971): 311-20.

Wojtyła, K. *Miłość i Odpowiedzialność.* Znak: Kraków, 1962.

*Marital Sexuality*

Abbott, W. and J. Gallagner. *The Documents of Vatican II.* New York: Association Press, 1966.

Bernardin, Most Rev. Joseph L. Letter of. Washington, D.C.: National Conference of Catholic Bishops (April 14, 1975).

Billings, J. *Natural Family Planning: The Ovulation Method*, Collegeville, Minn.: Liturgical Press, 1972.

Curran, C. *Contemporary Problems in Moral Theology.* Notre Dame, Ind.: Fides Publishers, 1970.

Dedek, J. *Contemporary Medical Ethics.* New York: Sheed and Ward, 1975.

*Ethical and Religious Directives for Catholic Health Facilities.* Washington, D.C.: USCCm 1971.

Haring, B. *Medical Ethics*, ed. by L. J. Gabrielle, Notre Dame, Ind.: Fides Publ., 1972.

———, *Contraception: Authority and Dissent*, ed. by C. E. Curran. New York: Herder and Herder, 1969.

———. *What Does Christ Want*. South Bend, Indiana: Ave Maria Press, 1968.

Hoyt, R., ed. *The Birth Control Debate*. Kansas City, Mo.: NCR, 1968.

Kelly, G. "Pope Pius XII and The Principle of Totality," *Theological Studies* 16 (1955): 373-96.

Kippley, J. and S. *The Art of Natural Family Planning*. Cincinnati: The Couple to Couple League International Inc., 1975.

Kubiś, A., ed. "Les Fondements de la Doctrine de L'Eglise Concernant les Principes de la vie Conjugale," *Analecta Cracoviensia*, 1 (1969): 194-230.

Noldin, H. "De Sexto Praecepto et De Usu Matrimonii," *Theologiae Moralis*, Austria, 1922.

Paolillo, L. and A. Walsh. *Emerging Attitudes Toward Alternate Family Forms*. Portland, Oregon. 13 April 1972.

*Policy Manual for Committee to Advise on Requests for Obstetrical/Gunaecological Sterilization Procedures*. London, Ontario: St. Joseph's Hospital, 1973.

Pope Paul VI, *Humanae Vitae*. Rome (July 25, 1968).

Pope Pius XI, *Casti Connubii*. Rome (1930).

Schillebeeckx, E. *Marriage Human Reality and Saving Mystery*. New York: Sheed and Ward, 1965.

Schulte, J. *The Phenomena of Child Free Marriage in American Society Today: A Theological Appraisal*, incomplete dissertation, Marquette University.

Skrzydlewski, W. "Problem Celów Małżeństwa," *Analecta Cracoviensia* 3 (1971): 321-61.

Thompson, T. D. "Some Legal Problems in the Book of Ruth," *Vetus Testamentum* 18 (1968).

Uricchio, W., ed. *Proceedings of a Research Conference on Natural Family Planning*. Washington, D.C.: The Human Life Foundation, 1973.

Vorgrimler, H., ed. *Commentary on the Documents of Vatican II*, vol. 5. New York: Herder and Herder, 1969.

Wassmer, T. *Christian Ethics for Today*. Milwaukee: Bruce, 1969.

*Variant Patterns*

Bell, R. R. and M. Gordon, ed. *The Social Dimension of Human Sexuality*. Boston: Little, Brown and Co., 1972.

Constantine, L. L. and J. *Group Marriage*. New York: Macmillan, 1973.

Casler, L. *Is Marriage Necessary?* New York:. Human Sciences Press, 1974.

Delora, J. and J. *Intimate Life Styles*. Pacific Palisades, Calif.: Goodyear, 1972.

Ethical Forum, *The Humanist* March/April 1974, and Readers Forum, July/Aug. 1974.

Gagnon, J. and W. Simon, ed. *The Sexual Scene*. Aldine Publishing Co., 1970.

Juhasz, McCreary A., ed. *Sexual Development and Behavior*. Homewood, Ill.: The Dorsey Press, 1973.

McCary, J. L. *Human Sexuality*. New York: Van Nostrand Co., 1973.

Morrison, E. S. and V. Borosage. *Human Sexuality: Contemporary Perspectives*. Palo Alto, Calif.: National Press Books, 1973.

Roy, R. and D. *Honest Sex*. New York: New American Library, 1968.

Schur, E. M. ed. *The Family and the Sexual Revolution*. London: George Allen and Unwin, Ltd., 1966.

*Non-Marital Sexuality*

Agterberg, M. *Ecclesia-virgo. Etudes sur la virginité de l'eglise et des fideles chez Saint Augustin*. Heverle-Louvain: Institut Historique Augustinien, 1960.

Aquinas, T. *Summa Theologica*, American Edition. New York: Benziger, 1947.

Balz, H. "Sexualitat und christliche Existenz," *Kerygma und Dogma* 14 (1968): 263-306.

Bassett, W. and Huizing, P., eds. *Celibacy in the Church*. New York: Herder and Herder, 1972.

Blenkinsopp, J. *Celibacy, Ministry, Church*. New York: Herder and Herder, 1968.

Bouranna, F. *La virginité chrétienne*. Montreal: L'Immaculee Conception, 1952.

Carre, A. M. Intro. *Celibacy: Success or Failure?*, trans. by Una Morrissey. Cork, Ireland: Mercier Press, 1960.

Colaianni, J., ed. *Married Priests and Married Nuns*. New York: McGraw-Hill, 1968.

Colloque du Centre Catholique des Medecins Francais. *Celibat et Sexualité*. Paris: Editions du Seuil, 1970.

Coppens, J., A. M., Charue et autres. *Sacerdoce et Celibat*. Gembloux: Editions Duculot, 1971.

Crouzel, H. *Virginité et Mariage selon Origene*. Paris: Desclée de Brouwer, 1962.

Davis, H. *Moral and Pastoral Theology*, vol. 2. London: Sheed and Ward, 1936.

de Kruijf. *The Bible on Sexuality*. Wisconsin: St. Norbert Abbey Press, 1966.

Denzinger, H. and A. Schönmetzer. *Enchiridion Symbolorum*, 32nd edition. New York: Herder, 1963.

Ford, J. Hassingberd. *A Trilogy on Wisdom and Celibacy*. Notre Dame: University of Notre Dame Press, 1967.

Francoeur, R. *Eve's New Rib*. New York: Harcourt Brace Jovanovich, 1972.

Frazier, C. A. "Origins of Clerical Celibacy in the Western Church," *Church History* 41 (June 1972): 149-67.

Frein, G., ed. *Celibacy: The Necessary Option*. New York: Herder and Herder, 1968.

Fuchs, J. *De Castitate et Ordine Sexuali*, 3rd edition. Rome: Gregoriana, 1963.

Funk, F. S. *Celibat und Priesterehe im Christlichen Altertum*, in *Kirchengeschlichtliche Abhandlungen und Untersuchungen*. 3 vols. Paderborn, 1897-1907.

Galot, J. "La motivation evangelique du celibat," *Gregorianum*. 53 (1972): 731-58.

Goergen, D. *The Sexual Celibate*. Evanston: The Seabury Press, 1975.

Görres, Ida Friederika. *Is Celibacy Outdated,* trans. by B. Waldstein-Wartenberg. Cork, Ireland: Mercier Press, 1965.

Greeley, A. *The Catholic Priest in the United States: Sociological Investigations*. Washington, D.C.: The USCC, 1972.

Gründel, J. "Voreheliche Sexualität aus der Sicht der Moraltheologen," *Lieben ver der Ehe*, F. Oertel, ed., Essen: Fredebeul und Koenen, 1969.

Gryson, R. *Les Origines du Celibat Ecclésiastique du Premier au Septieme Siecle*. Gembloux: Editions J. Duculot, 1970.

Guitard, A. and Marie-George Bulteau. *Bibliographie internationale sur le sacerdoce et le ministère*. Montreal: Centre de Documentation et de Recherche, 1971.

Harkx, P. *The Fathers on Celibacy*, L. McGraw, ed.; trans. by International Publishing Consultant. De Pere, Wisconsin, 1968.

Hermand, P. *The Priest: Celibate or Married?* Baltimore: Helicon, 1965.

Kean, P. "The Meaning and Functioning of Sexuality in the Lives of Celibates and Virgins," *Review for Religious* 34 (1975): 277-314.

Klimisch, M. J. *The One Bride.* New York: Sheed and Ward, 1968.

Küng, H. *Life in the Splirit.* New York: Sheed and Ward, 1968.

Laeuchli, S. *Power and Sexuality.* Philadelphia: Temple University Press, 1972.

Lea, H. *History of Sacerdotal Celibacy in the Christian Church,* 4th ed., revised. London: Watts, 1932.

Legrand, L. *The Biblical Doctrine of Virginity.* New York: Sheed and Ward, 1963.

L'Huillier, P. "Clerical Celibacy," trans. by G. Every. *Eastern Churches Review,* vol. 3 (Spring, 1971).

Liguori, A. *Theologia Moralis.* Rome: Vaticana, 1905.

Lombard, P. *Libri IV Sententiarum.* Florence: St. Bonaventure, 1916.

Matura, T. *Celibacy and Community: The Gospel Foundations for Religious Life,* trans. by P. J. Oligny. Chicago: Franciscan Herald Press, 1968.

Matura, T. "Le Célibat dans le Nouveau Testament d'après l'exégèse recente," *Nouvelle Revue Théologique* 97 (June, July-August, 1975).

McCary, J. *Human Sexuality.* New York: Van Nostrand, 1973.

McKenna, M. *Women of the Church.* New York: P. J. Kenedy, 1967.

Morrison, E. and V. Borosage. *Human Sexuality: Contemporary Perspectives.* Palo Alto, Calif: National Press Books, 1973.

National Conference of Catholic Bishops. *Statement of Celibacy.* Washington, D.C. (Nov. 14, 1969).

Noldin, H. *De Sexto Praecepto et de Usu Matrimonii.* Rome: Pustet, 1920.

Oraison, Marc. *The Celibate Condition and Sex,* trans. by L. Mayhew. New York: Sheed and Ward, 1967.

Pope Paul VI. *On Priestly Celibacy* (Sacerdotalis caelibatus), Washington, D.C.: USCC (June 24, 1967).

Perrin, J. *Virginity,* trans. by K. Gorder. Westminster, Maryland: Newman Press, 1956.

Phipps, W. *Was Jesus Married?* New York: Harper and Row, 1970.

Raguin, Y. *Célibat pour notre temps. Supplément à Vie Chrétienne,* n. 151 (November 1972).

Ramsey, P. "A Christian Approach to the Question of Sexual Relations outside of Marriage," *Journal of Religion* 45 (1965): 100-18.

Roy, R. and D. *Honest Sex*. New York: The New American Library, 1968.

Roy, R. "Is Monogamy Outdated?" *The Humanist* 30 (March, April, 1970): 19-26.

Schillebeeckx, E. *Celibacy*, trans. by C.A.L. Jarrate. New York: Sheed and Ward, 1968.

Schlegelberger, B. *Vor- und Aussereheliche Geschlechtsverkehr.* Remschied: St. Paulus Mission, 1970.

Semple, M. and M. McGriffin, and B. Puzon, "Chastity and Celibacy," *Sisters Today*, 43 (June-July, 1972).

Snoek, C. J. "Marriage and the Institutionalization of Sexual Relations," in *The Future of Marriage as an Institution*, F. Bockle, ed., *Concilium*. New York: Herder and Herder, 1970.

Strätling, B. "Lieben vor der Ehe?—Zur Frage vorehelicher Sexualbezienhungen," *Moral braucht Normen*, F. Schlosser, ed. Limburg: Lahn, 1970, pp. 135-62.

Thomas, J. L. "The Catholic Tradition for Responsibility in Sexual Ethics," *Sexual Ethics and Christian Responsibility*, J. C. Wynn, ed. New York: Association Press, 1970, 114-37.

Trevett, R. F. *The Church and Sex*. Twentieth Century Encyclopedia of Catholicism. New York: Hawthorn Books, 1960.

Vacandard, E. "Célibat ecclésiastique," *Dictionnaire de théologie catholique*, vol. 2, cols. 2068-88.

Vermeersch, A. *De Castitate et de Vitiis Contrariis*, Rome, 1921.

Von Hildebrand, D. *Celibacy and the Crisis of Faith*, trans by J. Crosby. Chicago: Franciscan Herald Press, 1971.

Wade, J. *Chastity, Sexuality and Personal Hangups*. Staten Island, New York: Alba House, 1971.

*Way*, Supplement no. 10—Celibacy (Summer 1970).

*Homosexuality*

*A Guide to Formation in Priestly Celibacy*. Washington: USCC, 1974.

Bailey, D. S. *Homosexuality and the Western Christian Tradition*. London: Longmans, Green and Co., 1955.

Baum, G. "Catholic Homosexuals," *Commonweal* 99 (1974): 479-81.

*Blue Book—1970*. Chicago, Ill: General Assembly of the U.S. Presbyterian Church in the United States of America, 1970.

Buckley, M. *Morality and the Homosexual, A Catholic Approach to a Moral Problem*. Westminster: Newman Press, 1959.

Cole, W. *Sex and Love in the Bible*. New York: Association Press, 1959.

Curran, C. *Catholic Moral Theology in Dialogue*. Notre Dame, Ind.: Fides Press, 1972.

*Declaration on Certain Questions Concerning Sexual Ethics*. Rome: Sacred Congregation for the Doctrine of the Faith (January 22, 1976).

*Dieu les aime tels qu'ils sont: Pastorale pours homophiles*. trans. from the Dutch by Hans Witte. Points Chauds: Fayard, 1972.

Episcopal Diocese of Michigan. *The Report and Recommendations of the Commission on Homosexuality*. Detroit, Mich (July, 1973).

Epstein, L. *Sex Laws and Customs in Judaism*. New York: KTAV, 1968.

Gottschalk, J. B. F., ed. *Kirche und Homosexualität*. Munich: Eric Wewel Verlag, 1973.

*Homosexualité*. trans. from the Dutch by Y. Huon. Tours: Maison Mame, 1967.

Jones, K. *Toward a Christian Understanding of the Homosexual*. New York: Association Press, 1966.

Karlen, A. *Sexuality and Homosexuality*. New York: W. W. Norton, 1971.

Kennedy, E. *The New Sexuality Myths Fables and Hang-ups*. New York: Doubleday and Co., 1972.

Kuss, O. *Der Römerbrief*. Regensburg: Pustet, 1963.

Livingston, J. M., ed., *National Institute of Mental Health Task Force on Homosexuality: Final Report and Background*. Rockville, Md.: National Institute of Mental Health, 1972.

Marmor, J., ed., *Sexual Inversion*. New York: Basic Books, Inc., 1965.

National Institute on Mental Health. *Final Report of Task Force on Homosexuality: The Hooker Report*. Chevy Chase: National Institute of Health, 1969.

McNeill, J. "The Christian Male Homosexual." *Homiletic and Pastoral Review* 70 (1970): 667-77; 747-58; 828-36.

_____ *The Church and The Homosexual*. Kansas City: Sheed, Andrews and McMeel, 1976.

Noth, M. *The Laws in the Penteteuch and Other Studies*. Philadelphia, Fortress Press, 1967.

Noth, M. *Leviticus, A Commentary*. London: SCM Press, 1965.

Nouwen, H. *Intimacy*. Notre Dame, Ind.: Fides Publ., 1969.

Phillips, A. *Ancient Israel's Criminal Law, A New Approach to the*

*Decalogue*. Oxford: Basil Blackwell, 1970.

*Principles to Guide Confessors in Questions of Homosexuality.* Washington, D.C.: National Conf. of Catholic Bishops, 1973.

Rad, G. Von, *Genesis, A Commentary.* Philadelphia: Westminster Press, 1961.

Rashke, R. A series of articles in the NCR on Homosexuality. Kansas City, Mo.: NCR (March 26, April 2, 9, 23. 1976).

Schoeps, H. & J. "Homosexualität und Bibel," *Zeitschrift für Evangelische Ethik,* vol. 6 (1962), pp. 369-74.

Sengers, W. J. *Se reconnaitre homosexuel? Vers une situation nouvelle.* trans. from the Dutch by M. Claes. Tours: Maison Mame, 1970.

Snaith, N. H. *Leviticus and Numbers. The Century Bible,* London, Nelson, 1967.

Thielicke, H. *The Ethics of Sex.* New York. Harper and Row, 1964.

*The Wolfenden Report,* Report of the Committee on Homosexual Offenses and Prostitution. New York: Stein and Day, 1963.

Weinberg, M. *Society and the Healthy Homosexual.* New York: St. Martin's Press, 1972.

Weinberg, M. and A. Bell. *Homosexuality: An Annotated Bibliography.* New York: Harper and Row, 1972.

Williams, L. *Is Gay Good?* D. Oberholtzer, ed. Philadelphia: The Westminster Press, 1971.

Zalba, M. *Theologiae Moralis Summa,* vol. 1. Madrid: Biblioteca de Autores Cristianas, 1957.

*Masturbation*

Abate, R. *Sex Sanity in the Modern World—A Guidebook for Everyone.* Missouri: Liguorian Pamphlet Books, 1975.

*A Guide to Formation in Priestly Celibacy.* Washington: USCC, 1974.

Bausch, W. *A Boy's Sex Life: Handbook of Basic Information and Guidance.* South Bend, Ind.: Fides, 1969.

Curran, C. *A New Look at Christian Morality.* Notre Dame, Ind.: Fides Press, 1968.

*Declaration on Certain Questions Concerning Sexual Ethics.* Rome: Sacred Congregation for the Doctrine of the Faith (January 22, 1976).

Dedek, J. *Contemporary Sexual Morality.* New York: Sheed and Ward, 1971.

deKruijf, T. C. *The Bible on Sexuality.* Wisconsin: St. Norbert Abbey Press, 1966.

Desinger, H. and A. Schonmetzer. *Enchiridion Symbolorum,* 33rd ed. Rome: Herder, 1965.

Fuchs, J. *De Castitate et Ordine Sexuali*, 3rd ed. Roma: Gregoriana, 1963.

Noldin, H. *De Sexto Praecepto et De Usu Matrimonii*. Austria, 1922.

*Pornography and Obscenity*

Clor, H., ed. *Censorship and Freedom of Expression*. Chicago: Rand McNally and Co., 1971.

————, *Obscenity and Public Morality*. Chicago: University of Chicago Press, 1969.

Coogan, J. "Some Meanings of Pornography," *Marriage* 51 (February 1969): 25-9.

Kilpatrick, J. *The Smut Peddlers*. Garden City, N.Y.: Doubleday and Co., 1960.

Klausler, A. *Censorship, Obscenity, and Sex*. St. Louis: Concordia Publ. House, 1967.

Kyle-Keith, R. *The High Price of Pornography*. Washington, D.C.: Public Affairs Press, 1961.

Lawrence, D. H. *Pornography and Obscenity, in Sex, Literature and Censorship*. New York: Harper and Row, 1953.

Lockhart, W. and R. McClure. "Censorship of Obscenity: The Developing Constitutional Standards," *Minnesota Law Review* 45 (November 1960): 5-121.

Mead, M. "Sex and Censorship in Contemporary Society," *New World Writings*. New York: The American Library of World Literature, 1953.

"Pornography: The Ethical Aesthetic Dimension," *Continuum* 5 (Summer 1967): 304-6.

*The Report of the Commission on Obscenity and Pornography*. New York: Bantam, 1970.

Robinson, J. *Christian Freedom in a Permissive Society*. Philadelphia: Westminster Press, 1970.

Ryan, M. and J. Julian. *Love and Sexuality: A Christian Approach*. New York: Holt, Rinehart and Winston, 1967.

*Programs of Sex Education*

Arnsteum, H. *Your Growing Child and Sex*. Avon Paperbacks.

Barnhouse, R. and U. Holmes, III, eds. *Male and Female*. New York: Seabury Press, 1976.

Bass, M. S. "Marriage, Parenthood and Prevention of Pregnancy," *American Journal of Mental Deficiency* 68 (1963): 318-33.

———— "Marriage, Parenthood and Prevention of Pregnancy for the Mentally Retarded," *Eugenic Quarterly* XI (June 1964): 96-111.

————, ed. *Sexual Rights and Responsibilities of the Mentally Retarded.* Ardmore, Pennsylvania: Author, 1973.

Bleinstein, R. "Getrubte Aufklarung: Zu neueren Publikationem uber die Sexualerziehung," *Stimmen der Zeit* (June 1972).

Bulckens, J. "Seksuele epvoeding en voorlichting in de lagere school," *Collentanea mechliniensia* 55 (1970).

Burger, R., ed. *Sexualerziehung in Unterricht an weiterfuhrenden Schulen.* Freiburg: Herder, 1970.

Burleson, D. "Use and Abuse of Audio-Visuals in Sex Education," *Siecus Report* (March 1974).

————. "Who is a Sex Educator—the Certification Dilemma?" *Siecus Report* (July 1974).

Calderone, M. "Sex Education for the Society: The Real Stumbling Block," *Pastoral Psychology* 21 (November 1970).

The Child Study Association of America. *What to Tell Your Child About Sex.* New York: Pocket Books, 1970.

Committee on Sex Education—Diocese of Rochester. *Education in Love—Handbook for Parents.* New York: Paulist Press, 1971.

Corrigan, J. "Sex Education—A Nonprint Bibliography," *Catholic Library World* 43 (November 1971): 141-8.

Cosse, L. "L'enseignement privé français voudrait dispenser une véritable education sexuelle," *Informationes catholiques internationales* (15 February 1974).

Dillon, V. and W. Imbiorski. *Your Child's Sex Life.* Chicago: Delaney Publ., 1966.

Driver, H., ed. *Sex Guidance for Your Child.* P.O. Box 3222, Madison: Monsona Publications, 1960.

"Education in Love?" *Social Justice Review* 65. (September, 1972): 162-67.

Flood, J. "The Human Body," *Homiletic and Pastoral Review* 74 (July 1974): 50-7.

Fox, R. "Sex Education without Morality," *Priest* 29 (Sept. 1973): 19-22.

Fraser, S., ed. *Sex, Schools and Society: International Perspectives.*

Gastonguay, P. "Sex for Salvation," *Today's Parish* 5 (Nov.-Dec. 1973).

Gavern, A. "Non-print Media on Sex Education (Grades K-6," *Collectanea mechliniensia.* 55 (1970).

Giovanazzi, G. "Educazione sessuale nella scuola: Come? quando? da chi?" *Religione e scuola* (February 1973).

*Growth Patterns and Sex Education: An Updated Bibliography, Pre-School to Adulthood.* Kent, Ohio: American School Health Association, 1972.

*Gruppi misti e educazione alla castita.* Turin: Gribaudi, 1970.

"Guidelines for Sex Education (issued by the bishops of New Jersey)" *Catholic Mind* 69 (April 1971): 7-10.

Harrison, B. Grizzuti. *Unlearning the Lie: Sexism in School.* New York: Liveright, 1973.

Hastings, V. and M. Moore. "Sex Education and the Role of the Doctor," *Catholic Medical Quarterly* (1973).

Haughton, R. *Religious Education and Sex Education.* New York: Paulist Press, 1973.

―――, "Sex Education and Religion," *New Catholic World* 215 (Jan.-Feb. 1972).

Howell, J. "Responsible Sex Education," *Review and Expositor* 48 (1971).

"Humane Sexualitat als Aufgabe des Sexualpadogogik," *Diakonia.* Austria (1971).

Italy, Bishops of Lombardo and Triveneto. "Principi morali e orientamenti pastorali perll'educazione sessuale," *Palestria del clero.* (1974).

Johnson, E. *Love and Sex in Plain Language.* Philadelphia: Lippincott, 1973.

Johnson, W. "Sex Education and the Mentally Retarded," *The Journal of Sex Research*, vol. 5.

Kentler, H. *Sexualerziehung.* Reinbek: Rowehlt, 1970.

Kratter, F. E. and G. Thorne. "Sex Education of Retarded Children," *American Journal of Mental Deficiency* 62 (1957).

Larsen, E. *Not My Kid.* Missouri: Liguorian Paperbacks.

Lentz, G. *Raping Our Children: The Sex Education Scandal.* New Rochelle: Arlington, 1972.

Leonfeld, M. "Sexual-Ethik: Eine Anfrange an Religions-padagogen und Moraltheologen sur Sexualerziehung der katholischen Kirche," *Religionspadagogik an berufsbildenden Schulen*, 1974.

Likoudis, J. "The Sex Educationists Fight God," *Social Justice Review* 64 (1971): 261-7.

Marcotte, M. "Amour, attente et sacrifice: Pour une education chrétienne des jeunes à l'amour," *Relations* (1972).

Mok, P. *Pushbutton Parents and the Schools.* Laurel Paperback.

Myre, J. and G. St-Denis. " 'Homme et femme il les créa' " Un document catéchetique sur la exualité destiné aux adolescents de 15-16 ans," *Communauté chrétienne* (January-April, 1971).

O'Reilly, S. "Formal Sex Education: Fact and Fancy," *Homiletic and Pastoral Review* 73 (April 1973): 20-9.

"Parents and Sex Education," *Pastoral Life* 19 (December 1970).

Peck, J. R. and Stephens, W. B. "Marriage of Young Adult Male

Retardates" *American Journal of Mental Deficiency* 69 (May 1965): 818-27.

Pole, K. F. "The Doctor's Role in Sex Education," *Linacre Quarterly.* 37 (November 1970): 262-67.

Sabagh, G. and R. B. Edgerton. "Sterilized Mental Defectives Look at Eugenic Sterilization," *Eugenic Quarterly.* 9 (1962): 213-22.

Salinas, J. "La formacion en la castidad," *Palabra* (October 1970).

Salk, Dr. L. *What Every Child Would Like His Parents to Know.* New York: Warner Paperback Division, 1973.

Sallee, L. K. "Sex Education is Your Responsibility," *Marriage and Family Living* 56 (September 1974): 2-5.

"Sexualerziehung—Entwicklung und personale Integration der Sexualitat," *Arzt und Christ* (1972): 8-17.

"Sexuality and Sex Education: An Interview with Mary Calderone," *Humanist* 33 (May-June 1973).

Sex Information and Education Council of the United States, ed. *Sexuality and Man.* New York: Charles Scribner's Sons, 1970.

S.I.E.C.U.S. *A Resource Guide in the Education for the Mentally Retarded,* 1971.

Shaw, C. H. and G. H. Wright. "The Married Mental Defective: A Follow-up Study," *The Luscet* 30 (1960): 273.

Thomas, L. and N. Moreada, eds. *Love, Marriage and Morals.* New York: Readers Digest Life Value Series, 1971.

Thorne, G. D., "Sex Education of Mentally Retarded Girls," *American Journal of Mental Deficiency*, vol. 62 (       ).

Tierney, J. "Sex Education Books for Children," *Catholic Library World* 42 (April 1971): 499-503; (May-June 1971): 567-70.

Tormey, J. "Sex and the Teenage Girl," *Religion Teacher's Journal* (November-December, 1972).

Trevijano, P. "Orientacion cristiana de la sexualidad juvenil," *Sal terrae* (1972).

Venditti-Milot, R. and H. Acoulon. "Catechèse et sexualité—á propos d'un manuel contesté," *Relations* (1973).

Walker, W. L. "Problems of Sex Education," *Catholic Medical Quarterly* (1972).

Whitehead, K. D. "From Abortion to Sex Education," *Homiletic and Pastoral Review* 74 (November 1973): 60-9.

Whitehouse, M. "Sex Education," *Learning for Living* (September 1970).

Wilke, J. and B. *The Wonder of Sex: How to Teach Children.* Cincinnati: Hiltz Publ., 1964.

# Appendix 1
## METHODS OF CONTRACEPTION

| METHOD | EFFECTIVENESS | REQUIREMENTS | MODE OF OPERATION |
|---|---|---|---|
| Birth Control Pill | .5 - 3% *<br><br>* No. of pregnancies per yr. per 100 women using the method. | Take a pill daily for 20 (21) days, and take placebos or no pills for the next 7 days. Do not break the 27 (28) day cycle. Repeat the process every 27 (28) days. There are more than 20 brands of the pill available consisting of varying amounts of synthetic estrogen and progesterone. Physician's prescription is needed. | Suppresses the ovaries preventing ovulation. Synthetic estrogen prevents the pituitary gland from releasing a follicle stimulating hormone (which stimulates growth of egg) and a luteinizing hormone (which stimulates ovulation). Synthetic progesterone changes normal mucus pattern, making sperm migration to uterus difficult, and changes uterine lining preventing normal implantation of fertilized egg. |
| Ovulation | .5 - 5% * | Abstain from all sexual contact on fertile mucus days and three days after last fertile mucus. | Vagina is free of sperm from time that fertile mucus may keep them alive (3-5 days) till two days following ovulation. |
| Progesterone Pill | 2 - 10% * | Take a progesterone pill at the same hour every day. Doctor's prescription is needed. | Changes mucus, making sperm migration to uterus difficult; changes uterine lining preventing implantation. |
| Intra Uterine Device | 2 - 10% * | IUD is placed inside uterus through cervical canal by a physician. Local anesthesia may be used. Woman checks weekly for IUD presence. | Irritates uterine lining preventing normal implantation. Stimulates entry of white cells which destroy fertilized egg. Increases uterine muscle motion forcing out fertilized egg. Copper acts as poison, preventing normal division of cells. Copper makes tubes contract more, forcing egg to enter uterus prematurely. |
| Diaphragm | 2 - 15% * | Individually fitted diaphragm & cream placed inside vagina. Need prescription for diaphragm. | Diaphragm blocks entrance of uterus. Spermicidal cream applied to diaphragm kills sperm in vagina. |

| | | | |
|---|---|---|---|
| Condom | 2 - 15% * | Rubber is unrolled over erect penis before any flow of semen. | Prevents sperm from entering vagina. |
| Basal Temperature | 3 - 15% * | Have sexual contact only on pre-determined "safe" days. | Absence of sperm when egg is fertile. |
| Foams, Jellies, etc. | 5 - 25%* | Foam, jelly, etc, is inserted into vagina before ejaculation. | Kills sperm in the vagina. One application is effective for one ejaculation. |
| Rhythm | 5 - 25% * | Abstain from all sexual contact on predetermined "unsafe" days. | Absence of sperm when egg is fertile. |
| Withdrawal | 10 - 40% * | Ejaculation occurs away from the area of the vagina. | Sperm do not enter vagina. |
| Morning After Pill (DES) | | Within 24 hrs. after ejaculation take pill every 12 hrs. for 5 days. | NOT KNOWN. It is known that metabolism is violently affected. |
| Sterilization | | Physician cuts and ties vas deferens (male) or fallopian tubes (female). | No sperm (male) or egg (female) can reach the uterus. |
| Abstinence | | Total abstention from marital intercourse. | Sperm and ovum never meet. |

# METHODS OF CONTRACEPTION (continued)

| METHOD | ADDITIONAL INFORMATION | OTHER CONSIDERATIONS |
|---|---|---|
| Birth Control Pill | Normal body metabolism changes when using the pill. The following have been experienced: Increase in rate of production of enzymes and blood clotting proteins (may result in thromboembolism, pulmonary embolism, and stroke). Rise in blood pressure. Increase of cholesterol and other fats in blood stream. Different use of proteins causes a deficiency resulting in depression. Bile fluid combines with other chemicals forming solid gall stones. Reduction of insulin hormone hastens onset of diabetes. Breast milk is decreased in quality and quantity, and will contain hormones. Amount and kind of cortisol is altered causing side effects like: nausea, fluid retention, breast growth, weight gain, oily skin, spotting, decreased bleeding, etc. Pregnancy is not advised for 1 yr. after last pill. | Uncertainty and anxiety regarding long-range effects upon human system; unknown long-range genetic implications; requires relatively intelligent and responsible people to follow directions faithfully; fear of possible pregnancy or other consequences (thrombophlebitis); diminished peace of mind and affects capacity for interrelationship. |
| Ovulation | Effectiveness is determined by couple's ability to abstain five to eight consecutive days guided by mucus symptom. Recognizing fertile mucus is easily learned. | Possible stress and tension on marital relationship resulting from required abstinence or greater risk of pregnancy. Advantages: economical, no biological interference, prescription unnecessary though competent guidance advised. |
| Progesterone Pill | Synthetic progesterone can cause irregular cycles, spotting between cycles, or no menstruation. Delay of a few hours in taking the pill lessens its effectiveness. | Same considerations as with birth control pill with realization that this form produces fewer undesirable consequences but is less effective. |
| Intra Uterine Device | Closed ring and stainless steel IUD's are no longer used. Plastic IUD is generally used. Plastic IUD covered with fine copper wire recently developed. IUD may result in: infection of uterus and fallopian tubes, perforation of uterine wall, miscarriages, heavier menstrual bleeding, cramps, irregular bleeding, backaches. Insertion of IUD is usually painful and followed by cramps. Spontaneous explusion of IUD occurs in 10-12% of women in first year. Replace plastic IUD within 5 years, copper IUD within 2 years. If pregnancy occurs, doctors advise removal of IUD. | Scientific doubt regarding precise manner in which IUD achieves its effect; possibly an abortifacient rather than a contraceptive; long-range medical and genetic effects unknown; increased moral concern in view of possible destruction of human life. |
| Diaphragm | Allergic reaction may be experienced by either partner. Insert 2 hours or less before and keep in place 6 hours or more after ejaculation. Repeat for each ejaculation. | Greater risk of pregnancy resulting in greater fear with corresponding effect on peace of mind and capacity for interrelationship: too |

great an inconvenience to insert or aesthetically unacceptable for some. Advantages: simplicity, economy, minimal undesirable side-effects.

| Method | Description | Considerations |
|---|---|---|
| Condom | Local irritation may occur. Condom should be carefully removed after ejaculation and before erection subsides. | Interferes with spontaneity and naturalness of the love-act; aesthetically and psychologically unacceptable to some, anxiety resulting from greater risk of pregnancy; economic expense. |
| Basal Temperature | Ovulation is determined by wife's basal body temperature rise (difficult to detect). Abstain from 5th day of period till 2 days after this rise. | Same consideration as with ovulation. |
| Foams, Jellies, etc. | Allergic reaction may be experienced by either partner. Insert 1 hour or less before and let remain 6 hours or more after ejaculation. | Same considerations as with condom. |
| Rhythm | Ovulation is estimated from a history of past cycles. For an average 27 to 30 day cycle abstain from 9th day following period until 20th day. | Same considerations as with ovulation method but decidedly less effective and requiring longer period of abstinence; unreliable with irregular cycle. |
| Withdrawal | Semen may flow unnoticed from penis before and after ejaculation. Sperm deposited near vagina can work their way up to the uterus. | Least effective and psychologically frustrating often rendering whole sexual relationship unsatisfying. |
| Morning After Pill (DES) | Contains synthetic estrogen DES (Diethylstilbestrol). Causes severe nausea, vomiting, and metabolism change. Serious complications may result. | Strong contrary medical considerations to user and offspring; long-range effects unknown; possibly abortive. |
| Sterilization | In most cases this process is irreversible. Injury to blood vessels or other organs is possible during the sterilization procedure. | Radical termination of procreative freedom of response; major surgical procedure for women; possible adverse after-effects for men; possible psychological and moral consequence affecting marital relationship. |
| Abstinence | No harmful physical effects as such but this method is generally regarded as impractical for any extended period of time since it often adversely affects the interpersonal relationship of the couple. | Most effective but most difficult to implement without harmful effect on marriage relationship. |

# APPENDIX 2

## A DOCUMENT ABOUT STERILIZATION IN CATHOLIC HOSPITALS

Responses to Questions of the Episcopal Conference

of North America (Prot. 2027/69)

### UNOFFICIAL TRANSLATION

This Sacred Congregation has diligently considered not only the problem of contraceptive sterilization for therapeutic purposes but also the opinions indicated by different people toward a solution, and the conflicts relative to requests for cooperation in such sterilizations in Catholic hospitals. The Congregation has resolved to respond to these questions in this way:

1. Any sterilization which of itself, that is, of its own nature and condition, has the sole immediate effect of rendering the generative faculty incapable of procreation, is to be considered direct sterilization, as the term is understood in the declarations of the Pontifical Magisterium, especially of Pius XII.[1] Therefore, notwithstanding any subjectively right intention of those whose actions are prompted by the care or prevention of physical or mental illness which is foreseen or feared as a result of pregnancy, such sterilization remains absolutely forbidden according to the doctrine of the Church. And indeed the sterilization of the faculty itself is forbidden for an even graver reason than the sterilization of individual acts, since it induces a state of sterility in the person which is almost always irreversible. Neither can any mandate of public authority, which would seek to impose direct sterilization as necessary for the common good, be invoked, for such sterilization damages the dignity and inviolability of the human person.[2] Likewise, neither can one invoke the principle of totality in this case, in virtue of which principle interference with organs is justified for the greater good of the person; sterility intended in itself is not oriented to the integral good of the person as rightly pursued "the proper order of goods being preserved."[3] in as much as it damages the ethical good of the person, which is the highest good, since it deliberately deprives foreseen and freely chosen sexual activity of an es-

296

sential element. Thus article 20 of the medical-ethics code promulgated by the Conference in 1971 faithfully reflects the doctrine which is to be held, and its observance should be urged.

2. The Congregation, while it confirms this traditional doctrine of the Church, is not unaware of the dissent against this teaching from many theologians. The Congregation, however, denies that doctrinal significance can be attributed to this fact as such, so as to constitute a "theological source" which the faithful might invoke and thereby abandon the authentic Magisterium, and follow the opinions of private theologians which dissent from it.[4]

3. In so far as the management of Catholic hospitals is concerned:

(a) Any cooperation which involves the approval or consent of the hospitals to actions which are in themselves, that is, by their nature and condition, directed to a contraceptive end, namely, in order that the natural effects of sexual actions deliberately performed by the sterilized subject be impeded, is absolutely forbidden. For the official approbation of direct sterilization and, *a fortiori*, its management and execution in accord with hospital regulations, is a matter which, in the objective order, is by its very nature (or intrinsically) evil. The Catholic hospital cannot cooperate with this for any reason. Any cooperation so supplied is totally unbecoming the mission entrusted to this type of institution and would be contrary to the necessary proclamation and defense of the moral order.

(b) The traditional doctrine regarding material cooperation, with the proper distinctions between necessary and free, proximate and remote, remains valid, to be applied with the utmost prudence, if the case warrants.

(c) In the application of the principle of material cooperation, if the case warrants, great care must be taken against scandal and the danger of any misunderstanding by an appropriate explanation of what is really being done.

This Sacred Congregation hopes that the criteria recalled in this letter will satisfy the expectations of that Episcopate, in order that, with the uncertainties of the faithful cleared up, the Bishops might more easily respond to their pastoral duty.

ROME, *Sacred Congregation for the Doctrine of the Faith,*
13 March 1975

*Notes*

1. Cf. especially the two Allocutions to the Catholic Union of Obstetricians and to the International Society of Hematology; in:

AAS 43, 1951, 843-844; 50, 1958, 734-737 and in the encyclical of Paul VI *Humanae Vitae* n. 14cf. AAS 60, 1968, 490-491.

2. Cf. Pius XI, the encyclical *Casti Connubii,* in AAS 22, 1930, 565.

3. Paul VI, the encyclical *Humanae Vitae*, in AAS 60, 1968, 487.

4. Cf. Vatican Council II, Const. *Lumen Gentium,* n. 25, 1 (in AAS, 57, 1965, 29-30); Pius XII, Allocution to the Most Reverend Cardinals, ibid, 46, 1954, 672; the encyclical *Humani generis*, ibid, 42, 1950, 568; Paul VI, Allocution to the Meeting regarding the theology of Vatican Council II, ibid, 58, 1966, 889-896 (especially 890-894); the Allocution to the Members of the Congregation of the Most Holy Redeemer, ibid, 59, 1967, 960-963 (especially 962).

## DECLARATION ON CERTAIN QUESTIONS
## CONCERNING SEXUAL ETHICS

(Taken from *L'Osservatore Romano*, January 22, 1976)

**1.** According to contemporary scientific research, the human person is so profoundly affected by sexuality that it must be considered as one of the factors which give to each individual's life the principal traits that distinguish it. In fact it is from sex that the human person receives the characteristics which, on the biological, psychological and spiritual levels, make that person a man or a woman, and thereby largely condition his or her progress towards maturity and insertion into society. Hence sexual matters, as is obvious to everyone, today constitute a theme frequently and openly dealt with in books, reviews, magazines and other means of social communication.

In the present period, the corruption of morals has increased, and one of the most serious indications of this corruption is the unbridled exaltation of sex. Moreover, through the means of social communication and through public entertainment this corruption has reached the point of invading the field of education and of infecting the general mentality.

In this context certain educators, teachers and moralists have been able to contribute to a better understanding and integration into life of the values proper to each of the sexes; on the other hand there are those who have put forward concepts and modes of behavior which are contrary to the true moral exigencies of the human person. Some members of the latter group have even gone so far as to favor a licentious hedonism.

As a result, in the course of a few years, teachings, moral criteria and modes of living hitherto faithfully preserved have been very much unsettled, even among Christians. There are many people today who, being confronted with so many widespread opinions opposed to the teaching which they received from the Church, have come to wonder what they must still hold as true.

**2.** The Church cannot remain indifferent to this confusion of minds and relaxation of morals. It is a question, in fact, of a matter which is of the utmost importance both for the personal lives of Christians and for the social life of our time (1).

The Bishops are daily led to note the growing difficulties experienced by the faithful in obtaining knowledge of wholesome moral teaching, especially in sexual matters, and of the growing difficulties experienced by pastors in expounding this teaching effectively. The Bishops know that by their pastoral charge they are called upon to meet the needs of their faithful in this very serious matter, and important documents dealing with it have already been published by some of them or by Episcopal Conferences. Nevertheless, since the erroneous opinions and resulting deviations are continuing to spread everywhere, the Sacred Congregation for the Doctrine of the Faith, by virtue of its function in the universal Church (2) and by a mandate of the Supreme Pontiff, has judged it necessary to publish the present Declaration.

**3.** The people of our time are more and more convinced that the human person's dignity and vocation demand that they should discover, by the light of their own intelligence, the values innate in their nature, that they should ceaselessly develop these values and realize them in their lives, in order to achieve an ever greater development.

In moral matters man cannot make value judgments according to his personal whim: "In the depths of his conscience, man detects a law which he does not impose on himself, but which holds him to obedience . . . For man has in his heart a law written by God. To obey it is the very dignity of man; according to it he will be judged" (3).

Moreover, through his revelation God has made known to us Christians his plan of salvation, and he has held up to us Christ, the Savior and Sanctifier, in his teaching and example, as the supreme and immutable Law of life: "I am the light of the world; anyone who follows me will not be walking in the dark, he will have the light of life" (4).

Therefore there can be no true promotion of man's dignity

unless the essential order of his nature is respected. Of course, in the history of civilization many of the concrete conditions and needs of human life have changed and will continue to change. But all evolution of morals and every type of life must be kept within the limits imposed by the immutable principles based upon every human person's constitutive elements and essential relations—elements and relations which transcend historical contingency.

These fundamental principles, which can be grasped by reason, are contained in "the divine law—eternal, objective and universal—whereby God orders, directs and governs the entire universe and all the ways of the human community, by a plan conceived in wisdom and love. Man has been made by God to participate in this law, with the result that, under the gentle disposition of divine Providence, he can come to perceive ever increasingly the unchanging truth" (5). This divine law is accessible to our minds.

**4.** Hence, those many people are in error who today assert that one can find neither in human nature nor in the revealed law any absolute and immutable norm to serve for particular actions other than the one which expresses itself in the general law of charity and respect for human dignity. As a proof of their assertion they put forward the view that so-called norms of the natural law or precepts of Sacred Scripture are to be regarded only as given expressions of a form of particular culture at a certain moment of history.

But in fact, divine Revelation and, in its own proper order, philosophical wisdom, emphasize the authentic exigencies of human nature. They thereby necessarily manifest the existence of immutable laws inscribed in the constitutive elements of human nature and which are revealed to be identical in all beings endowed with reason.

Furthermore, Christ instituted his Church as "the pillar and bulwark of truth" (6). With the Holy Spirit's assistance, she ceaselessly preserves and transmits without error the truths of the moral order, and she authentically interprets not only the revealed positive law but "also . . . those principles of the moral order which have their origin in human nature itself" (7) and which concern man's full development and sanctification.

Now in fact the Church throughout her history has always considered a certain number of precepts of the natural law as having an absolute and immutable value, and in their transgression she has seen a contradiction of the teaching and spirit of the Gospel.

5. Since sexual ethics concern certain fundamental values of human and Christian life, this general teaching equally applies to sexual ethics. In this domain there exist principles and norms which the Church has always unhesitatingly transmitted as part of her teaching, however much the opinions and morals of the world may have been opposed to them. These principles and norms in no way owe their origin to a certain type of culture, but rather to knowledge of the divine law and of human nature. They therefore cannot be considered as having become out of date or doubtful under the pretext that a new cultural situation has arisen.

It is these principles which inspired the exhortations and directives given by the Second Vatican Council for an education and an organization of social life taking account of the equal dignity of man and woman while respecting their difference (8).

Speaking of "the sexual nature of man and the human faculty of procreation", the Council noted that they "wonderfully exceed the dispositions of lower forms of life" (9). It then took particular care to expound the principles and criteria which concern human sexuality in marriage, and which are based upon the finality of the specific function of sexuality.

In this regard the Council declares that the moral goodness of the acts proper to conjugal life, acts which are ordered according to true human dignity, "does not depend solely on sincere intentions or on an evaluation of motives. It must be determined by objective standards. These, based on the nature of the human person and his acts, preserve the full sense of mutual self-giving and human procreation in the context of true love" (10).

These final words briefly sum up the Council's teaching—more fully expounded in an earlier part of the same Constitution (11)—on the finality of the sexual act and on the principal criterion of its morality: it is respect for its finality that ensures the moral goodness of this act.

This same principle, which the Church holds from divine Revelation and from her authentic interpretation of the natural law, is also the basis of her traditional doctrine, which states that the use of the sexual function has its true meaning and moral rectitude only in true marriage (12).

**6.** It is not the purpose of the present Declaration to deal with all the abuses of the sexual faculty, nor with all the elements involved in the practice of chastity. Its object is rather to repeat the Church's doctrine on certain particular points, in view of the urgent need to oppose serious errors and widespread aberrant modes of behavior.

**7.** Today there are many who vindicate the right to sexual union before marriage, at least in those cases where a firm intention to marry and an affection which is already in some way conjugal in the psychology of the subjects require this completion, which they judge to be connatural. This is especially the case when the celebration of the marriage is impeded by circumstances or when this intimate relationship seems necessary in order for love to be preserved.

This opinion is contrary to Christian doctrine, which states that every genital act must be within the framework of marriage. However firm the intention of those who practice such premature sexual relations may be, the fact remains that these relations cannot ensure, in sincerity and fidelity, the interpersonal relationship between a man and a woman, nor especially can they protect this relationship from whims and caprices. Now it is a stable union that Jesus willed, and he restored its original requirement, beginning with the sexual difference. "Have you not read that the creator from the beginning made them male and female and that he said: This is why a man must leave father and mother, and cling to his wife, and the two become one body? They are no longer two, therefore, but one body. So then, what God has united, man must not divide" (13). Saint Paul will be even more explicit when he shows that if unmarried people or widows cannot live chastely they have no other alternative than the stable union of marriage: ". . . it is better to marry than to be aflame with passion" (14). Through marriage, in fact, the love of married people is taken up into that love which Christ irrevocably has for the Church, (15) while dissolute sexual union (16) defiles the temple of the Holy Spirit which the Christian has become. Sexual union therefore is only legitimate if a definitive community of life has been established between the man and the woman.

This is what the Church has always understood and taught, (17) and she finds a profound agreement with her doctrine in men's reflection and in the lessons of history.

Experience teaches us that love must find its safeguard in the stability of marriage, if sexual intercourse is truly to respond to the requirements of its own finality and to those of human dignity. These requirements call for a conjugal contract sanctioned and guaranteed by society—a contract which establishes a state of life of capital importance both for the exclusive union of the man and the woman and for the good of their family and of the human community. Most often, in fact, premarital relations exclude the possibility of children. What is represented to be conjugal love is not able, as it absolutely should be, to develop into paternal and maternal love. Or, if it does happen to do so, this will be to the detriment of the children, who will be deprived of the stable environment in which they ought to develop in order to find in it the way and the means of their insertion into society as a whole.

The consent given by people who wish to be united in marriage must therefore be manifested externally and in a manner which makes it valid in the eyes of society. As far as the faithful are concerned, their consent to the setting up of a community of conjugal life must be expressed according to the laws of the Church. It is a consent which makes their marriage a Sacrament of Christ.

**8.** At the present time there are those who, basing themselves on observations in the psychological order, have begun to judge indulgently, and even to excuse completely, homosexual relations between certain people. This they do in opposition to the constant teaching of the Magisterium and to the moral sense of the Christian people.

A distinction is drawn, and it seems with some reason, between homosexuals whose tendency comes from a false education, from a lack of normal sexual development, from habit, from bad example, or from other similar causes, and is transitory or at least not incurable; and homosexuals who are definitively such because of some kind of innate instinct or a pathological constitution judged to be incurable.

In regard to this second category of subjects, some people conclude that their tendency is so natural that it justifies in their case homosexual relations within a sincere communion of life and love analogous to marriage, in so far as such homosexuals feel incapable of enduring a solitary life.

In the pastoral field, these homosexuals must certainly be treated with understanding and sustained in the hope of overcoming their personal difficulties and their inability to fit into society. Their culpability will be judged with prudence. But no pastoral method can be employed which would give moral justification to these acts on the grounds that they would be consonant with the condition of such people. For according to the objective moral order, homosexual relations are acts which lack an essential and indispensable finality. In Sacred Scripture they are condemned as a serious depravity and even presented as the sad consequence of rejecting God (18). This judgment of Scripture does not of course permit us to conclude that all those who suffer from this anomaly are personally responsible for it, but it does attest to the fact that homosexual acts are intrinsically disordered and can in no case be approved of.

**9.** The traditional Catholic doctrine that masturbation constitutes a grave moral disorder is often called into doubt or expressly denied today. It is said that psychology and sociology show that it is a normal phenomenon of sexual development, especially among the young. It is stated that there is real and serious fault only in the measure that the subject deliberately indulges in solitary pleasure closed in on self ("ipsation"), because in this case the act would indeed be radically opposed to the loving communion between persons of different sex which some hold is what is principally sought in the use of the sexual faculty.

This opinion is contradictory to the teaching and pastoral practice of the Catholic Church. Whatever the force of certain arguments of a biological and philosophical nature, which have sometimes been used by theologians, in fact both the Magisterium of the Church—in the course of a constant tradition—and the moral sense of the faithful have declared without hesitation that masturbation is an intrinsically and seriously disordered act (19). The main reason is that, whatever the motive for acting in this way, the deliberate use of the sexual faculty outside normal conjugal relations essentially contradicts the finality of the faculty. For it lacks the sexual relationship called for by the moral order, namely the relationship which realizes "the full sense of mutual self-giving and human procreation in the context of true love" (20). All deliberate exercise of sexuality must be reserved to this regular relationship. Even if it cannot be proved that Scripture condemns this sin by name, the tradition of the Church has rightly understood it to be condemned in the New Testament when the latter speaks of "impurity", "unchasteness" and other vices contrary to chastity and continence.

Sociological surveys are able to show the frequency of this disorder according to the places, populations or circumstances studied. In this way facts are discovered, but facts do not constitute a criterion for judging the moral value of human acts (21). The frequency of the phenomenon in question is certainly to be linked with man's innate weakness following original sin; but it is also to be linked with the loss of a sense of God, with the corruption of morals engendered by the commercialization of vice, with the unrestrained licentiousness of so many public entertainments and publications, as well as with the neglect of modesty, which is the guardian of chastity.

On the subject of masturbation modern psychology provides much valid and useful information for formulating a more equitable judgment on moral responsibility and for orienting pastoral action. Psychology helps one to see how the immaturity of adolescence (which can sometimes persist after that age), psychological imbalance or habit can influence behavior, diminishing the deliberate character of the act and bringing about a situation whereby subjectively there may not always be serious fault. But in general, the absence of serious responsibility must not be presumed; this would be to misunderstand people's moral capacity.

In the pastoral ministry, in order to form an adequate judgment in concrete cases, the habitual behavior of people will be considered in its totality, not only with regard to the individual's practice of charity and of justice but also with regard to the individual's care in observing the particular precepts of chastity. In particular, one will have to examine whether the individual is using the necessary means, both natural and supernatural, which Christian asceticism from its long experience recommends for overcoming the passions and progressing in virtue.

**10.** The observance of the moral law in the field of sexuality and the practice of chastity have been considerably endangered, especially among less fervent Christians, by the current tendency to minimize as far as possible, when not denying outright, the reality of grave sin, at least in people's actual lives.

There are those who go as far as to affirm that mortal sin, which causes separation from God, only exists in the formal refusal directly opposed to God's call, or in that selfishness which completely and deliberately closes itself to the love of neighbor. They say that it is only then that there comes into play the fundamental option, that is to say the decision which totally commits the person and which is necessary if mortal sin is to exist; by this option the person, from the depths of the personality, takes up or ratifies a fundamental attitude towards God or people. On the contrary, so-called "peripheral" actions (which, it is said, usually do not involve decisive choice), do not go so far as to change the fundamental option, the less so since they often come, as is observed, from habit. Thus such actions can weaken the fundamental option, but not to such a degree as to change it completely. Now according to these authors, a change of the fundamental option towards God less easily comes about in the field of sexual activity, where a person generally does not transgress the moral order in a fully deliberate and responsible manner but rather under the influence of passion, weakness, immaturity, sometimes even through the illusion of thus showing love for someone else. To these causes there is often added the pressure of the social environment.

In reality, it is precisely the fundamental option which in the last resort defines a person's moral disposition. But it can be completely changed by particular acts, especially when, as often happens, these have been prepared for by previous more superficial acts. Whatever the case, it is wrong to say that particular acts are not enough to constitute mortal sin.

According to the Church's teaching, mortal sin, which is opposed to God, does not consist only in formal and direct resistance to the commandment of charity. It is equally to be found in this opposition to authentic love which is included in every deliberate transgression, in serious matter, of each of the moral laws.

Christ himself has indicated the double commandment of love as the basis of the moral life. But on this commandment depends "the whole Law, and the Prophets also" (22). It therefore includes the other particular precepts. In fact, to the young man who asked, ". . . what good deed must I do to possess eternal life?" Jesus replied: ". . . if you wish to enter into life, keep the commandments. . . . You must not kill. You must not commit adultery. You must not steal. You must not bring false witness. Honor your father and mother, and: you must love your neighbor as yourself" (23).

A person therefore sins mortally not only when his action comes from direct contempt for love of God and neighbor, but also when he consciously and freely, for whatever reason, chooses something which is seriously disordered. For in this choice, as has been said above, there is already included contempt for the divine commandment: the person turns himself away from God and loses charity. Now according to Christian tradition and the Church's teaching, and as right reason also recognizes, the moral order of sexuality involves such high values of human life that every direct violation of this order, is objectively serious (24).

It is true that in sins of the sexual order, in view of their kind and their causes, it more easily happens that free consent is not fully given; this is a fact which calls for caution in all judgment as to the subject's responsibility. In this matter it is particularly opportune to recall the following words of Scripture: "Man looks at appearances but God looks at the heart" (25). However, although prudence is recommended in judging the subjective seriousness of a particular sinful act, it in no way follows that one can hold the view that in the sexual field mortal sins are not committed.

Pastors of souls must therefore exercise patience and goodness; but they are not allowed to render God's commandments null, nor to reduce unreasonably people's responsibility. "To diminish in no way the saving teaching of Christ constitutes an eminent form of charity for souls. But this must ever be accompanied by patience and goodness, such as the Lord himself gave example of in dealing with people. Having come not to condemn but to save, he was indeed intransigent with evil, but merciful towards individuals" (26).

**11.** As has been said above, the purpose of this Declaration is to draw the attention of the faithful in present-day circumstances to certain errors and modes of behavior which they must guard against. The virtue of chastity, however, is in no way confined solely to avoiding the faults already listed. It is aimed at attaining higher and more positive goals. It is a virtue which concerns the whole personality, as regards both interior and outward behavior.

Individuals should be endowed with this virtue according to their state in life: for some it will mean virginity or celibacy consecrated to God, which is an eminent way of giving oneself more easily to God alone with an undivided heart (27). For others it will take the form determined by the moral law, according to whether they are married or single. But whatever the state of life, chastity is not simply an external state: it must make a person's heart pure in accordance with Christ's words: "You have learned how it was said: You must not commit adultery. But I say this to you: if a man looks at a woman lustfully, he has already committed adultery with her in his heart" (28).

Chastity is included in that continence which Saint Paul numbers among the gifts of the Holy Spirit, while he condemns sensuality as a vice particularly unworthy of the Christian and one which precludes entry into the kingdom of heaven (29).

"What God wants is for all to be holy. He wants you to keep away from fornication, and each one of you to know how to use the body that belongs to him in a way that is holy and honorable, not giving way to selfish lust like the pagans who do not know God. He wants nobody at all ever to sin by taking advantage of a brother in these matters. . . . We have been called by God to be holy, not to be immoral. In other words, anyone who objects is not objecting to a human authority, but to God, who gives you his Holy Spirit" (30). "Among you there must not be even a mention of fornication or impurity in any of its forms, or promiscuity: this would hardly become the saints! For you can be quite certain that nobody who actually indulges in fornication or impurity or promiscuity—which is worshipping a false God—can inherit anything of the kingdom of God. Do not let anyone deceive you with empty arguments: it is for this loose living that God's anger comes down on those who rebel against him. Make sure that you are not included with them. You were darkness once, but now you are light in the Lord; be like children of light, for the effects of the light are seen in complete goodness and right living and truth" (31).

In addition, the Apostle points out the specifically Christian motive for practicing chastity when he condemns the sin of fornication not only in the measure that this action is injurious to one's neighbor or to the social order but because the fornicator offends against Christ who has redeemed him with his blood and of whom he is a member, and against the Holy Spirit of whom he is the temple. "You know, surely, that your bodies are members making up the body of Christ . . . All the other sins are committed outside the body; but to fornicate is to sin against your own body. Your body, you know, is the temple of the Holy Spirit, who is in you since you received him from God. You are not your own property; you have been bought and paid for. That is why you should use your body for the glory of God" (32).

The more the faithful appreciate the value of chastity and its necessary role in their lives as men and women, the better they will understand, by a kind of spiritual instinct, its moral requirements and counsels. In the same way they will know better how to accept and carry out, in a spirit of docility to the

Church's teaching, what an upright conscience dictates in concrete cases.

**12.** The Apostle Saint Paul describes in vivid terms the painful interior conflict of the person enslaved to sin: the conflict between "the law of his mind" and the "law of sin which dwells in his members" and which holds him captive (33). But man can achieve liberation from his "body doomed to death" through the grace of Jesus Christ (34). This grace is enjoyed by those who have been justified by it and whom "the law of the spirit of life in Christ Jesus has set free from the law of sin and death" (35). It is for this reason that the Apostle adjures them: "That is why you must not let sin reign in your mortal bodies or command your obedience to bodily passions" (36).

This liberation, which fits one to serve God in newness of life, does not however suppress the concupiscence deriving from original sin, nor the promptings to evil in this world, which is "in the power of the evil one" (37). This is why the Apostle exhorts the faithful to overcome temptations by the power of God (38) and to "stand against the wiles of the devil" (39) by faith, watchful prayer (40) and an austerity of life that brings the body into subjection to the Spirit (41).

Living the Christian life by following in the footsteps of Christ requires that everyone should "deny himself and take up his cross daily" (42) sustained by the hope of reward, for "if we have died with him, we shall also reign with him" (43).

In accordance with these pressing exhortations, the faithful of the present time, and indeed today more than ever, must use the means which have always been recommended by the Church for living a chaste life. These means are: discipline of the senses and the mind, watchfulness and prudence in avoiding occasions of sin, the observance of modesty, moderation in recreation, wholesome pursuits, assiduous prayer and frequent reception of the Sacraments of Penance and the Eucharist. Young people especially should earnestly foster devotion to the Immaculate Mother of God, and take as examples the lives of the Saints and other faithful people, especially young ones, who excelled in the practice of chastity.

It is important in particular that everyone should have a high esteem for the virtue of chastity, its beauty and its power of attraction. This virtue increases the human person's dignity and enables him to love truly, disinterestedly, unselfishly and with respect for others.

**13.** It is up to the Bishops to instruct the faithful in the moral teaching concerning sexual morality, however great may be the difficulties in carrying out this work in the face of ideas and practices generally prevailing today. This traditional doctrine must be studied more deeply. It must be handed on in a way capable of properly enlightening the consciences of those confronted with new situations and it must be enriched with a discernment of all the elements that can truthfully and usefully be brought forward about the meaning and value of human sexuality. But the principles and norms of moral living reaffirmed in this Declaration must be faithfully held and taught. It will especially be necessary to bring the faithful to understand that the Church holds these principles not as old and inviolable superstitions, nor out of some Manichaean prejudice, as is often alleged, but rather because she knows with certainty that they are in complete harmony with the divine order of creation and with the spirit of Christ, and therefore also with human dignity.

It is likewise the Bishops' mission to see that a sound doctrine enlightened by faith and directed by the Magisterium of the Church is taught in Faculties of Theology and in Seminaries. Bishops must also ensure that confessors enlighten people's consciences and that catechetical instruction is given in perfect fidelity to Catholic doctrine.

It rests with the Bishops, the priests and their collaborators to alert the faithful against the erroneous opinions often expressed in books, reviews and public meetings.

Parents, in the first place, and also teachers of the young must endeavor to lead their children and their pupils, by way of a complete education, to the psychological, emotional and moral maturity befitting their age. They will therefore prudently give them information suited to their age; and they will assiduously form their wills in accordance with Christian morals, not only by advice but above all by the example of their own lives, relying on God's help, which they will obtain in prayer. They will likewise protect the young from the many dangers of which they are quite unaware.

Artists, writers and all those who use the means of social communication should exercise their profession in accordance with their Christian faith and with a clear awareness of the enormous influence which they can have. They should remember that "the primacy of the objective moral order must be regarded as absolute by all", (44) and that it is wrong for them to give priority above it to any so-called aesthetic purpose, or to material advantage or to success. Whether it be a question of artistic or literary works, public entertainment or providing information, each individual in his or her own domain must show tact, discretion, moderation and a true sense of values. In this way, far from adding to the growing permissiveness of behavior, each individual will contribute towards controlling it and even towards making the moral climate of society more wholesome.

All lay people, for their part, by virtue of their rights and duties in the work of the apostolate, should endeavor to act in the same way.

Finally, it is necessary to remind everyone of the words of the Second Vatican Council: "This Holy Synod likewise affirms that children and young people have a right to be encouraged to weigh moral values with an upright conscience, and to embrace them by personal choice, to know and love God more adequately. Hence, it earnestly entreats all who exercise government over people or preside over the work of education to see that youth is never deprived of this sacred right" (45).

At the Audience granted on 7 November 1975 to the undersigned Prefect of the Sacred Congregation for the Doctrine of the Faith, the Sovereign Pontiff by divine providence Pope Paul VI approved this Declaration "On certain questions concerning sexual ethics", confirmed it and ordered its publication.

Given in Rome, at the Sacred Congregation for the Doctrine of the Faith, on 29 December 1975.

FRANJO Card. SEPER
*Prefect*
✠fr. JEROME HAMER, O.P.
*Titular Archbishop of Lorium*
*Secretary*

NOTES

1. Cf. Second Vatican Ecumenical Council, Constitution on the Church in the Modern World *Gaudium et Spes*, 47:*AAS* 58 (1966), p. 1067.

2. Cf. Apostolic Constitution *Regimini Ecclesiae Universae*, 29 (15 August 1976): *AAS* 59 (1967), p. 897.

3. *Gaudium et Spes*, 16: *AAS* 58 (1966), p. 1037.

4. Jn 8:12.

5. Second Vatican Ecumenical Council, Declaration *Dignitatis Humanae*, 3: *AAS* 58 (1966), p. 931.

6. 1 Tim 3:15.

7. *Dignitatis Humanae*, 14: *AAS* 58 (1966), p. 940; cf. Pius XI, Encyclical Letter *Casti Connubii*, 31 December 1930; *AAS* 22 (1930), pp. 579-580; Pius XII, Allocution of 2 November 1954: *AAS* 46 (1954), pp. 671-672; John XXIII, Encyclical Letter *Mater et Magistra*, 15 May 1961; *AAS* 53 (1961), p. 457; Paul VI, Encyclical Letter *Humanae Vitae*, 4, 25 July 1968: *AAS* 60 (1968), p. 483.

8. Cf. Second Vatican Ecumenical Council, Declaration *Gravissimum Educationis*, 1, 8: *AAS* 58 (1966), pp. 729-730; 734-736. *Gaudium et Spes*, 29, 60, 67: *AAS* 58 (1966), pp. 1048-1049, 1080-1081, 1088-1089.

9. *Gaudium et Spes*, 51: *AAS* 58 (1966), p. 1072.

10. *Ibid.*; cf. also 49: *loc. cit.*, pp. 1069-1070.

11. *Ibid.*, 49, 50: *loc. cit.*, pp. 1069-1072.

12. The present Declaration does not go into further detail regarding the norms of sexual life within marriage; these norms have been clearly taught in the Encyclical Letters *Casti Connubii* and *Humanae Vitae*.

13. Cf. Mt 19:4-6.

14. 1 Cor 7:9.

15. Cf. Eph 5:25-32.

16. Sexual intercourse outside marriage is formally condemned: 1 Cor 5:1; 6:9; 7:2; 10:8; Eph 5:5; 1 Tim 1:10; Heb 13:4; and with explicit reasons: 1 Cor 6:12-20.

17. Cf. Innocent IV, Letter *Sub catholica professione*, 6 March 1254, *DS* 835; Pius II, *Propos. damn, in Ep. Cum sicut accepimus*, 14 November 1459, *DS* 1367; Decrees of the Holy Office, 24 September 1665, *DS* 2045; 2 March 1679, *DS* 2148. Pius XI, Encyclical Letter *Casti Connubii*, 31 December 1930: *AAS* 22 (1930), pp. 558-559.

18. Rom 1:24-27: "That is why God left them to their filthy enjoyments and the practices with which they dishonor their own

bodies, since they have given up divine truth for a lie and have worshipped and served creatures instead of the creator, who is blessed for ever. Amen! That is why God has abandoned them to degrading passions: why their women have turned from natural intercourse to unnatural practices and why their menfolk have given up natural intercourse to be consumed with passion for each other, men doing shameless things with men and getting an appropriate reward for their perversion." See also what Saint Paul says of *masculorum concubitores* in 1 Cor 6:10, 1 Tim 1:10.

19. Cf. Leo IX, Letter *Ad splendidum nitentis*, in the year 1054: *DS* 687-688, Decree of the Holy Office, 2 March 1679: *DS* 2149; Pius XII, *Allocutio*, 8 October 1953: *AAS* 45 (1953), pp. 677-678; 19 May 1956: *AAS* 48 (1956), pp. 472-473.

20. *Gaudium et Spes*, 51: *AAS* 58 (1966), p. 1072.

21. ". . . if sociological surveys are useful for better discovering the thought patterns of the people of a particular place, the anxieties and needs of those to whom we proclaim the word of God, and also the opposition made to it by modern reasoning through the widespread notion that outside science there exists no legitimate form of knowledge, still the conclusions drawn from such surveys could not of themselves constitute a determining criterion of truth", Paul VI, Apostolic Exhortation *Quinque iam anni*, 8 December 1970, *AAS* 63 (1971), p. 102.

22. Mt 22:38, 40.

23. Mt 19:16-19.

24. Cf. note 17 and 19 above: Decree of the Holy Office, 18 March 1666, *DS* 2060: Paul VI, Encyclical Letter *Humanae Vitae*, 13, 14: *AAS* 60 (1968); pp. 489-496.

25. 1 Sam 16:7.

26. Paul VI, Encyclical Letter *Humanae Vitae*, 29: *AAS* 60 (1968), p. 501.

27. Cf. 1 Cor 7:7, 34; Council of Trent, Session XXIV, can. 10: *DS* 1810; Second Vatican Council, Constitution *Lumen Gentium*, 42, 43, 44: *AAS* 57 (1965), pp. 47-51; Synod of Bishops, *De Sacerdotio Ministeriali*, part II, 4, b: *AAS* 63 (1971), pp. 915-916.

28. Mt 5:28.

29. Cf. Gal 5:19-23; 1 Cor 6:9-11.

30. 1 Thess 4:3-8; cf. Col 3:5-7; 1 Tim 1:10.

31. Eph 5:3-8; cf. 4:18-19.

32. 1 Cor 6:15, 18-20.

33. Cf. Rom 7:23.

34. Cf. Rom 7:24-25.

35. Cf. Rom 8:2.
36. Rom 6:12.
37. 1 Jn 5:19.
38. Cf. 1 Cor 10:13.
39. Eph 6:11.
40. Cf. Eph 6:16, 18.
41. Cf. 1 Cor 9:27.
42. Lk 9:23.
43. 2 Tim 2:11-12.
44. Second Vatican Ecumenical Council, Decree *Inter Mirifica*, 6: *AAS* 56 (1964), p. 147.
45. *Gravissimum Educationis*, 1: *AAS* 58 (1966), p. 730.

# Index

Abelard, 251 n. 56
Abstinence, sexual, 34, 102, 292-95
Adler, Alfred, 74
Adultery, 30, 43, 88, 148-49; empirical sciences on, 148, 149; Jesus on, 24, 103; Old Testament on, 14
Albert the Great, 41, 42, 251 n. 56
Alexander VII, pope, 271 n. 175
Alphonsus Liguori, 44, 154, 155, 157
American Medical Association, 140
American Psychiatric Association, 70, 74, 211, 232
American Psychological Association, 232
*Amplexus reservatus*, 44
Animal behavior, 57, 61-64
Anthropology, Christian, 1-5
Aquinas, Thomas, 4, 41-42, 88, 251 n. 57; on: homosexuality, 197-99; premarital sex, 153, 155, 157; unnatural sin, 266 n. 72
Artificial insemination, 137-40
Asceticism, 26-27, 34-35, 102, 104, 249 n. 38
Augustine, 4, 36-37, 196, 248 n. 34, 249 n. 36

Baum, Gregory, 204, 206
Behavior modification, 73
Bernardin, Joseph, archbishop, 131-32
Bestiality, 61, 88, 229-30
Bible, 2-3, 103-04; and human sexuality, 7-32; on: contraception, 123; premarital sex, 155; sterilization, 129. *See also* New Testament and Old Testament
Birth control; *See* Contraception
Bisexuality, 257; *See also* Homosexuality
Body, 243 n. 3, 4, 5
British Council of Churches, 161, 262 n. 24

Call to Action Conference (1976), 241

Canon Law, 42, 85, 141
Carnegie Report, 74
*Casti Connubii. See* Pius XI
Catholic Theological Society, ix, 183, 241
Celibacy, 26-28, 183-86
Chastity, 100-02
Child-free marriage, 140-43
Christic dimension of sexuality, 95
Chrysostom, John, 196
Church teaching. *See* Magisterium
Cicero, 245 n. 23
Clement of Alexandria, 34, 247 n. 14
Common law marriage, 145
Communal living, 146-47
Concubinage, 13, 14, 30
Concupiscence, 24-25, 145. *See also* Pleasure
Congregation for the Doctrine of the Faith, 129-30, 221
Conscience, 115, 134
Contraception, 114-28, 135; methods of, 116-21, 292-95
Courtly love, 42
Courtship, 170-75
Covenant, 269 n. 141
Creation, 29
Cultic prostitution, 190
Cultic purity, 9-11
Curran, Charles E., 53, 120-21, 202-03, 220
Cyprian, 35

Dating. *See* Courtship
Davis, Henry, 158-59, 252 n. 60
*Declaration on Sexual Ethics*, 50-52, 81, 86-87, 100; on: homosexuality, 201; masturbation, 223; premarital sexuality, 159-60. *See* Appendix 3 for full text.
Deviant sexual behavior, 64-74
Dualism, 4, 26
Dulles, Avery, S.J., 240
Divorce, 20, 21, 26

Elvira, Council of, 36, 197
Empirical sciences, 53-77

*317*

Obscenity. *See* Pornography
Old Testament, 7-17, 96, 102-03, 111. *See also* Bible
Onan, 15, 112. *See also* Masturbation

Paci, E., 64
Palmieri, 156
Papal Commission, 47, 119-20, 133
Parenthood, 46, 111-40
Parousia, 104
Partnership, 102-11, 126-28, 202-04
Patriarchal Society, 11-15
Paul VI, pope, 48, 117-18, 122, 131
Paul, saint, 22-29, 31, 96; on: marital fidelity, 144; parenthood, 112; partnership, 104
Penitentials, 38, 39-40, 42, 88, 250 n. 50
Personhood, 15-17, 83-88, 99-100
Peter Lombard, 267 n. 82
Pius XI, pope, 45, 48, 106, 117, 129
Pius XII, pope, 46, 48, 132, 141; on: artificial insemination, 137; Christian Education of Youth, 221; contraception, 117; principle of totality, 130
Pleasure, 37, 42, 76, 164. *See also* Concupiscence
Polygamy, 13, 14, 30, 111
*Porneia*, 23-24, 25
Pornography, 234-37
Premarital sex, 88, 152-69; empirical sciences on, 58, 61, 66-69
Presbyterian Report, 162, 202
Procreation, 37, 85, 262 n. 25; dominant norm, 39, 43; frustration of, 105-06
Promiscuity, 166, 215
Prostitution, 23-24, 144. *See also* *Porneia*
Psychotherapy, 73
Pythagoras, 244 n. 7

Renshaw, Domeena, 274 n. 221
Revelation, 243 n. 1
Rhythm, 46. *See also* Contraception
Rosenzweig, S., 70

Sacred Congregation for Catholic Education, 222, 228

Sacred Congregation for Religious, 221
Sacred Penitentiary, 221
Salvatorian Gay Task Force, 204
Sanchez, Thomas, 44
Scholasticism, 41, 42
Scripture. *See* Bible, Old Testament and New Testament
Sex clinics, 231-32
Sex education, 237-39
Sexual behavior, 64-74, 88-89
Sexual variants, 229-31
Sexuality, definition of, 80-83
Single state, 175-83
Social responsibility, 93-94
Sodom, 191-92, 193, 197
Sodomy, 88. *See also* Homosexuality
Sterilization, 128-36, 296-98
Stoicism, 2, 39-40, 112, 198; influence on Church Fathers, 34; influence on St. Paul, 18, 24-25
Supreme Court of the United States, 236
Swinging, 147

Taboos, 10, 30, 56-57, 189
Talmud, 20, 190
Tamburini, 156
Temple prostitutes, 9
Tertullian, 247 n. 13
Theology of Human Sexuality, 78-98
Tradition, Christian, 33-77
Transsexualism, 232
Transvestism, 10, 230-31, 244 n. 8
Trial marriages, 58
Tubal ligation, 136. *See also* Sterilization

University of Indiana Sex Research Institute, 75

Values, 92-95
Variant patterns, 143-52
Vasectomy, 136. *See also* Sterilization
Vatican II, 48, 78-79, 89, 134; on: chastity, 100; marriage, 49; procreative and unitive aspects of sexuality, 85, 112-14, 115, 119; on responsible partnership, 107-09

### Catholic Theological Society of America
### Committee on the Study of Human Sexuality

WILLIAM CARROLL is married and the father of two children. He has graduate degrees from the Catholic University of America and Duquesne University, a doctorate in philosophy from the University of Strasbourg, France, a doctor of law degree from Northwestern University, and has done post-doctoral studies in religion and psychology at the University of Chicago. Both a certified psychologist and a trial lawyer, he has taught theology, psychology, and law at a variety of colleges and universities and is presently a professor of law at the John Marshall School of Law in Chicago.

AGNES CUNNINGHAM, a member of the Servants of the Holy Heart of Mary, is associate professor of patrology and Church history at Saint Mary of the Lake Seminary, Mundelein, Illinois. She has a master's degree from Marquette University and a doctorate in sacred theology from the Facultes Catholiques in Lyon, France. She has served as a consultant to the National Council of Churches' Ad Hoc Committee on the Role of Women and has lectured widely in the areas of patristics, spirituality, and women in the Church. After serving as a member of the Board of Directors of the Catholic Theological Society of America and then as its Secretary, she was elected its Vice-President in 1976. She is a co-author of *La Femme* (1968) and *Widening the Dialogue* (1974) and has published in *Chicago Studies, Emmanuel, Spiritual Life*, and *Worship*.

ANTHONY KOSNIK, a priest of the Archdiocese of Detroit, is professor of moral theology and dean at Saints Cyril and Methodius Seminary, Orchard Lake, Michigan. He has a doctorate in sacred theology from the Angelicum University and a bachelor's degree in canon law from the Gregorian University in Rome. He has served as a theological consultant to the Advisory Committee of the American Bishops' Committee on Health Affairs, as a synodal judge, and as a member of the Theological Commission of the Archdiocese of Detroit. He has lectured widely in the areas of medical and sexual ethics and has published in a variety of journals, including *The Jurist, Linacre Quarterly*, and the *Catholic Mind*.

RONALD MODRAS, a priest of the Archdiocese of Detroit, is associate professor of systematic theology at Saint John's Seminary, Plymouth, Michigan. He has a bachelor's degree in sacred theology from the Catholic University of America, a master's degree in philosophy from the University of Detroit, and a doctorate in theology from the University of Tübingen, Germany. He has served as a member of the Theological Commission of the Archdiocese of Detroit and as an advisor to the editorial board of *Concilium*. His published writings include two books, *Paths to Unity* (1968) and *Paul Tillich's Theology of the Church, A Catholic Appraisal* (1976), as well as articles and reviews in *America, Commonweal, Concilium,* and the *Journal of Ecumenical Studies.*

JAMES SCHULTE, is director of instruction at the Saint Joseph's Hospital School of Nursing in Marshfield, Wisconsin. He studied theology at Saint Francis Seminary, Milwaukee and is presently completely a doctorate in theology at Marquette University with a dissertation on child-free marriage. His pastoral experience includes parish ministry and teaching on both the secondary and college levels. He has served as an advisor to the Tribunal of the Archdiocese of Milwaukee and has lectured and written widely in the areas of marriage and sexuality.